D1348771

TWO WHEEL SHOWDOWN!

By the same author

AYRTON SENNA
The second coming

TORVILL AND DEAN
The full story

JAMES HUNT
Portrait of a champion

GERHARD BERGER
The human face of Formula 1

GRAND PRIX SHOWDOWN!
The full drama of the races which decided
the World Championship 1950–92

NIGEL MANSELL
The making of a champion

AYRTON SENNA
The hard edge of genius

HONDA
The conquest of Formula 1

HONDA
Conquerors of the track

ALAIN PROST

A MAN CALLED MIKE

Patrick Stephens Limited, an imprint of Haynes Publishing, has published authoritative, quality books for enthusiasts for more than 25 years. During that time the company has established a reputation as one of the world's leading publishers of books on aviation, maritime, military, model-making, motor cycling, motoring, motor racing, railway and railway modelling subjects. Readers or authors with suggestions for books they would like to see published are invited to write to: The Editorial Director, Patrick Stephens Limited, Sparkford, Nr. Yeovil, Somerset BA22 7JJ.

TWO WHEEL SHOWDOWN!

**The full drama of the races which decided the
World 500cc Motor Cycle Championship from 1949**

CHRISTOPHER HILTON

Patrick Stephens Limited

First published in 1994

British Library Cataloguing-in-Publication Data:
A catalogue record for this book is
available from the British Library

ISBN 1 85260 456 5

Library of Congress catalog card no. 93 81189

Patrick Stephens Limited is an imprint of Haynes Publishing
Sparkford, Nr Yeovil, Somerset BA22 7JJ

Typeset by G&M, Raunds, Northamptonshire
Printed in Great Britain by
Butler & Tanner Ltd of London and Frome

Contents

Prologue

THE HOUSE IS very Bavarian, large and full of shadows. Pairs of antlers loom along one wall. From its deep windows you can see the Alps; and you can almost see Salzburg just over the border in Austria. The man who lives in this house is also very Bavarian – easy, natural and unhurried, full of chuckling, rumbling laughter. 'I will be 66 in eight days,' Walter Zeller says, the laughter rising as if he can't believe it. It is Sunday, 5 September 1993.

He first raced in 1947, two years before the World 500cc Championship began, and in time almost won it. On the wall of his study there's a framed scroll officially recognizing his second place to John Surtees in 1956. Zeller had never been so close to the great prize before, and never would be again. He points to the scroll – he has a bike rider's hands, enlarged, chunks of muscularity but softly sensitive – with pride, and no regrets visible.

We talk of his career, of that wild and improbable season of 1956, and he moves through the prism of memory: how in slipstreaming he over-revved his BMW and it blew in the crucial race; how his mechanics cried; how, the Championship finally lost, he found himself drawn into Irish folk dancing at a Belfast hotel, and he remembers it as much as the disappointment. 'Very nice, very funny.'

Zeller is becalmed among the memories, but not confined to them. 'Every year there is an old-timer's race in Misano. I have my old BMW mechanic, and in the winter time he makes up my engine. In June we go to the race at Misano. John Surtees is there on his very fast works Norton, but he can ride what he wants. The Italians give him MVs with three cylinders, four cylinders, six cylinders. We go faster than in my competition days because the bikes are faster! At Misano it is always a very hard fight with John.'

Some few minutes after the interview ended, Wayne Rainey led the Italian Grand Prix – at Misano – and moved, as it seemed, smoothly and easily towards another victory; another step to his fourth World Championship equalling the total of Surtees and placing him in the most exalted company: Geoff Duke, Mike Hailwood and Eddie Lawson (four, too). Only the Italian Giacomo Agostini would be ahead with eight. *That* exalted company.

On lap 10 Rainey crashed, damaging his spinal column. The medical bulletins were sombre and disturbing, the word paralysis repeatedly mentioned. The crash essentially made Kevin Schwantz the World Champion for the first time, but in a way no man could have wished.

And that was Sunday, 5 September 1993, an uncanny and haunting conjunction of past, present and future. The coincidence of events spans virtually the whole of this book.

Before the Second World War the European Championship had been judged a great success, and after it the sport's governing body, the Federation of International Motorcycling (FIM), created the World Championship in 1949. In time the Championship embraced six categories (50/80cc, 125, 250, 350, 500 and sidecars) although the 500 represented, and represents, the summit. No disrespect to riders in the other categories, but to cover all their *showdown* races might better be tackled as a complete modern history of the sport. This book is uniquely about the 500s, and the other categories make their entrances only if they exercised a bearing on that.

There is, however, a difference of emphasis between the book and its predecessor *Grand Prix Showdown* (also Patrick Stephens) which recreated the deciding races in the World Formula One car Championship. The difference wasn't intended – it simply evolved. Year after year many pivotal moments in the 500cc Championship happened during races before the decider, precisely like Rainey's crash. Schwantz did not secure the title *finitely* until the race after – the American at Laguna Seca. As a result I've let the stories of the seasons unfold, often in detail, with the deciding race as the natural (or sometimes unnatural) climax.

I thank many people for their time, help and memories. They are, in no particular order: Franco Uncini, Walter Zeller, Wayne Rainey, Kenny Roberts, Freddie Spencer, Giacomo Agostini, Charlie Rous, Ralph Bryans, Iain Mackay of Honda, Geoff Duke, Jack Findlay, David Fern of Donington Park, John Dodds, Andrew Marriott of CSS, Jim Redman, Nobby Clark, Monica Meroni of Scuderia Italia, for conducting a superb interview, Gabriella Strauss and Hans Sautter of BMW, Tommy Robb, Stuart Graham (for background and foreground assistance and lending an evocative photograph), Tommy Robb, Jimmy Walker of the *Belfast Telegraph,* Phil Read, John Surtees, Mick Duckworth of *Classic Bike* magazine, Umberto Masetti, and John Brown.

Particular gratitude goes to Nick Harris for several kindnesses, the Rothmans Honda Press service for a bedrock of information and pictures, and Marlboro's Motor Sport Media Service, Proaction.

Wherever possible I've used original sources and race reports because they give both an immediacy and a flavour of the times; so thanks to Brian Woolley for permission to quote from the magazine *Motor Cycling;* Rob Munro-Hall, Editor, for *Motor Cycle News;* James H. Gray, Managing Editor, *Belfast Telegraph* for *Ireland's Saturday Night;* Richard Poulter for *Motocourse;* Motor Racing Publications for *No Time to Lose* by Alan Peck; Ted Macauley for *Hailwood* (Cassell) and *Yamaha* (Cadogan Books); Michael Scott for *Barry Sheene: A Will to Win* (Star); Redman for *Wheels of Fortune* (Motoraces Book Club); Harris for *Fast Freddie* co-authored by Peter Clifford (MRP); Nick Hartgerink for *The Wayne Gardner Story* (Fairfax Magazines, Australia).

I've consulted and drawn from the *Rothman's Grand Prix Motorcycle Yearbook; Marlboro's Grand Prix Guide; Suzuki* by Jeff Clew (Haynes); *John Surtees, World Champion* by Surtees and Alan Henry (Hazleton); *Motor Cycling Today* by Bob McIntyre (Arthur Barker); *In Pursuit of Perfection* by Geoff Duke (Osprey); *The Art and Science of Motor Cycle Road Racing* by Clifford (Hazleton); *Freddie Spencer* in the Champions series by Michael Scott (Kimberley's); *Directory of Classic Racing Motorcycles* by Woolley (Aston); *The Story of Honda Motorcycles* (PSL) and *Great Motor-cycle Riders* (Hale), both by Peter Carrick.

Duke Marketing have a superb (and to the historian, necessary) catalogue of video titles, and I thank Peter Duke for permission to avail myself of them: in the Champions series, *Giacomo Agostini, Geoff Duke and Mike Hailwood; Czech Bike GP '88, Bike GP Highlights '86, Italian Finale, To The Limit, Rainey's Year. Bike Hero, The Story of Kevin Schwantz* (Front Runner) was illuminating, as were the Rothmans compilations of the 1987 and 1989 seasons.

1949

Les Graham – the first

Ulster Grand Prix, Clady

THAT SATURDAY MORNING, bright but with enough humidity to soften any glare from the sun, the pilgrimage began early towards the narrow, uneven, dangerous place. The local newspaper, *Ireland's Saturday Night*, caught the mood perfectly:

The Ulster Transport Authority had special bus services scheduled to commence at 9 a.m. from College Square, Belfast to Nutt's Corner and from Smithfield to Templepatrick to cater for the race crowds. So great was the early morning rush, however, that by 9 a.m. 20 buses had already been filled and despatched to the Clady circuit. In addition the Authority also operated a rail service from York Road station to Muckamore. By mid-morning traffic reached a peak. Motorists, motorcyclists and pedal cyclists formed a solid stream on all routes leading to Clady.

The beginning: full of bustle, charged with currents of movement; an energy evident. It was 21 August 1949.

They came to Clady, a circuit of ordinary roads, although *Motor Cycling* magazine described the surface as 'in excellent condition'. It did not mean the same, surely, as it would now.

Jimmy Walker, a youngster who'd become a noted journalist, sets Clady into simple words. 'It used to be $21^1/2$ miles but had been reduced to $17^1/2$. It was north of Belfast with a place called Clady Corner the nearest point to the city. The Corner was by the village of Liganiel, the terminus for trams to and from the city. Spectators would go to the race on the trams in literally thousands. Clady would be black with people.

'The course started about three miles up the road from Clady Corner on a very straight patch, featureless, no village or anything, just in the middle of a field you might say. It was a country road about eight or ten yards wide with no white lines, no cat's eyes. You went through Ballyhill, famous for its bumps. Bikes took off like they were scramblers. You turned right at Nutt's Corner, Belfast's airport until it moved to Aldergrove . . .'

The riders ran a couple of miles to Killead Bridge – a left kink – then three miles to a V-shaped corner at Muckamore. That fed onto the seven-and-a-half-mile straight, spectators sitting on banks which ran alongside it, the surface harsh here. It brought them to Clady Corner, a hard right some half-a-mile from the start-finish.

Strong men waited. Les Graham had been a bomber pilot and would harness his British twin AJS to the demands of the circuit against Artie Bell, the 'local hero' on a Norton, Johnny Lockett on another, Nello Pagani – face like a mask, eyes sharp and flinty – on a Gilera, Arcisio Artesiani on another, Carlo Bandirola – wrist bandaged from a crash in the Swiss – on a third, Bob Foster on a Guzzi. As the pilgrimage flowed in – and by now the buses had made five return journeys – the riders readied themselves.

Robert Leslie Graham, born at Wallasey, Cheshire in 1911, had been competing since the 1920s – he started at the Stanley Speedway track in Liverpool – but, like so many others in all walks of life, the Second World War cut into his career. His son Stuart says 'my father joined the RAF as a Lancaster pilot and did his stint at that. He was awarded the DFC, although we never quite found out why. He dismissed it as "well, they were dishing a few out so they thought they'd send me one." It arrived in the post.

'We still have his log books at home, and bit by bit the picture emerged that he'd done one or two secret sorties, I believe staying behind after bombing raids to photograph various things like the U-boat pens, but I don't really know because he didn't say. After the War he picked up his career by going to work for AJS and they picked him up immediately because he'd shown such potential before the War.'

The magazine *Classic Motorcycling Legends* catches the mood of Graham and his era nicely enough. 'Win or lose, Les enjoyed the competition and the friendship of other riders. He was a professional with an amateur's delight in the sport.'

He waited with the other strong men. *Ireland's Saturday Night* reported:

Smartest set up in the pits was that of the Gilera team. They followed the Continental manufacturer's custom by bringing along a brightly coloured mobile workshop, which seemed to carry everything from a small washer to a complete reserve machine. Shortly before the start a director of the Gilera company arrived by plane accompanied by his wife. Several small camping parties had taken up position close to Clady Corner late on Friday night. The new 1,100 seater tubular steel stand, which was booked out in a day, was occupied for almost two hours prior to the commencement of the race.

The strong men had already contested four rounds of this first World 500cc Championship. They'd begun at the TT on the Isle of Man in June where Graham set fastest lap but didn't finish in the points. Graham won the Swiss Grand Prix at Berne from Artesiani, and Pagani won the Dutch Grand Prix at Assen from Graham.

For 1949 and almost three decades after it the Championship would be decided by counting a specified number of a rider's best finishes – in 1949 three out of the six rounds – and this acted like a ratchet, tightening and tightening on the leader and those hounding and hunting him. In the Belgian Grand Prix at Spa, Graham scored no points, Artesiani finished second and Pagani fifth. Artesiani had 24 points, Pagani 22 and Graham 20, totals which favoured Graham because of the ratchet. He'd set fastest lap at the TT, worth a single point. If he won the Ulster and set fastest lap there he'd have 11 more points and only drop the one from The Island. There were permutations, but if Graham won at Clady he could scarcely be caught whatever happened at the final race – the Nations Grand Prix at Monza – two weeks later.

The scoring: 10 for a win, then 8, 7, 6, 5 with the 1 for fastest lap. What chance had Graham? *Motor Cycling* reported that Ulster Motor Cycling Club's . . .

. . . own timing over a kilometre past the grandstand, where a 'good' 500 is still approaching its maximum performance, suggested that the Gileras at 121 mph were a shade faster than the Guzzis, about 2 mph up on the AJS and around 5 mph quicker than the fastest Norton.

To the tune of 'McNamara's Band', blared over the loudspeakers, Sig. G. Curli and other notables from Italy arrived at the grandstand. They were a few among thousands because the beautiful morning had brought more people than ever before to the course. With half an hour to go to the 'off', officials and police were at last clearing the stragglers from the road near the start to enable competitors to come out for the warming up. The '500s' led the way.

Three races would be run concurrently, the 500s setting off on 15 laps (247$\frac{1}{2}$ miles/398 km), two minutes later the 350s on 13 laps (214$\frac{1}{2}$ miles/345 km), two minutes after that the 250s on 12 laps (198 miles/318 km). *Ireland's Saturday Night* reported:

The clock showed 11.55 a.m. The riders were motionless on the grid – ready and eager. Ten seconds . . . five . . . go. There was an ear-splitting roar as the 30 riders chased away along the straight to Ballyhill. Pagani, the Italian, was out in front on the Gilera, with Les Graham (AJS) in behind, and A. J. Bell not far behind.

By Muckamore, Graham had taken Pagani and led. The strong men of the 350 class waited.

Just out of hospital after his crash in the Temple '100', Ernie Lyons, Kildare agricultural engineer, had his official Velocette taken over by C. F. Salt, a Lancashire jam manufacturer. Freddy Frith, the Grimsby stonemason, headed the Velocette aces who expected the main opposition challenge from the Works AJS piloted by Frend, Armstrong, of Dublin, and M'Pherson, a New South Wales rider. Frith shot into the lead . . .

As the 350 riders set off *Motor Cycling* reported:

First news of the 500 race progress came from Muckamore, where Graham was ahead of Bell and Pagani third. The AJS man was still in front at the end of the seven-mile Clady straight, with Pagani's reputedly faster Gilera-four some way back, but now lying second. A course record! Graham's standing lap was covered in 10 minutes 20 seconds, an average speed of 95.86 mph (154.2 kph) and he had a considerable lead over Pagani. Bell, as he passed the grandstand, was completely surrounded by the red Italian machines with Pagani in front, Bandirola overtaking and Bob Foster on the Guzzi coming up fast.

A tone had been set to endure across the eras: pace. *Ireland's Saturday Night* reported that . . .

Graham has broken the lap record. The record had stood since Bell set it in 1947 – 94.79 mph (152.5 kph), 10 minutes 27 seconds. Les Graham was giving the big AJS 'everything'. Tucked down behind the visor on the bars he flashed past the stand at 115 mph! (185 kph), Pagani was twenty yards away with Bell 'tailing' him closely.

On Graham's second lap he lifted the record to 97.45 mph (156.8 kph), 10 minutes 10 seconds. *Motor Cycling* reported that . . .

Bell was ahead of Bandirola – in fact the latter had dropped right back – at the end of the second lap and held off Foster's challenge, but Artesiani was now boring along in pursuit, right on the tail of Lockett. A distant roar on the straight! Graham was through and away on his third lap well ahead of Pagani with Foster third and Bell a bad fourth. Graham now averaged 97.70 mph (157.2 kph) with Pagani 96, and Foster 95.69. Foster took up the record breaking. He set up 10 minutes 8 seconds (97.43 mph/156.7 kph). Graham was well ahead at the end of the third lap with Pagani second. The order was unchanged in the fourth with Foster in third place. Graham had broken it this time – 10 minutes 7 seconds (97.92 mph/157.5 kph).) The 100 mph seemed in sight.

On lap 5 Foster took Pagani for second place, but two laps later missed his pit signal, a goggle lens having been fractured by a stone. He ran out of petrol before reaching the pits again. By then Graham had lifted the record to 98.08 mph (157.8 kph). *Ireland's Saturday Night* reported:

Graham, keen, confident, his machine holding perfectly, was 40 seconds ahead on lap 7. Pagani was certainly moving – 121 mph on the measured mile. The leader board suddenly changed. Graham was still out in front with 45 seconds in hand, but Pagani was back to second position and Bell third.

At this point, with more than half the 15 laps completed, Artesiani made his move, accelerating hard. The order – Graham, Pagani, Artesiani, Bell – became Graham, Artesiani, Bell, Pagani on lap 10. Bell made his move, too, and passed Artesiani at Muckamore, having a fleeting glimpse of Graham on the distant crest of a hill. That was all. When they reached the start-finish line Artesiani had re-taken him and held second place until the last lap before disappearing somewhere between Muckamore and Clady.

Motor Cycling reported:

Despite the fact that he was almost certainly a few mph down, Bell managed to keep ahead of Pagani along the straight – the latter apparently finding his very light, very powerful Gilera just a little too much of a handful over the undulations and bumps of this gruelling seven miles.

Graham finished in 2 hours 34 minutes 52.5 seconds (averaging 96.49 mph/155.2 kph), Bell at 2 hours 35 minutes 44.2, Pagani at 2 hours 35 minutes 54.0.

And that was the beginning.

Postscript

I point out to Stuart Graham that in its coverage of the race *Ireland's Saturday Night* does not mention his father had become World Champion. 'I am not sure if people knew. They probably had more important things on their minds in 1949. Motor cycle racing really was a relatively obscure sport. Motor racing in general did not sit at the top of people's priorities.'

You were only around six years of age but, even so, did *you* realize your father came back from Ulster as World Champion? 'No, no. My earliest recollections are of his having to go away a lot to dinners and so forth, the usual social functions, but I didn't have a sort of *my dad's World Champion* feeling.'

Stuart Graham does now, all these years later.

1950

Masetti – magnifico

Nations Grand Prix, Monza

HE COVERED A few laps in a Vanguard car. That gave him a feel for the contours of the place – the angle of the corners, the braking points. Then he and a man by the name of Joe Craig parked the Vanguard and walked the circuit, stopping here and there, discussing, noting, remembering. They had a decision to make and it must be the right decision.

Geoff Duke, nearing the end of his first season of World Championship racing, and Craig, long-time Norton team manager, decided that yes, they'd enter the 'lion's den'. Norton and Duke would contest the Nations Grand Prix against the mighty Gileras. This may seem curious now; that, the Championship at stake, a decision was needed at all, but the pride and prestige of Norton was also at stake and the lions could devour both.

Duke had just ridden in the Swiss Grand Prix at Geneva which Graham (AJS) won, an Italian, Umberto Masetti, behind him, and Duke fourth. Duke took the opportunity to motor down and have a look at Monza. He'd not been to Italy before and, even in 1950, the contrast between the neatness of neutral Switzerland and the war ravages of northern Italy struck him hard.

He returned to Britain to contest the Ulster Grand Prix three weeks before the race at Monza. Jimmy Walker remembers that . . . 'I was a kid and I lay in the grass at the side of the course listening to this roar which became louder and louder and then into view came Les Graham. He had a handkerchief round the lower part of his face, one of those spotted handkerchiefs like speedway riders wore. He looked a bandit! He came weaving round on the AJS followed by Duke and Pagani and they were all in a rush.

'This, incidentally, was the first year of the 125 class, and Carlo Ubbiali rode his bike with his legs stretched out behind him on two footrests above the rear wheel. He lay in a sort of prone position as if he was on his stomach on a stretcher. Incredible . . .'

Duke won the 500 race from Graham, with Masetti sixth. Masetti had

23 points, Duke 19, Graham 17, but the ratchet tightened: the best four finishes from the six rounds. Duke and Graham had only three, so whatever they got at Monza they'd keep. Masetti had four but faced dropping only the single point from Ulster. The scoring (which changed from 1949 and remained unaltered until 1969): 8, 6, 4, 3, 2, 1, nothing for fastest lap. Duke needed to win Monza and Masetti to come no higher than third. Graham could still do it *but* needed to win and Masetti to finish no higher than fourth.

Umberto Masetti, born Parma on 4 May 1926, came inevitably to racing. 'My father, who rode a 500, was a Gilera distributor, and so from my birth I inhaled the smell of tyres and burnt oil. It stirred in me a passion for bikes. My "career" began one birthday – a Sunday, I remember – when my father said "do you want to come on the bike with me?" I curled up on the seat behind him. If my career was pushed by my father it was obstructed by my mother. She informed my father she'd abandon him if I kept on riding!'

Masetti kept on riding.

Duke and Craig approached the jaws of the den quietly, methodically and guarding secrecy, although driving the van down they'd experienced a 'spot of bother' at the Italian customs. These customs had, and would have, a quixotically nationalistic view of how quickly visitors could proceed through if those visitors might damage Italy's chances in motor sporting events, and this reached all the way to 1976 when James Hunt (Marlboro McLaren) duelled with Niki Lauda *(Ferrari)* and, before the Italian Grand Prix at Monza, the customs held up for a long time the lorry carrying McLaren's fuel.

Duke and Craig arrived a couple of days before practice and made full use of the 'peace and quiet', Duke lapping and lapping and lapping on the Norton. This allowed him to do a minimum of actual qualifying and spend time watching the opposition – particularly at the first corner – accompanied by Dickie Dale, another Norton rider. At one moment, as Duke recalls in his autobiography, a Briton, Ted Frend, (who'd been in the 350 race at the 1949 Ulster) got into a broadside and Dale sprang behind a tree. Duke would have done the same but, stopwatch in hand, happened to be looking the other way. *Motor Cycling* reported that . . .

Those who arrived early at Monza during the pre-race week found an atmosphere very different from that prevailing at a similar period last year, when only the AJS team and a handful of 'circus' riders represented Britain's bid for the World Championship titles – mainly against Italy – on a high speed track ideally suited to both the temperament and racing technique of the latter country.

The track, a boomerang-shaped 3.9 mile circuit, stills favours the Italian school but since the first post-war Monza Grand Prix of Nations in 1949, Britain's chief adversaries – Gilera, MV and Guzzi, whose stablimenti *are all virtually on Monza's doorstep – have by no means enjoyed a run of unbroken success. Harried, and in some cases beaten, in previous events forming the 1950*

Championship series, the Contintentals now face stern opposition in this, the final event of the season.

One hears that the odds are in favour of Duke. Stop-watches have been clicking busily during the two practice days; people have rumoured laps by Geoff in the region of 2 minutes 17 seconds, but Joe Craig in his shrewdness just smiles enigmatically and says he 'hasn't been able to notice it!' What one has noticed is that lights have been ablaze in each camp far into the night, clearly in the effort to bring Duke's existing 19 marks [points!] or Graham's 17 in excess of the Italian Masetti's total of 23.

In fact, Duke covered only five laps in practice, and on three of them Masetti followed him. Duke did do 2 minutes 17 seconds, but entirely to try to shed Masetti. He didn't shed him. This fastest lap offered no particular encouragement because Masetti had been able to stay behind – clinging or teasing or simply observing? 'I studied Duke during practice,' Masetti says enigmatically, 'and I saw he was fast, so with Piero Taruffi, the Gilera sporting manager, and my team-mates – Bandirola and Pagani – we decided they'd help me. Unfortunately it didn't work out like that.'

Artesiani (MV Agusta) looked very good in that first corner as Duke observed *him*. Worse, Duke felt his tummy wobbling. In 1950, and well after, the British nurtured themselves on plain food, the Italians adoring rich, succulent variety overlaid with equally rich, succulent sauces.

The day before the meeting Duke did something extremely British and restricted himself to bread rolls.

Duke contested the 350 race, although without any particular intention of winning – he'd save himself for the 500 – but at the start someone ran over his foot. By a paradox Duke won it despite the foot and, the 500 a couple of hours away, returned to his hotel to nap. *Motor Cycling* reported:

What a grand day it is! The sun climbs up into a cool, blue sky but by noon we shall be grilled. Racing is to start at 9 a.m. and at the early hour of 8 motor coaches, cars and thousands of excited Italians choke the approach roads to Monza park. Seven flags come on parade and they represent the cream of motorcycle racing.

Taruffi said to Masetti: 'If you win the race, that is marvellous, but don't forget that if you finish in the first three you win the Championship.' Masetti himself felt 'afraid' the Championship might be lost 'if my Gilera abandoned me', which is a delightful way of expressing anxiety about mechanical failure. 'No, I was never nervous *preparing* for a race, and that was one of my values. Ten minutes before, I'd always eat a sandwich. However, when only 30 seconds were left my heart beat like a fool because I worried I'd fail to start: I was very thin ($8^1/2$ stone/56 kg) and pushing the bike presented a constant problem. Because of the tension which that worry caused, my blood froze, and if you'd put a needle into me you'd have found water!'

The race: 31 laps. *Motor Cycling* reported that . . .

With a great crescendo the riders get under way and at once it is noted that, apart from Geoff Duke, the Britishers have little, or no, advantage over the mass of red-tanked, foreign machines.

The AJS 'Porcupines' are particularly unlucky. Between them and the leaders is a block of Gileras. C. Bandirola heads them. Not far behind is A. Artesiani on an MV and mixed up with the Italians is Duke, a situation which the Norton rider appears to resent and which he rectifies before three laps are finished. At the beginning of the fourth lap he is in the lead – an almost imperceptible lead, constantly challenged by Masetti and Bandirola.

Duke understood that Masetti tucked in behind and bided his time, clinging or teasing or simply observing. Masetti knew the power of the Gilera. On lap 10 *Motor Cycling* reported that . . .

Masetti's Gilera comes screaming at maximum revs way past the grandstand in front of the Norton. Masetti, to achieve it, pushes the 500cc lap record up to 105.4 mph! (169.6 kph)

Duke remembers the moment Masetti went by. Never had he seen anything so potent. Meanwhile . . .

Graham and Lockett are both moving up but they have a stiff task in piercing the Bandirola-Pagani 'defence' line.

Duke reasoned that, by overtaking him, Masetti satisfied himself that he could do it again whenever he liked towards the end of the race. Duke decided he must re-take Masetti and break him. Duke selected the two corners before the start-finish straight (a hard-right immediately followed by another hard-right, then called the Curva di Vedano, now the Parabolica) and took him there, swiftly. *Motor Cycling* mused . . .

How much has either Masetti or Duke in reserve? That question crops up continuously because, with the race a little more than half completed, only 50 yards separate potential Champions. For some minutes the position remains unchanged: one or other had to fall back or press on. Which?

Duke remembers Masetti drawing up alongside 'sitting up!' Was this psychology to prove to Duke – crouched in the tuck position and squeezing the Norton – that Masetti could afford to sit up? 'I didn't want to sacrifice my chance of the Championship,' Masetti says 'but if I had the possibility to beat Duke, that was mine. I loved the battle with Duke, always a challenge between him and me, a . . . contest!'

Geoff Duke, quiet Lancastrian, knew his trade intimately, knew what you could make a motor bike do, and how. The mark of that is shown easily enough. In a long career riding many circuits in many conditions he won and won, became the bench-mark by which other riders judged themselves, and fell so rarely that people still speak of the times he did. Around the loops of Monza he seemed finally to break Masetti. It remains the gesture of a racer, no matter that by holding second place Masetti also held the Championship. *Motor Cycling* reported . . .

With 13 laps to go it becomes obvious that Masetti's four is tiring. Duke now has more than a hundred yards in hand. Joe Craig steps out and gives him man the 'grif' [slang for information] that the Gilera's pace is slackening; the distance between the two machines is now nearly 500 yards. Craig signals again and the board tells a very significant story. How quiet the crowd has become, and understandably so. Their idol, Masetti, has the almost impossible job of recapturing something like thirty five seconds in the five remaining laps if he is to win the race.

Masetti had not surrendered but, with two laps to run, 'at the big corner after the finishing line a marshal or a member of the public crossed the track. Trying to avoid him I went off and struck a straw bale. I hurt my foot and this provoked a terrible pain when I braked for the rest of the race.'

Duke stroked the Norton round the loops, steady, steady, Masetti falling away so that Duke won it by slightly more than 50 seconds. Won it? Well . . .

With a large figure 'One' still showing on the lap-scorer's board the man with the chequered flag steps on to the track as Geoff flashes by. Yes, a mistake has been made but the organisers stand by their decision and, despite an appeal, it is confirmed by the jury that the position of the riders at the end of the 31st lap constitutes the final result.

'I didn't know the situation,' Masetti says, 'and the question was really debated afterwards. I remember two of the riders – Les Graham and one other – staying on their bikes and completing another lap, believing they had to.'

Curious, or perhaps not so curious. Masetti might have broken down on that mythical lap 32 which never was and in the moment Duke would have had the Championship.

Postscripts

'My victory was celebrated at the restaurant Gilera Sant Eustorgio at Arcore, not far from Monza, with all my friends, and then we went to Commendatore Gilera's home with his son Ferruccio, one of my best friends. That evening was nice, Ferruccio, the Commendatore, his wife Ida. The Commendatore laughed all the time because he put some pepper into my wine and I started to sneeze. I had to leave the room to wash my mouth out. Then I went home because my little daughter Giordana Gloria was due to be born. The choice of names? I chose Giordana because I wanted to be reminded of Giordano Aldrighetti, who I'd seen riding a 500 Gilera in a race when I was eleven, and that impressed me a lot. I chose Gloria for the glory of the victory.'

During this season of 1950 Walter Zeller went to Munich railway station and exchanged some money. For each Deutschmark he received 20 East-marks. He was travelling to the other part of his own country to ride a BMW but not in a World Championship round, just a race. When he reached the other part of his own country 'the people were afraid to say a wrong word. They were very afraid. When you talked to them they were thinking about every word they said, and you could tell. We stayed at a hotel called the Chemnitzerhof where, because of the exchange rate, we ate caviar and drank champagne and generally lived like kings. We always called the town Chemnitz, [it had been renamed Karl-Marx-Stadt] and whenever we did the local people opened their eyes wide and didn't say one word.'

The circuit he was to ride on? The Sachsenring, home of the German Grand Prix before the War, a place he found 'difficult, a lot of trees right and left, although I was young then and I liked every course.' The significance? The Sachsenring would host six World Championship *showdowns,* a total equalled only by Monza. Legendary, amazing and sinister are the tales woven around the Sachsenring, but you'll have to wait a while for them.

1951

Duke finds the balance

Ulster Grand Prix, Clady

RAIN HAD FALLEN for days, fallen so hard that the leaden skies seemed to have emptied themselves, but now, on the Saturday, the wind stirred from the south-west. Invariably that meant more rain coming in from the tattered grey clouds.

Moving past ten o'clock – the Ulster Grand Prix, second last round of the season, still two hours away – the crowds gathered at Clady Corner, gathered at Ballyhill and at Muckamore so far out into the country, gathered along the seven mile straight. Four hundred marshals tried to direct their flow, but the starting area, where the little grandstand stood, became so choked they almost lost control. *Ireland's Saturday Night* reported that . . .

The grandstand, booked out for many days before, presented a colourful spectacle.

The colour was provided by ladies wearing bright summer frocks. A mistake, as they'd discover. Shortly before midday the rain began, not heavy but enough to douse those ladies and flood the carburettor of Dubliner Reg Armstrong's AJS. Riding was dangerous in the dry then, never mind the wet – as the build-up to the meeting proved.

On the Wednesday two Italians, Sante Geminiani and Gianni Leoni, crashed riding the circuit before official practice began. The details are obscure, but evidently Leoni pulled a long way ahead, turned and returned to find Geminiani. Because the roads weren't closed Geminiani found himself face to face with Leoni on what to him was the 'wrong' side. *Motor Cycling* suggested Geminiani 'momentarily forgot the British rule of the road.' They struck head on and were killed.

A strange as well as a sad build-up. On the Thursday Geoff Duke won the 350 race on a Norton, the first World Championship of his life and potentially enabled him to become the first man to achieve the 350 and 500 double. The ratchet: five best finishes from the eight rounds, and

Duke had 26 points from four, Milani 26 from three. If Duke won the Ulster he had the Championship even if Milani came second and won the final round – the Nations at Monza. They could both total 34 but Duke led on wins, 4-1.

On that Thursday evening Les Graham neared the end of a deeply frustrating season with MV. They entered for races and didn't show up, or if they did they broke down. *Ireland's Saturday Night* reported that . . .

Graham spent several pounds on telephone calls and telegrams to the MV Agusta Works in Italy concerning his machine and also asking for permission to switch to another make now that the Agusta machines are not likely to arrive. He is very keen to go to the line.

A rumour insinuated that Graham might be getting on a Gilera, and might be the man to beat Duke.

On the Friday a plane left a local airport taking the bodies of Geminiani and Leoni to Italy for burial. Now, the wind risen and the rain hardening on the Saturday morning, they would not be forgotten. The Gilera personnel had a special corner to themselves in the riders' paddock and made last minute adjustments under the direction of their managers. At 11.30 tannoys echoed 'clear the paddock', and 45 bikes were wheeled on to the grid, and sorted themselves out. Graham, no MV and no Gilera either, took his place in the grandstand.

The battle lines: a contest between three factories, Norton with Duke, Jack Brett and Lockett; AJS with Armstrong and Bill Doran, Gilera with Masetti, Alfredo Milani and Pagani. *Ireland's Saturday Night* reported that . . .

The only bearded rider was 45-year-old Manchester man Leo Starr, a stage and screen actor. Leo, who is now with the Manchester Repertory Theatre, has as his hobbies motor-cycle racing and scenery designing.

He'd ride an AJS. The sky had become slightly overcast and the breeze whipped the flags on top of the scoreboard. A brief moment of silence was observed in memory of Geminiani and Leoni. On the grid the Gilera personnel shielded their bikes with umbrellas – creature comforts worthy of mention in 1951. The National Anthem was played and, as that melted into the rain, every rider watched for the starter's flag. *Motor Cycling* caught the moment.

Midday, and the starter is ready with his Union Jack. Down it sweeps and riders splash forward over the wet road. Duke, Ken Kavanagh (Norton), Pagani, Armstrong and Doran are particularly quick off the mark. C. Gray's brilliant red helmet and yellow overalls bring colour to the rear of the pack.

Another contemporary account caught the moment, too:

Off the grid came the riders – a noisy, competent company. The 'works' men were away in sonorous unison down the straight to Ballyhill.

While the mechanics and team managers cleared the grid the tannoy echoed 'Kavanagh's first at Muckamore.'

Of Kavanagh, Duke says: 'A strange chap, Australian, who had on-days when he was absolutely superb and off-days when you'd probably lap him. I don't know how you can explain that, except to say perhaps he was temperamental on a bike. I've seen him literally sliding a bike in the wet in perfect safety, and in other races, wet and dry, be completely out of form. That's how he was. If he'd been consistent . . .'

Somewhere down the seven mile straight Duke drew up to Kavanagh, and at Clady Corner he inched ahead. Crossing the line to complete the first of the 15 laps Duke and Kavanagh were so close that the stop watches in the pits recorded them at the same speed – 94.04 mph (151.3 kph) – with Milani some 50 metres behind at 'only' 92.29 mph (148.5 kph).

The wind still rose, the rain fell harder. Duke led by some three seconds at the end of lap 2, Milani so blinded by spray that he pitted for new goggles. Duke appeared untroubled, and as he came down from Clady on his third lap a contemporary account describes how he 'flayed the Norton to great effect'. A harsh description. Geoff Duke didn't do anything like that to a machine; he nursed it, and rarely won races by using more than the minimum necessary. *Ireland's Saturday Night* reported that . . .

The biting rain with a cold wet wind drove spectators from the course and out of the grandstand from the third lap. Ulster Transport Authority buses were returning to Belfast with wet-through passengers, as other vehicles were on their way to the course. Newspapers, cardboard and sacking were pressed into service by enthusiasts who, determined to see the race through, sat huddled by the roadside or in the open stand.

Even riders were not immune from the desire to keep out of the rain. Charlie Gray, who later retired, swept past the stand with a billowing yellow mackintosh covering his riding leathers. [So much for the yellow overalls Motor Cycling *reported.] Women were the hardest hit. Bright summer frocks were drenched by the searching rain. Few of those who came to see the race brought umbrellas, and those who did shared them with less fortunate friends. Occupants of cars stayed in the parks and followed the race from the* [BBC] *commentary.*

Those who stayed witnessed a master and his work. 'In many ways,' Duke says, ' it was a miserable race, although, strangely enough, I enjoyed it because I settled down to the conditions, and anyway when you're winning you do enjoy races more (chuckle). I remember subsequently watching some film and you could actually see a reflection of the bike on the road in the water. That's how smooth and slippery it was.'

This film repays scrutiny; a section of ordinary road flanked by grassy verges and trimmed hedgerows. People crouch and sit in the grass. Puddles have gathered by the verges, and puddles lie in the undulations of the road, too. Duke is approaching a right-hander. He turns in very erect, leaning the bike only a little and, at the apex of the corner, there it is, a startling mirror-image beneath the bike, the wheels clearly visible and the shadows of dark leather nestled above them. Duke hugs the rim of the verge, emerges from the corner on to a sort of straight (the road bends in the distance) and takes his time, plenty of time, bringing the bike from the lean to vertical again, no sudden movement. The rear wheel slices light spray.

There's another moment further on: a stone cottage, the road carving directly round it and feeding to a kink, solid walls at either side, before the rider turns hard right. The road glistens and the mirror-image is here again, so clear that the wheels are not distorted in it. Again Duke remains upright, hardly a lean and, as he emerges, the momentum carrying the bike far to the other side of the road, he's faced by the lip of a pavement rearing at him. He moves into the tuck position and caresses the bike perhaps two feet away from the lip, the tyres cutting a narrow path through the surface water and leaving a furrow.

At periods during the race Duke tip-toed; at others he went fast. On lap 4 he raised his average speed to 95.75 mph (154.0 kph), Kavanagh still hustling away at 94.83 mph (152.6 kph). And the rain fell heavier. Doran came in to change his goggles for a second time, Pagani came in to change his goggles. On lap 7 Duke, Kavanagh and Masetti pitted for fuel and goggles – 'in such a long race you had to stop for fuel,' Duke says. *Ireland's Saturday Night* reported that . . .

Masetti's stop was a frantic affair. Half a dozen pairs of hands shot out. The bunch of pit attendants encircled him. He was away in 22 seconds! Duke took on fuel in 19 seconds without losing the lead. He was now a minute in front.

Of the 45 who set out only 19 finished, Brett not among them. He began to fall back, pitted and *Motor Cycling* reported that . . .

It is obvious he is in a bad way, crippled by cramp. Mechanics help him to the First-Aid hut and his machine is wheeled away.

In absolute contrast Duke pressed his average speed to 97.11 mph (156.2 kph) setting fastest lap, but on lap 9 Milani moved up to fifth and stretched the fastest lap to 97.27 mph (156.5 kph). *Ireland's Saturday Night* reported that . . .

Bill Doran had improved to fill fourth place but Milani, the slender Gilera man, was out to pull something out of the bag. He whisked round in 97.27 mph (156.5 kph), 10 mins 11 secs. He was in tigerish form. A flash of red and a screech from a well-tuned engine and he was through.

On lap 12 – Duke leading by a long way from Kavanagh, Masetti third, Doran fourth, Milani fifth, Lockett sixth – Doran's brakes were water-logged and at Muckamore he went up the escape road, falling while he turned the bike round. He remounted and struggled forward. *Ireland's Saturday Night* reported that . . .

Duke completed the thirteenth lap but called at the pits, where he topped up with fuel, chatted with Joe Craig and left after losing 35 seconds.

He could afford to. A lap later Kavanagh came in to top up, too. *Motor Cycling* reported that . . .

He has been taking some punishment, has Ken Kavanagh, and is so exhausted that only at the second attempt does he manage to bump his engine over compression. To a chorus of cheers he goes out of sight, still side-saddle and unable to muster energy enough to heave his numbed body astride the machine.

Taruffi hoisted 'go faster' signals to Masetti and Milani and, although they responded as best they could, it was too late. Duke, easing the pace, completed the race in 2 hours 36 minutes 6 seconds. Because of the conditions, riders were flagged down wherever they happened to be on the course when Duke crossed the line. Kavanagh, however, kept on to the finish.

Duke remembers that, 'Kavanagh had had great difficulty re-starting his bike after that pit stop because he was shattered, he could hardly push it. At the end of the race he had to be lifted off the bike. Ken was quite a small bloke, you know, and 2 hours 30-odd minutes is a long time. I was pretty shattered, too, although I didn't have to be lifted off.' Duke beat Kavanagh by almost 3 minutes.

Doran saw the flags on the seven mile straight and we have two accounts of what happened next. One says he 'made a gallant attempt to get up among the leaders but towards the end, with still a lap to go, was reported as having left the straight and was on his way to his hotel in Belfast. He had enough of it.' Another says 'all riders are flagged as soon as the winner has crossed the line – mercifully, because many others are as dead-beat as Kavanagh – and Doran, a lap and a few hundred yards behind Duke, motors on straight for his hotel at Antrim and for the hot bath he has been thinking of for the past three hours!'

Leo Starr had covered ten laps when the flags were waved. Since Clady measured $17^1/2$ miles, Geoff Duke beat him by $87^1/2$ miles (140 km).

Postscripts

Forty two years later Duke is an honoured guest at the British Grand Prix, Donington. He sits in the Gilera hospitality area. The lingering, warming Lancashire accent remains, the sense of humour, the innate politeness of another generation. If he'd raised his voice (never mind used an oath) you'd have been shocked.

'That first Championship was my greatest year, a double championship, and I was riding better than at any time in my career – still young and dashing but I'd developed a certain amount of common sense (chuckle). It was the right balance, and I was on a bike which handled superbly, a bike which suited my riding style. At that time, fortunately, Gilera hadn't got their bikes completely reliable, although towards the end of that season they were becoming harder to beat.'

How did you hold your concentration for more than two and a half hours? 'The TT on the Isle of Man was 254 miles and the Ulster always a long race. I think, incidentally, the prize was £20! It is possible to hold your concentration if you need to because if you allow it to lapse at all you have real problems. I was very fit, always kept very fit, and that helped. I believe physical and mental fitness go hand in hand. It's something you're born with, not something you create. Apart from leaving nothing to chance and keeping fit, concentration just came naturally. It sounds a bit much to say it was easy; I mean it wasn't easy, but . . .'

That afternoon of 18 August 1951 as Duke went off to find shelter, went to try to dry himself, he'd taken a step towards becoming the first genuinely great 500cc rider of the Championship.

Mind you, two weeks before the Nations Grand Prix at Monza Duke rode in a race at Thruxton and (of course) won. Charlie Rous, who'd become a noted journalist after a short but active sidecar career, remembers 'Duke rode a Norton but the race proved to be a very, very close run thing.' The man Duke beat, only 18, rode a Vincent. He was called John Surtees and, as Rous adds, 'this brought Surtees to the public's notice because the race was broadcast on the radio.'

Surtees had taken a tentative (if you get my meaning) step towards becoming the second genuinely great 500cc rider of the Championship.

1952

Encore, Masetti

Spanish Grand Prix, Barcelona

'THE 1952 SEASON was my busiest of all. I managed the Gilera team in the Grands Prix of Holland, Belgium, Ireland, Spain and Italy, of which we won the first three and brought off a Championship "double", winning both the World Championship with Umberto Masetti and the Manufacturers' Championship. I also took part in 16 car races – although this was not much for a professional driver, who normally reckons on 20 or more a year unless he is like Stirling Moss, racing in England on Saturday and Italy on the Sunday, and doing 50 or more. However, 16 was a record for me. This increased activity enabled me to keep in practice and to come third in the Formula One World Championship, which was won decisively by Alberto Ascari.'

The speaker is Taruffi, then 48, and his words reflect the era; not that a 48-year-old might contest Formula 1 (and win the Swiss Grand Prix) but that he might successfully manage the leading motor bike team at the same time. The world was less rigid then, less consuming, less technical, but what remains fascinating is that a man thought it quite natural to do both and pass off the achievements in such a dried, dispassionate way.

During the winter before the season, MV Agusta worked hard, thinking of beating the Gileras. MV, soon to become an echoing, thunderous name, contested the 500cc Championship in 1950 and 1951 with minimal success, despite Les Graham forcing the pace. He insisted the bikes' transmissions were converted to chain drive although, as Brian Woolley records in his *Directory of Classic Racing Motorcycles,* he also insisted on 'singularly hideous pivoted swinging arm front forks made under Earles patents, which did absolutely nothing for its appearance and probably little more for the roadholding and steering.'

Duke (Norton) led the first race, the Swiss at Berne – Graham out with mechanical trouble. He couldn't re-start after a pit stop. At the TT on the Isle of Man Duke led but dropped out (clutch), passing the lead to Graham, but Armstrong (Norton) won it. At Assen at the Dutch Grand

Prix Graham retired (engine) and Masetti held off Duke. At the Belgian Grand Prix at Spa Graham retired (engine) and Masetti held off Duke. Of the contenders, only Graham – fourth – scored in the West German Grand Prix at Solitude. By then Duke had crashed heavily in a non-Championship continental race, removing him from the run-in. Graham won the Nations at Monza from Masetti. The ratchet: five best finishes from the eight rounds and only the Spanish Grand Prix at Barcelona remained.

Masetti had 22 points, Graham 17 and both from only three finishes. They'd keep whatever they got, but Graham had to win with Masetti no higher than fifth, or Graham finish second and Masetti not finish. 'I faced the race quietly,' Masetti says. 'It was a good, varied circuit and I chose a spare bike for it – not the best bike we had overall, but good on acceleration!' *Motor Cycling* reported that . . .

In a blaze of sunshine which makes one forget that it is almost winter back in England (race day, 5 October) the year's Championship series enters its final stages this morning. The Spanish Grand Prix, due to take place shortly at Montjuich Park in the centre of this great city, will comprise 24 lap races for the 125cc and sidecar classes and a 48 lap 500cc event.

The 2.6 mile (4.1 km) circuit is shorter than last year's but longer than that used in 1950, and is going to give all competitors a punishing ride. With the local custom of dining at 10 p.m. and then embarking upon the evening's social round, it is not surprising that the grandstands lining each side of the 400-yard finishing straight are almost empty as the 9.30 a.m. zero hour for the first race, the 125, approaches.

Just past midday, and now there isn't a vacant seat or even a place to stand around the circuit. The 29 competitors in the 500 race are on the line, and in a few minutes a terrific struggle will be on between the Norton (Ken Kavanagh), MV and Gilera camps. AJS are unfortunately absent. The start is as spectacular as it is noisy and leading from the outset are C. Bandirola (MV) S. Wunsche (350 DKW), Graham (MV), S. Lawton (Norton) and U. Masetti (Gilera).

The start-finish appeared like a gully between the grandstands with, behind the grandstand on the right, a giant edifice of a museum or mausoleum looming stately and immense.

Graham led, crossing the line to complete lap 1, from Belgian Auguste Goffin (Norton) by some hundred yards; Masetti third. Goffin 'literally' dropped out of third place – *Motor Cycling* didn't specify why – on the third lap. By then Masetti had overtaken him. At the end of lap 8 (of 48) Graham led Masetti by half a minute – Graham averaging more than 60 mph (96.6 kph) on this street circuit. Bandirola challenged Masetti, and so did Pagani, Lomas and Kavanagh (both Bandirola and Lomas could help their MV team-mate Graham to the title). *Motor Cycling* reported:

Oh, ho! He's done it. Bandirola has bitten the dust, hurt his hand and put his MV out of action on the thirteenth lap. With a third of the race run, Graham is still slightly increasing his lead over Masetti, some 400 yards behind, while Kavanagh holds third place by a few lengths from Lomas and Pagani. Masetti is making a determined effort to narrow the gap between himself and the leader and has put in the fastest lap in two minutes 35.57 seconds (61.21 mph/98.5 kph). Kavanagh is making an equally determined effort to catch Masetti. By the thirty first lap, on which the exhaust note of Graham's MV changes abruptly as he passes the stand, the leader had almost a minute in hand once more over Masetti, who is only five seconds ahead of Kavanagh.

You can only imagine what Graham felt, his MV down to three cylinders. He could not influence Masetti in any way, only run, or try to run, to the end.

Lap 40 – only eight more to go and it is now obvious that, try as he will, Ken Kavanagh just cannot oust the fleet Masetti from second place. On the other hand, despite the fact that his machine is definitely running on only three cylinders, Graham still has 40 seconds in hand.

Would the MV last? Agonizingly he slowed as Masetti came – slowed as Masetti came – but he'd built up enough lead and won it by just under 27 seconds. Masetti, second, had his second Championship. 'Unfortunately,' Masetti says, ' my team only gave me pit signals about Graham's plight two laps from the end. If the signals had come earlier – even perhaps four or five laps from the end – I could have been stronger by a couple of seconds a lap. Perhaps I still wouldn't have won but I could have profited from any mistake he made. Who knows?'

Postscripts
This time Masetti celebrated at the Sant Eustorgio restaurant in Arcore *and* the Giannino Restaurant in Milan – 'nice moments with the mechanics, lots of jokes. Mrs Ida Gilera presented me with a silver plate.'

Graham explained to *Motor Cycling* that a plug lead had come adrift but 'the corners come in such quick succession on this circuit that I never had a chance to peer down to see what was wrong!'
   His son Stuart was becoming aware. 'I remember much more clearly as I got older, I remember him winning Grands Prix and being second in the World Championship. We moved to Italy, a little place up in the mountains, a villa owned by the Agusta family in a village near Lake Como just over the hill from Lugano. They put us up in it until we found a place of our own. I've always wanted to go back and find the place. I hope they haven't knocked it down. A lovely little village, a lovely summer house.
   'I do recall my father being extremely disappointed in 1952 because he looked back and remembered how much work he'd put into the bike with this special frame. He'd done the hard development work and it came good in the end. He dominated the last couple of races, but it was too late.

I wasn't at Monza when he won the Nations Grand Prix, but my mother told me all about it because he'd become a national hero in Italy. When he'd won Monza on the MV it caused a genuine sensation. Mother didn't see him for an hour afterwards and she was terrified, but you know what the crowd at Monza is like, mobbing the winners.

'We couldn't travel anywhere without him being recognized. We'd stop at traffic lights and people said *ah ha, ah ha, Graham!* Italians are wonderful. My father had a black Mark 7 Jaguar, one of only three in Italy, and that was terrific.

'Anyway, he was pipped for the Championship in Barcelona at the end of what had obviously been a hard year, and a year which must have been pretty tough. But that was him; he shrugged his shoulders, and off he went and got on with it. He tested all winter, spent a lot of time at Monza testing, testing, testing, and the bike got better and better. We'd spend days down there, me playing around while dad worked.

'Maserati and Ferrari would be there testing cars at the same time. You'd have Fangio and Eugenio Castellotti and those sorts of people around, you'd have Alfa Romeos going round, the odd Gilera going round. I was just a kid amongst all this lot and I treated it as normal. Life is what you grow up with, whether that's deprived or very privileged, it's what's natural. Until you get older and experience different things you don't always understand differences.

'The tragedy of it all is that in my view 1953 would have been *the* year. The bike was brilliant, dad was on top of the job . . .'

1953

Duke in full flow

Nations Grand Prix, Monza

'I GREATLY STRENGTHENED the Gilera side by signing two wonderful riders, the Irishman Reg Armstrong and the unique, the incomparable Geoff Duke. The latter was convinced that Gilera made the best bike and I, for my part, wanted him on our side. My job as competitions manager that year consisted mainly of keeping the peace and enforcing discipline amongst my riders, all of them strong personalities – mostly with big names and reputations to keep up.

'Masetti, who had been World Champion in 1950 and '52, did not like playing second fiddle to Duke, who at that time was virtually unbeatable. A champion hates to admit that he can be even fractionally inferior to someone else, and will stave off the admission as long as possible. He will say his machine is not so good as the others and plague the mechanics to alter the gear ratios, swop engines and make a hundred and one little alterations to improve the road holding or riding position.'

Taruffi again, a sympathetic man, the kind you'd like to work for, but that alone did not influence Duke's decision to leave Norton, itself something which demands exploration.

Taruffi wrote an 'unexpected' letter to Duke towards the end of 1950 inviting him to Gilera in 1951, but Duke declined for patriotic reasons. Norton bestrode racing in the 1930s, and during the post-War period manufactured bikes which still had a resonance, notably when Duke mounted them.

Duke knew, and Norton knew, that to match Gilera they needed a 'four' but, although one was under development, Norton's managing director, Gilbert Smith, explained it would take time. Nor did Norton pay Duke much. In 1950, for example Duke's contract stipulated that Norton kept his TT prize money! Duke says that by joining Gilera he doubled his income.

He reasoned, too, that he might serve the prestige of Britain better by 'winning on a foreign bike, in this case Italian, than coming second on a British bike.' He flew to Milan, where Taruffi (who he hadn't met before) charmed and impressed him, and signed. A strong combination, this: Armstrong, Dale and Milani, but not Masetti because, as *Motor Cycling* noted, 'it appeared he went off in a huff when he found he had Geoff Duke as a Gilera team-mate.' To which Masetti says: 'You have to understand that in 1952 I won the Championship, and in 1953 the team enlisted my rival!!! I almost never spoke with Duke, although of course there were language problems, too. Gilera had too many good riders, me, Duke, Milani, Liberati, four or five little fighting cocks.' Masetti sat out the season.

Duke wanted to win the TT on the Isle of Man, the opening round, to vindicate his decision, but Les Graham crashed fatally at Bray Hill and that hung heavy as a shroud over everything. Duke himself fell after skidding on melting tarmac, so that paradoxically Ray Amm won on a Norton, with Brett second on a Norton. Deceptive. Duke took the Dutch at Assen, Milani the Belgian at Spa (Duke's engine lost a cylinder and he retired after breaking the lap record twice). Duke took the French at Rouen and finished second to Kavanagh's Norton at the Ulster – clutch problems. (The Ulster had moved from Clady to Dundrod – something explored in the chapter on 1955.) Duke took the Swiss Grand Prix in Berne.

The ratchet: five best finishes from the eight rounds and two remained, the Nations at Monza and Spain at Barcelona. Approaching Monza, Duke had 30 points from only four races, Armstrong 27 but from six, Milani 18 from three, Kavanagh 18 from four.

If Duke scored no points in these last two and Armstrong won both he'd end on 32 points against Duke's 30. *If* Duke and Armstrong scored no points in the last two and Milani won both, he'd have 34. *If* Duke, Armstrong and Milani scored no points in the last two and Kavanagh won them both he'd have 31. Duke travelled to Monza in a position anything but impregnable. The mathematics altered immediately. Norton stayed away from the lion's den altogether, taking Kavanagh's chance with them. Nor did AJS go, something which *Motor Cycling* reported was 'none too well received by the Italian Press or Public.'

The riders practised for three 'swelteringly hot' days before the meeting. After the practice, race eve, Gilera took Duke's bike back to the factory at Arcore not far from Monza, and in Duke's words a 'major fault was found to be developing' which forced Gilera to build a new engine overnight.

Giuseppe Gilera supervized in person the running of this engine on the test bed during the early hours of the morning and, when fitted, they summoned Duke from his hotel to try it. He did that on the road in front of the factory. Early risers glimpsed the master at work in the most unlikely surroundings. Duke was and is a very British figure, and in his autobiography he writes phlegmatically that 'all was well so I returned to the hotel for breakfast.'

All would not be well for long. *Motor Cycling* reported that . . .

There has been the nearest thing to a riders' strike, settled only at the eleventh hour, over the matter of whether foreign (British) riders employed by Italian factories should be paid starting money by the promoters. The privateers, not directly involved, lent their support to the factory men.

Duke carries clear memories of it, and with reason. 'Virtually all the private riders signed a petition.' The gesture of solidarity was appreciated but would come back to haunt Duke two years later, thrust him deep into a moral dilemma and cost him a World Championship. The events before the Nations Grand Prix on 6 September 1953 cast a shadow so long that even today Duke ruminates on the magnitude of them.

The warm-up for the race completed, Armstrong, Pagani and Duke moved to the pits to have plugs changed. Monza was, and is, emotion driven and the emotion sometimes reached to the man with the flag. Many are the legends of chaotic starts to car races when the competitors weren't exactly ready (Graham Hill insisted you always kept your eye on the starter's flag because you never really knew when it would fall).

While Armstrong, Pagani and Duke were in the pits . . . *Motor Cycling* reported:

At the moment all the excitement is engendered by the enormous amount of hissing and whistling directed at the flag marshal, who set the race in motion without waiting for Armstrong or Pagani to complete their plug changes.

The reporter didn't mention Duke – also left behind – but his change happened to be further advanced and he slotted into the mid-field as the riders passed. Bruno Francisci (MV) led from Cecil Sandford (also MV) but, as *Motor Cycling* said, 'a race like this takes a lap or two to sort itself out.' Thirty two laps and 125.2 miles (201.4 km) stretches a long way. However . . .

Soon Geoff Duke moves into his accustomed first place and by the end of lap five it is Duke, tailed by Dale, who leads the race with Sandford on the rival MV a good third. Then come Liberati, Anderson on the Guzzi, Giani, Pierre Monneret, Francisci – and Reg Armstrong, already among the leaders despite his wretched luck at the start. By quarter distance Duke and Dale are almost neck-and-neck out in front with Sandford still a close third and Anderson fourth.

Of Dale, Peter Carrick writes in *Great Motor-Cycle Riders* that his 'record is far less impressive (than Bill Lomas) though he was constantly in demand by the Italian factories in the 1950s to ride their exciting machines. In 1949, as a member of Guzzi's four man squad on the Isle of Man, he might well have won the Lightweight 250cc but on the last lap, while in the lead, his engine failed. After four years with Guzzi he moved to Gilera in 1953, riding their exotic four-cylinder machines alongside Geoff Duke and Reg Armstrong.'

This was the man who now, as low cloud hovered over the circuit and a cooling breeze caressed the crowd, challenged Duke in the Nations Grand Prix. He could not sustain the challenge. Few could. Crossing the line to complete lap 14 Duke had flowed to a 10 second lead over Dale and almost 30 over Sandford. While Sandford, Liberati, Monneret and

Armstrong struggled and duelled so far back, Duke flowed on, flowed away, alone at the front.

He beat Dale by more than 40 seconds.

Postscripts
On the same page of *Motor Cycling* as the 500cc report there's an item headed *East Anglian Racing – Airfield Meeting at Snetterton*. If this is not the most riveting headline ever written, never mind. Under it is this paragraph:

Having established, with J. Surtees, a record lap speed in the first heat of the Senior 500cc event, it was unfortunate that R. McIntyre was unable to start in the final, owing to mechanical troubles.

Surtees we've already met in a postscript and, like R. McIntyre, we'll be meeting him again. But now in September 1953 we'll have to content ourselves with imagining the two of them flogging round the old American bomber base in deepest Norfolk in a meeting with the astonishing name of the Open-to-Eastern Centre ACU.

Les Graham remains lamented. His son Stuart says 'reading some of the things that Damon Hill is now having to contend with I can very much relate to the same thing. I cannot, however, remember an awful lot because I was 10 or 11 when dad was killed. Up to then it had been like any childhood. He was daddy who was away a lot racing, came back, and whenever he appeared again the first question would be *have you brought me anything?* I've been told he was a quiet man, but it's difficult at that age to judge your parents.'

In 1953 Umberto Masetti took part in the inauguration of the Imola circuit, bike people and car people. 'I was a good friend of Enzo Ferrari and he'd heard of my exploits: for example an uphill mountain challenge at Parma with a car against a bike and for the first time a bike won. At Imola, Enzo asked if I wanted to do two laps – Ascari and Luigi Villoresi (both Ferrari Formula 1 drivers) were there, too. I drove a Ferrari 250, went out and did more than two laps, came in to the pits, went out again and set the same times as they had done. Enzo asked me to go to Modena (the Ferrari factory and test circuit) and try a Formula 1 car.

'I covered 100 laps and beat the record set by Froilan Gonzalez (an Argentine who'd been with Ferrari in 1951). However, at the end I was destroyed because on a bike we wore overalls, but in the car clothes under the overalls, and it was terribly hot!

'I drove a Ferrari in the Tour of Sicily but in the first part of it, Palermo to Trapani, I went off, broke the radiator and stopped. Enzo was angry. He couldn't bear his cars being damaged. And in the end I came to understand that I preferred to race on bikes. I never somehow appreciated wheels being completely covered by mudguards, as they were on sports cars and road cars . . .'

1954

A cradle at Bethlehem

Swiss Grand Prix, Berne

TWO WORLDS MET. From one came Duke, Ray Amm (described as a wild Rhodesian racer), Armstrong, Fergus Anderson, Kavanagh, Bob McIntyre and Eric Oliver the sidecar specialist; from the other, Juan-Manuel Fangio, Moss, Gonzalez and Mike Hawthorn. A third world existed nearby, itself trading in speed but of strictly human velocity – Roger Bannister and Vladimir Kuts. In August 1954 the normally placid city of Berne became a sporting epi-centre, the bike riders sharing the 4.52 mile (7.27 km) Bremgarten circuit with the Formula 1 cars (not simultaneously). Nearby, the European Athletics Championships unfolded. *Autosport*'s Gregor Grant reported:

Never has the picturesque city seen such tremendous crowds. Every available bit of accommodation was taken up weeks ago and, I am sorry to say, prices in many places soared to remarkable heights.

Another echo of the times: worth mentioning that hoteliers might capitalize on shortage. Duke, only second in the TT – a confused race run in bad weather and stopped after four laps – seized the mid-season, ticking off wins in Belgium, Holland and West Germany. The ratchet: five best finishes from the eight rounds. Duke had 30 points, Amm 14, Kavanagh 9. Duke could take the Championship at Berne. A wet weekend stirred Grant to comment:

Sunday dawned and it was still raining. Even the stolid Swiss are inclined to put credence into the theory that atom bombs have upset the world's weather. However, it cleared up later on. Having to be up at the circuit early turned out to be a good thing. We witnessed two excellent motorcycle races, the 350cc and the 500cc. Ken Kavanagh led the last-named till he blew up. A most exciting race dominated almost entirely by the skilful British riders.

Just before the start of the [car] *Grand Prix, Mercedes Benz supplied some comic relief. Artur Kesser, their PRO, presented several drivers with slices of cheese cut from a huge 100 kilograms affair. Stirling Moss carried off his muttering that we would be able to keep all the mice in England in luxury for weeks!*

The two engine-driven worlds came as near to joining as they ever would. *Motor Cycling* reported that . . .

In an absolute Bedlam, with the exhaust notes of single, twin and four-cylinder motorcycles mingling with that of the Grand Prix cars now coming into the paddock in readiness for the race to follow, warming up for the 500cc event takes place. There has been no rain for some time and the roads are drying as machines are brought to the grid.

Drying, yes, but not dry, and this on a road circuit of many perils. A great rider reveals himself in many ways, just as a great driver does, but mastery of conditions remains elusive if they are changing during a race; then you see the control, the thought-processes, the calculations and tactics at work. Invariably the great can out-think as well as out-perform any rivals.

The Swiss (bike) Grand Prix stretched 28 laps, 126.58 miles (203.7 km) and the Bedlam is still rising and rising – Gileras, Nortons, and AJSs here, Maseratis, Mercedes and Ferraris there.

Geoff Duke wore dark leathers, baggy at the knees. He had a serious sort of face, youthful, and a haircut of the day, a parting down one side like a slicing and it cut across the crown of the head; the hair nipped short and neat across the nape of the neck. He had natural proportions, the body in perfect harmony; not too tall, not too short, strong and yet not stocky.

He moulded onto a bike. Each photograph and the meagre footage of him in motion all demonstrate this. There's a balance you can't miss, the more because photographers tended to congregate at corners to get the bikes held at angles. He always seems at ease in these corners.

At the flag Anderson and Kavanagh (both Guzzis) moved marginally clear, with Duke, Armstrong and Frenchman Pierre Monneret (all Gileras) behind and McIntyre (Norton) holding on. Duke made an early thrust to take the lead from Anderson but, as *Motor Cycling* reported:

The Guzzis really get into their phenomenal stride and the lap is completed with Kavanagh right out in front, Anderson running a good second and then Amm, Duke, Armstrong and Coleman all in close company. The rain has come to nothing and there is a slight breeze drying the road.

Duke remembers that second lap, remembers the drying. He knew how to wait. Kavanagh completed lap 2 in 2 minutes 56 seconds, an average of over 90 mph (144 kph), with Amm second, and Duke, Coleman and Armstrong 'hard on his heels'. McIntyre went into the pits on lap 3 for a plug change which took a long time. A lap later he dropped out altogether. Bob Mac from Scotstoun, Glasgow was in his first season on the Continent and it disagreed with him. He felt isolated among these great riders, felt literally queasy so far from home.

Meanwhile, *Motor Cycling* reported that . . .

Quarter distance sees Kavanagh still in the lead with Amm second some ten seconds behind, followed again at a ten second interval by Duke. Armstrong has just taken fourth place from Coleman. Then comes Brett and Farrant, and Simpson keeping his Matchless ahead of Monneret's Gilera.

Duke knew how to wait. Here and there the circuit dried and he began to use 'more and more' power. *Motor Cycling* reported that . . .

This is the race of the year! At the end of 10 laps Amm is still only 15 seconds behind Kavanagh, and Duke – who has put in fastest lap so far in 2 minutes 52.9 seconds (94.13 mph/151.4 kph) is only three seconds behind Amm. Armstrong is within striking distance of all three while Brett, who has just passed Coleman, has Armstrong in sight.

On lap 11 Kavanagh's bike slowed – water in the carburettor. Amm led, Duke 50 yards behind. Duke knew how to wait. *Motor Cycling* reported that . . .

Another lap, and it is still Amm out in front, and Brett is within a few yards of Armstrong. So it goes on – Gilera chasing Norton, Norton chasing Gilera – for another two laps. For three laps. And four. The sun has broken through the clouds and the circuit is almost dry in the pit area, although it will remain wet in the wooded part of the course. It is Amm who still makes the pace, having clipped one second off Duke's best time. Both have already lapped Monneret and there are now only 13 riders left in the race.

Amm increased the pace and stretched the lead; Duke responded by increasing his pace, reducing the lead – stretch-contract, stretch-contract as they moved past the pits and on to the right-left semi-kink, the hard right at Eicholz, the kinks past the grandstand up towards Eymatt Corner, a curve-right and another right. Now past twin grandstands flanking the circuit and facing each other; to the right which flowed so urgently to Glasbrunnen where the track wiggled in front of three grandstands; the right-angle right at Forsthaus corner, and the right-curve immediately before the pits called Bethlehem; 4.52 miles in two and a half minutes, give or take a bit. The trees dripped but still the circuit dried.

Duke had waited.

It was nearly time; time to make a move, time to make *the* move. He covered the 4.52 miles in 2 minutes 48.1 seconds (96.82 mph/155.8 kph) on lap 21 and drew up to within 10 yards, feeding more and more power into the Gilera. Amm clung in front; clung until the 21st lap.

Duke remembers drawing up to 'within a few lengths of Amm's Norton. There I chose to stay, weighing up the situation and content to wait for the roads to dry more.' *Motor Cycling* reported:

Then Duke comes up alongside as they sweep through the full-bore curve in front of the grandstand and at last takes the lead as the pair go into the Bethlehem

Corner. That lap ends with Duke still in front. So does the next, and there are only two more to the end of the race. The last lap starts with Duke a good 50 yards in front and it concludes – in a burst of cheering – with exactly the same interval separating the pair who have fought so hard for the lead.

Duke 1 hour 21 minutes 4.6 seconds; Amm 1 hour 21 minutes 8.3 seconds.

Postscripts

Fangio won the Formula 1 car race in his mighty Mercedes-Benz, covering 66 laps in 3 hours 0 minutes and 34.5 seconds, an average speed of 99.20 mph (159.6 kph). Duke averaged 93.68 (150.7 kph). On the evening of 22 August 1954 Duke had won his third World Championship, Fangio his second.

Both had more to give, more to take. That's not an unfair way of putting it, particularly because in 1954 riders and drivers took so little except satisfaction. Nigel Mansell, I'll wager, earned more from each race of 1992 than Duke or Fangio from a lifetime, even allowing for inflation. Anyway, it's water under a bridge, water on a drying track.

Roger Bannister – a tall, angular man, bony knees and elbows, an entirely different balance from Duke (and Fangio) – came to Berne and that third world in August 1954 vastly famous. Three months before, at Iffley Road, Oxford he'd run the first four-minute-mile (3 minutes 59.4 seconds). Duke on the Gilera would have done the mile in something over 30 seconds, Fangio slightly quicker, and yes, yes, I know the comparison is unfair. Bannister won the 1500 metres at the European Athletics Championships, Berne, in 3 minutes 43.8 seconds. How fast was that? Does it matter? Not really, not with only foot power.

Masetti did contest the 1954 season on a Gilera, finishing joint tenth in the Championship table with six points. 'Then I moved from Gilera to MV Agusta. I think Commendatore Gilera suffered over this but me, too, I suffered. I loved the Gilera family as I loved my own. When Ferrucci died (in 1956 at the age of 26) it was one of the most terrible moments of my life. Gilera were opening a factory in Argentina and he contracted malaria. His death struck me in the same way as that of my parents . . . as that of Enzo Ferrari's son Dino.'

1955

Duke – striking out

Ulster Grand Prix, Dundrod

CLOUD HUNG OVER the Van Drenthe circuit masking a hot July sun, the sun which had burnished the quiet flatlands of Holland for two days. Among the immense crowd for the Dutch Grand Prix a pleasant sense of anticipation stirred. The Van Drenthe had been used for racing since 1925, but its 10.2 miles (18 km) – part of it over cobblestones, and the whole noted for being slippery – needed restructuring. An essentially new circuit of 4.79 miles (7.70 km) had been constructed sharing little with the old: the name Van Drenthe carried over and the start-finish laid at almost the same place.

Duke had a relatively straightforward run to here, although the season began in sadness when Amm, who'd joined MV, crashed in a 350 race – his first for them – at Imola at Easter, killing himself.

Duke's team-mate at Gilera, Armstrong, won the first round, the Spanish at Barcelona, Duke won the French at Reims, the TT and the West German at the Nürburgring. (A young man from Surrey rode a semi-works BMW in this race, the first time he'd seen The Ring. 'Duke won, Zeller second and I was up to third at one stage but my carburettor kept on flooding and finally it fell off.' The speaker: Surtees, who'd be tempted to sign for BMW but didn't.)

Duke broke down during the Belgian at Spa, timing-gear. The ratchet; five best finishes from eight rounds. Duke led with 23 points from Armstrong's 18, the rest nowhere. As the cloud hung over Assen, Duke could not lock up the Championship but make it extremely difficult for Armstrong to take it from him.

In the background, hidden from the crowd, great anger rose. The private entrants, particularly those in the 350 race, felt extremely unhappy about the amount of start money, so unhappy they prepared to do something about it. Duke insists that the organizers of the meeting, the K.N.M.V, knew how the privateers felt but chose to ignore it. The organizers insisted they knew nothing, and were caught by surprise.

The 250 race which opened the programme also opened controversy. Lomas (MV) led, but on lap 13 of 17 pointed to his fuel tank as he passed the pits, indicating he'd come in next lap. Contemporary accounts say Lomas, a dogger rider, spent nine seconds in a 'frantic' pit stop for more fuel, rejoined and within a lap and a half regained the lead. He crossed the line to win in front of a small, neat Swiss, Luigi Taveri (also MV). This result was protested on the grounds that Lomas hadn't switched his engine off during the pit stop. *Motor Cycling* phrased this cryptically:

Later it is announced that Lomas's time was 1 hour 4 min. 21.2 sec, a speed of 75.88 mph (122.1 kph) which, though faster than the winner's, still does not alter the ruling that he is the second man home.

By now the privateers, facing the 350 race, told the organizers they would complete a symbolic lap and peel off into the puts en masse, reducing the race to a farce. Duke believes the organizers judged the privateers were 'bluffing'. *Motor Cycling* reported:

On goes the light (a traffic-lamp start is used here) and into the lead goes Baltisberger on his over-bored NSU 'Sportmax' with Hobl in close company and Lomas on his heels. They complete one lap, with Hobl narrowly leading Lomas. Then come Lorenzetti (Guzzi), Kavanagh, Karl Hofmann (DKW) and a horde of private runners . . . but this is fantastic. Rider after rider pulls into the pits led by Jack Ahearn on his AJS. The private entrants are retiring. One after another they come in – Britons, Commonwealth and European alike (save for the few Dutchmen) – doff their helmets and retire! Finally only 13 men carry on out of an original three dozen!

The farce had to be played out, the 'race' run. By lap 3 Kavanagh led from Lomas but 'nobody seems to have much heart in it. Lomas is even sitting up.'

After the 350s, Ubbiali won the 125 and Willi Faust the sidecars. In the background Assen boiled. The privateers announced they'd repeat the 350 farce in the 500. One contemporary account says that . . .

. . . feelings ran high in the paddock and in the Committee there is a sullen atmosphere entirely foreign to our sport. There were rumours of private owners being refused fuel; of threats of FIM action.

Another account talks of 'angry demonstrations by the huge crowd.'

Duke, gazing back on it, judges: 'I wouldn't say it got ugly, but certainly a great buzz went round the crowd because they didn't really know anything except what they'd seen in the 350 race. If the 500 hadn't gone on I think there would have been trouble – 200,000 people and I'm sure some had been drinking beer.'

The haunting with the long shadow had come. Duke and Armstrong felt a strong obligation to support the privateers. 'The fact that two years earlier at Monza the privateers virtually all signed a petition supporting us made it very difficult for me. This was the main reason why I supported them now. Personally I've always been against strikes of any kind, I just don't believe in them, but what does one do in a situation like that?'

Duke remembers vividly a meeting between the K.N.M.V. and riders' representatives, and the compromise hammered out: an offer of £15 increased to £20 a race. Duke felt this 'unreasonable' if only because the privateers who'd covered the single lap in the 350 would now receive £20 for that.

At the start of the race Duke pushed but the Gilera wouldn't fire – Armstrong leading, he lay eighth. Reaching the back of the circuit he'd already overtaken four riders, and completing lap 1 lay second. Crossing the line a lap later he'd caught Armstrong, tracked him and taken him. He led decisively by lap 6, and across the remainder of the race lapped every rider up to fifth, beating Armstrong by 35 seconds. Duke 32 points, Armstrong 24, Masetti 11. If only it had been that simple . . .

Duke subsequently wrote apologizing for the near-strike to the secretary of the K.N.M.V. but, ominously, no reply came.

In theory, Armstrong could still win the Championship. Two rounds remained, Ulster and the Nations at Monza. Duke's 32 came from only four finishes, as did Armstrong's 24, but *if* Duke didn't finish the last two and Armstrong won he'd have 40, giving a counting total of 36. Then . . . Gilera decided that because they couldn't get what they considered proper start money for the Ulster they wouldn't go. It gave Duke the Championship. What did Armstrong make of that? We'll never know. Of him, Peter Carrick has written . . .

During the eight years he raced, the Dublin-born Armstrong had contracts with AJS, Norton, Gilera and NSU. Always neat and coolly calculating, there was nothing spectacular about Armstrong's style. His climb to top-class racing was steady and logical, and he always gave the impression of being happiest when riding as number two to a more obvious front man.

Like Geoff Duke, in fact.

Lomas (Moto Guzzi) won the Ulster from a rider called John Hartle in front of 100,000 people. *Ireland's Saturday Night* reported:

In a classic example of high-speed riding Lomas achieved the highest speed for a lap ever recorded on the course – 94.34 mph (151.8 kph), returning a lap of 4 mins 43 secs. The previous 'absolute' record was held by Giuseppe Farina in an Alfa Romeo racing car with 94 mph.

The Ulster was now at Dundrod, and while not strictly relevant to this chapter it will be subsequently. Jimmy Walker says: 'The Ulster Motor Cycle Club ran the event, but in 1952 the Northern Ireland government decided "we have had enough of this nonsense, you're closing too many roads. What we'll do is give you a course in the middle of nowhere and you can race to your heart's content." And that's what they gave them: Dundrod, no traffic on it whatsoever. Bear in mind that the Clady course had become the main route to Belfast Airport at Nutt's Corner, air traffic was building up and closing those roads became extremely inconvenient.

'So it was, and is, enshrined in an Act of Parliament that the Dundrod course remains there as long as they want it to be. That first race at Dundrod nobody knew where it was! There's a village called Dundrod and everybody went there thinking that's where it must be – nowhere near. The circuit was an Irishman's mile away, you know.'

No Duke and no Armstrong, perhaps, but Surtees contested the 350 on a Norton, the 250 on an NSU (which he won – his first Championship victory – and broke both the race and lap records). Thereby hangs one of Walker's tales. 'Surtees came down to scrutineering in the middle of Belfast as all the riders did. A friend of mine, a complete Surtees fan, went up and said "hello John" although he'd never spoken to him before. Surtees looked at him quizzically. Then as Surtees drove away my friend got in the passenger seat and I got in the back. My friend knew all about Surtees' career and started asking him some hard questions about races Surtees hadn't won, and the conversation became very animated! That was the atmosphere surrounding the Ulster.

'It was the biggest annual sporting event in Ireland. For example in 1955 Great Britain were playing a football match against Europe to mark the 75th anniversary of the Irish FA's founding. Billy McMaster, secretary of the Ulster Motor Cycle Club, was in the Central Hotel, Belfast – where the annual press conference was always held – and McMaster asked Fergus Anderson who all these people, football fans with scarves come for the match, were. McMaster went up to one and said "do you know who this is" and the fan replied "yes of course" and asked Fergus for his autograph.'

Postscripts
Ireland's Saturday Night reported:

Mike Hawthorn, motor racing star, who arrived in Belfast yesterday (Friday) was not at the Grand Prix. He was visiting in hospital his friend Julian Crossley, injured in the 350cc class on Thursday. World motor cycling ace Geoff Duke sat in the grandstand.

Masetti won the Nations from Armstrong and Duke, the formalities of a season completed. Duke 36, Armstrong 30, Masetti 19.

Some six weeks later the C.S.I (Commission Sportive of the FIM) met in London and announced that Duke and Armstrong were suspended for six months from 1 January 1956. Three Italians – Giuseppe Colnago, Masetti and Milani – got four months. The K.N.M.V. had struck back. 'My memory's a bit vague about whether I went in at the meeting,' Duke says. 'Some riders did, but the big point is that it was already a foregone conclusion. It didn't matter what anybody said and this influenced me I'm sure about going in and saying my piece. It would have been a complete waste of time.' An irony. Proposals were put forward to regulate starting money and they became mandatory.

Motorcycle News (then only two words, not three, and in their very first issue) covered Duke's suspension all over the front page. They restated the events of Assen and said:

Before the 500cc race commenced, the organizers of the meeting agreed to pay more money, and that race took place without any similar bout of first-lap retirements. To be fair, some of the riders concerned have agreed that there was planned strike action. Nor do Geoff Duke and Reg Armstrong deny that they showed sympathy for the 'independents' who wanted more money.

When one considers that the appearance payment at Assen is less than half made by the impecunious promoters of some of the smaller French races, while the paying customers for the Dutch 'classic' total well over the 100,000 mark (five or six times the attendance at a typical French town-circuit promotion) then one must have some sympathy for the strike. It was, however, an ill-judged move, and an infringement of the agreement (however hard its terms may have been) arrived at between each rider and the organizers when entering. Upon reflection, most of those involved would probably have admitted this, and, without prejudice to their claim that the starting money was totally inadequate, would have been prepared to make an apology.

The organizers, however (whose handling of the Lomas incident at the same meeting has scarcely covered them with glory) were determined to have their vengeance. Before any sort of FIM enquiry had been held they issued a manifesto to the Press giving their version of what happened and calling for severe punishments. All riders concerned have been adjudged guilty of 'conduct prejudicial to the sport of motorcycling' and the penalties imposed – against which it would appear there is no appeal – are savage. They deprive many of the men not only of their present means of livelihood but also of the most obvious alternatives, such as car racing. Owing to an agreement with other international bodies, their suspension will prevent them from taking part in any competitive events in the car, flying or motor boat world.

As savage as that.

In purely motor bike terms Duke would miss the TT on the Isle of Man and Assen, leaving only four Championship rounds. He'd already lost the 1956 Championship in London on 24 November 1955. The ratchet had already tightened.

There's a Stop Press item on that front page, in a little traditional box. 'Yesterday John Surtees left for Italy to consult with the MV Agusta factory about racing plans for next year.'

Geoff Duke never did win the World 500cc Championship again.

1956

Surtees – bowled over

West German Grand Prix, Solitude

THAT TUESDAY AT Headingley, Leeds, a tall, earthy Yorkshireman called Jim Laker ran a few, tight, economical steps and bowled to a rugged Australian, Ken Mackay. The ball, a full length, hit Mackay's middle stump. England had won the Third Test by an innings and 42 runs to level the Ashes cricket series.

That same day – 17 July – riders began to gather at Solitude, the tree-lined circuit near Stuttgart, although qualifying for the West German Grand Prix didn't begin until the Thursday. News from Leeds came through – the fate of the England cricket team a much more urgent topic of national concern than now – and *Motorcycle News* reported that . . .

Someone found a piece of wood and in no time at all we were having an impromptu game of cricket. The ball was an old milk tin. Soon an Aussie versus England spirit crept in and we decided to stage a full-blown match the following day. Pip Harris borrowed a scythe and, looking for all the world like a living replica of the famous weather vane at Lord's set about reducing the lush grass of the paddock to a suitable length. Cyril Smith and Bob Mitchell fabricated two excellent bats, complete with taped handles, from an old board whilst Eric Bliss cut six stumps from a nearby hedge.

John Surtees and Bill Hall, who were both going into town, were commissioned to purchase a ball apiece. We were taking no chances on such an important match being held up through a lost ball. When the pitch was 'mown', the stumps in position and the marking out done (with racing number paint!) we roped off the playing area and it looked fit for any match. England won the toss and after herding numerous puzzled Germans behind the boundary rope, batted first.

England made 62, Australia 32, and in Australia's second innings 'Surtees struck a blow for us when he took a wicket with the first ball and another wicket two balls later. The result was a win for England, numerous stiff bowling muscles and many mystified Germans.'

Surtees would never be able to bowl another ball.

Zeller, who didn't see the match, had been a long time reaching here. 'I was only interested in motor cycles. My brother had a very good friend who rode a BMW 500 in the mountains and on dirt tracks. When I was four or five the friend came with this BMW to our home, I saw the bike and from that moment I never imagined driving a car, I only thought about motor cycles. I first raced at Salzburg in 1947 and joined the BMW factory team in 1950, riding in the German Championships.' BMW flirted briefly with the World Championship in 1952, tried again – this time with Zeller – in 1955. Thus far into 1956 he'd been unable to hold Surtees, and no surprise about that.

The sequel to *Motorcycle News*'s Stop Press had been that Count Domenico Agusta, a busy man, summoned Surtees and stated almost bluntly he wanted him for MV. As Surtees sat, a woman in black entered and gazed at him, spoke briefly to Domenico and left. Surtees, naturally curious, asked what this was about and they informed him Domenico's mother had been surveying whether she 'liked the look' of Surtees, and whether he was 'suitable to be allowed into the Agusta family'.

He was.

'I'd nearly become Walter's team-mate,' Surtees says, 'after I rode the BMW at the Nürburgring in 1955. I had quite a feeling for BMW dating back to pictures of their Compressor bike winning the 1939 TT with George Meier. I thought it a beautiful bike. I'd been going about as quick as Walter at The Ring in 1955 and they said "ah, you must ride for us" but – a typical Teutonic-cum-English thing – they hesitated and delayed.

'My first option had been to stay with Norton. I'd a small amount of sponsorship from a newspaper which would just about pay for the mechanics. I offered that if Norton provided a bike I'd meet the expenses. They turned that down on the basis that if I won the World Championship I might earn more than a director of the company! I said goodbye. Geoff Duke had Gilera sewn up, no chance of going there. I tested the MV and thought: right. It represented the only ride available with a chance of the Championship.'

The season began at the TT in early June, but Zeller flew to the Isle of Man in March 1956 to familiarize himself. 'I rode a road BMW there for four weeks, every day going round the course for ten laps amongst normal traffic.' Surtees won the TT, with Zeller fourth. Surtees won Assen from Zeller's second. 'Against Surtees and MV,' Zeller says, 'we had only one problem – we were not fast enough! Not enough horsepower! In every race the same: the MVs and Gileras faster and they had the leading riders, Surtees and Duke and Bandirola and Masetti, and so on. Sometimes I could go faster than them, maybe because I was better (chuckle).'

Duke returned for the Belgian Grand Prix at Spa after his suspension and, based on practice times, Surtees judged Duke and the Gilera would be 'difficult to hold'. Surtees, moreover, had not ridden Spa before, something which Duke judged gave *him* an advantage. Duke tracked

Surtees for four laps and on a 'blind' left hand corner (which Duke knew intimately) closed, and went past on the exit. Surtees could not stay with him, but Duke broke down on the last lap, a piston disintegrating. Surtees won, Zeller second.

The ratchet: four best finishes from the six rounds. Surtees had a maximum score, 24 points, Zeller 15, and three rounds remain: the West German at Solitude, the Ulster at Dundrod and the Nations at Monza. *If* Surtees won Solitude he became Champion regardless.

Surtees remembers the circuit had been resurfaced, but sand lay 'at its edges'. In the 350 race he and Lomas duelled and it reached a great intensity, Surtees riding '110 per cent' to catch Lomas.

'I'd been in with a chance of the 350 Championship,' Surtees says, 'Lomas my main competitor. We had quite a dice in the race. I relied on catching him through the corners before the start because up the hill his super-lightweight Guzzi went a bit quicker, then on the flat downhill section I'd try to catch up again. Bill had to gain his advantage where he could and I had to gain mine where I could. It got fiercer and fiercer and I lost the front end. There are a number of theories about why, but I think it happened because we were going quicker and quicker and sand or something was on the road.

'There were boulders around and a little First-Aid post on the bank behind one of them. You'd be going up towards the ton at that point, I slithered across the road and bang, hit the boulder and it broke my arm. I was taken to hospital in Stuttgart and they decided to pin the arm.'

From nowhere a chance, a real chance, opened for Zeller to take the 500 Championship.

'Solitude was a very, very crazy and bad thing,' Zeller says. 'Surtees fell off in the 350 and I only had Duke on the Gilera and Bill Lomas on the eight-cylinder Guzzi to really worry about. Solitude was up the hills and down with one long straight of about two kilometres then right-left, right-left through a wood – boom, boom, boom. On the first lap I was behind Masetti (on an MV, of course) at the beginning of the straight and I thought *oh very fine, fantastic. I can slipstream him.* Masetti took me with him all along the straight.

'Normally in practice I'd get 10,000 revs. In Masetti's slipstream I reached about 11,500 – that was the difference between the BMW and four-cylinder machines, and again I thought *fantastic*. Then in the right-left, right-left I passed him and I was away. In front I had Duke and Lomas. Crossing the line to complete lap 1 they must have been 300, 400 metres ahead, but I was really fast and at the end of lap 2 the gap had come down to 200 metres. *Very fine,* I thought, *everything is going well.* On the straight on lap 3 – an explosion in my engine, piston broken in my right cylinder. I was very, very mad. With my left cylinder I rode back to the pits – whaang, whump, whaang, whump. Terrible.

'What did I see in the other pits? Bill and Geoff, both with broken engines. If I hadn't slip-streamed Masetti and over-strained the engine I could have *slept* on the bike and won. I would have been World Champion. My mechanics were in tears.'

Surtees remained in hospital in Stuttgart when Zeller went to the Ulster Grand Prix three weeks later. Zeller could still take the Championship but couldn't escape the ratchet: he *had* to be at least second in Ulster. *If* he finished there he'd have 21 points and if he won the final race, the Nations at Monza, he'd have 27. Dropping his lowest, the 3 from the Isle of Man, he'd total 26.

Jimmy Walker describes Dundrod as a 'very bumpy, hard circuit, there weren't the run-offs. And you were talking about 100,000 people there, which is a lot. Bear in mind that most of it was free because you couldn't charge admission to fields. The starting point, called the Flying Kilometre, was the fastest part of the course. Then the riders went down through a series of right- and left-handers, very quick, to a junction at Levenstown – a bridge spanning a river and they bounced over it – went down another fast section to Deer's leap, a one-in-four descent to Cochrane's Town, a sweeping bend, again very fast.

'They swung right to Ireland's Corner, a right-hander and interesting because a man owned a bungalow there and he had a "toy" windmill in the garden which fluttered round all day, and some riders took that to find their line. From there to a crossroads, straight over, through sweeping bends to a 70 degree left-hander down to a proper hairpin which turned back on itself. Quite a lot used to fall off. The riders soared through the most popoular part, Quarry Bends, left-right, left-right, left-right and if you watched the boys going through there it would take the light out of your eyes. That was a super place. Then a right-hand sweeping into the start-finish and they roared past the stands, and off they went again.

'People forget that in the early days no circuit commentary existed. The BBC covered it and that was the only way to find out. Graham Walker (father of Murray) did all the World Championship commentaries. You'd take radios but in those days they weren't transistors, they were big ones with handles on them like portable typewriters. Everybody gathered round that radio, and I remember doing it because otherwise you hadn't a clue what was happening when the bikes had gone by. You'd lie in the grass and hear Graham Walker saying "now, after such and such a number of laps the leader in the 500cc class is Hartle with Duke behind him."'

Zeller flew to Ulster in a private plane, the mechanics and bike travelling by road. Showery weather and *Motor Cycling* reported . . .

Altogether 34 riders come to the grid. Among them is Geoffrey Duke and probably the bulk of the crowd has come to see him and his Gilera. But conceivably a win is of less value to Duke than it would be to his team-mate H. R. Armstrong who at least had eight points towards the Championship against the 15 of the German, W. Zeller (BMW). He is also a competitor here today. But further speculation is interrupted by the starting siren and now a surge of sound as riders hare off to start a windy 205 mile (330 km) jaunt on which, if earlier form is maintained, more records are due to go sky-high.

The first seven laps – roughly a quarter of the race – is the scrapping phase. At the start John Hartle and Jack Brett make a Norton bloc to keep back Duke; Murphy follows, with Zeller and Brown close together. Duke then takes the lead – and Hartle reclaims it; Lomas passes both Brown and Zeller and then tours in to retire with carburettor trouble. Now it is Hartle again in front, and he puts in a terrific lap before falling back to be passed by Brett on lap 7. Duke, as if wearying of the scrap going on so near him, rockets up to a 4 minutes 22.6 seconds lap-time, and bang goes the 500cc record at 94.47 mph! (152.0 kph).

Zeller went soon after. 'I had great problems with my bike, and riding for the first time there was difficult in the wet. It wouldn't have been so difficult in the dry. I couldn't win, but maybe I could get second, but even that became impossible. The BMW was very difficult in the rain and I had clutch problems, I had to stop. That was the finish of the Championship.'

On lap 14 Duke crashed, hurting but not breaking his shoulder. 'Duke never won at Dundrod,' Jimmy Walker says, 'and he fell at Levenstown Bridge in '56 when he had such a lead he could have got off and pushed the bike home. He lost concentration apparently. Duke was superb at Clady, a miniature Isle of Man course where Duke was equally superb. Dundrod was shorter, faster and it took more knowing; so many kinks and bends in it. You really did have to be a short-circuit type of rider. Surtees was good there . . .'

But not of course on 11 August 1956. That day he was being good in hospital in Stuttgart. 'I waited to hear,' Surtees says. 'I relied on someone ringing through – no commentary or anything else to listen to, no television coverage in those days. I think my dad picked up the news, rang and told me. I stayed in hospital five weeks and my mother came over and drove me home.

'My right arm never quite straightened, the muscles never really got back to the point where I could throw again. I could use it very well, but trying to throw would give me very considerable pain. Cricket? I'd have to bowl underarm.'

Postscripts

'We stayed the night in a little hotel in Belfast,' Zeller says. 'People said *ah yes, German riders, come on with us*. They took us to a festival inside the hotel and we did special dances which we had to learn. It was very funny and very nice. You see, the whole atmosphere in the sport was that. I had good relationships with most of the riders. For instance, I got on extremely well with John Surtees. He's still a really good friend. OK, he had the fastest bike but he's one of the best riders of all and I just couldn't beat him. Geoff Duke the same. If I'd been on an MV then (chuckle) . . .

'You could see something, however, when Geoff got on the BMW racing bike after I retired. He couldn't ride it. Impossible. Terrible. He was the best on a Gilera but not on the BMW, it was too difficult for him. You needed much power in the arms, you had to be strong to ride it. Libero Liberati? I didn't have much contact with him, I don't know why. No reason, you know, no reason. I can't say what sort of a man he was.'

In the Nations Grand Prix at Monza a month after Ulster, a race academic to the Championship, the team-mates Duke and Liberati fought out the lead, the only time Duke had a real 'dice' with Liberati. 'Liberati had a slightly faster bike and he flew. He led for quite a bit of the way but then decided his safest plan was to let me get in front so that he could dictate the race on the last lap. I realized he was gradually easing back on the straight to try to make me overtake so I eased back too, and eventually he almost shut his bike off.

'I'd no choice but to go by him. He followed me with this slightly quicker bike that he had, and was going to *do* me after the Parabolica (on the rush to the finishing line) but, although for some reason my bike wasn't handling over well, I managed to persuade Liberati that my braking point for the Parabolica was around 280 metres. I braked there absolutely consistently every lap when he was behind me so that he thought "I can take that little bit more on the last lap."'

'On that last lap I went down to 250 metres before I braked, went round the Parabolica with everything screwed on and I beat him by a machine's length. There's a lot of psychology in racing, convincing the opposition you are better than they are.'

Or, on 9 September, 1956, convincing the opposition that they were better than you when you knew they weren't.

That psychology.

1957

The breaking of Bob Mac

Nations Grand Prix, Monza

THERE HAS BEEN a disappointment. The 22 riders who wait for the starter's flag do not include one of the strongest favourites – the doctors have decided that Bob McIntrye is not fit to race again today. But the Gilera contingent still contains last year's winner, Geoff Duke, and runner-up Libero Liberati, with World Champion John Surtees to head the MV challenge.

The paragraph stands not just as understatement but as a monument to the journalism of the time. The *Motor Cycling* reporter did not evidently trouble to find out why the doctors had decided what they had; or, if he did, didn't trouble to mention it. *Motor Cycle News* fared a little better . . .

Top event of the meeting is the 500cc race, despite several non-starters. Bob McIntrye cannot come to the line – thus losing the chance of winning the world title – because of a very painful headache (a consequence of his Dutch TT crash?) which developed during the 350 race.

At Monza on 1 September 1957 the struggle of a season climaxed and anti-climaxed. McIntyre would have gone into the 500cc race a mere two points behind Liberati.

McIntyre, his father a riveter, came to bike riding by chance. 'Cars and motor cycles interested me as they do most boys,' he would remember, 'but I was not excited by race meetings. My reason for seeking a job in a garage when I left school at 14 was to learn a useful trade, not because of any passion for motors. My father had not had an easy working life; he had suffered in the years of depression when there were no jobs in the shipyards. He did not want me to follow in his footsteps.

'I found my first job in a garage at Partick, the next borough to Scotstoun. It was a fairly big garage and employed 60 or 70 people in all. I could not be apprenticed until I was 16, so for two years I repaired punctures, washed and greased cars, sold petrol and did all the odd jobs. What I did not learn was anything about motor cycles. The garage dealt

with private cars and commercial vehicles. I bought my first motor cycle
when I became 16. It was a 500cc Norton of 1931 vintage. I paid £12 for it
and that was a lot of money to me. I think my wages were just over £1 a
week at that time. I bought the bike to take me between the garage and my
home in Harefield Drive, Scotstoun. When I came home with it I
discovered quickly that my mother did not share my enthusiasm for the
idea.'

Mothers rarely do. During McIntyre's National Service he became a
dispatch rider in North Africa, took part in scrambles and trials after de-
mob and by 1954 made a modest entry into the World 500cc
Championship, scoring four points on an AJS, and five points on a Norton
in 1955.

'The year 1954 was not a very happy one. Inevitably I felt rather a new
boy. I did not even enjoy the foreign travel. On my first trip I probably ate
the wrong things: at any rate I was sick and left with lingering mistrust of
the continental food.'

In September 1956 Gilera contacted McIntyre, who knew he needed
their bikes if he was to win Grand Prix races. He signed to partner
Liberati.

Liberati won the first round of 1957, the West German at Hockenheim,
with McIntyre just 0.3 of a second behind. Surtees remembers this damp
day; remembers leading Dale's Moto Guzzi until the engine let go;
remembers Masetti, third, slowing and Dale too, spreading a clear run
home before Liberati and McIntyre.

'It was a dreadful year,' Surtees says. 'We were subject to typical
complacency. MV sat back and did a couple of modifications, but I had
nothing but piston problems. I couldn't run the full fairings because the
engines didn't like that, and the pistons used to fail.'

Two weeks later McIntyre became the first man to lap the Isle of Man at
more than 100 mph (160 kph). 'The interest was all on the part of
journalists and spectators because, as far as the riders were concerned, we
just wanted to win. I told newspapermen that if I did the first 100 mph lap
it would be because I was forced to do it to win; my aim was to win at the
slowest possible speed.'

From a standing start McIntyre averaged 99.99 mph, which broke the
record of 99.97 mph set by Duke in 1955. On his second lap he did 100.54
mph (161.79 kph) – 'stopwatches were out all round the course, I heard
later, but my eyes were for that flashing ribbon of road. Down the sharp
slope of Bray Hill on full throttle at 140 mph (224 kph) . . .'

Third lap: 100.54 mph (161.79 kph).

Fourth lap: 101.12 mph (162.73 kph).

'I knew none of this. I knew I was going fast. I had expected from the
practice times that I would beat the 100 mph lap but, as I have said, I had
no particular interest in this. What did interest me was that at the end of
the fourth lap I had caught up with Surtees on his MV.' (A staggered
start, of course, Surtees going two minutes earlier than McIntyre.)

McIntyre won, from Surtees who crossed the line two minutes 7.2 seconds behind. Surtees, typically trenchant, pays his tribute to McIntyre for a 'faultless' race although he adds that MV didn't deserve better than to finish second. Duke, recovering from a crash at Imola, missed the TT but speaks of how McIntyre went to the limit and 'I suspect, occasionally chanced his hand.'

At Assen, the third round, McIntyre led Surtees but his Gilera developed a misfire; a plug oiled. He pitted and set off after Surtees hard; too hard. 'I left the road and went into the ditch. When John took the chequered flag I was on my way to hospital.' He'd injured his neck.

The ratchet: four best finishes from the six rounds, and Liberati, McIntyre and Surtees all had 14 points. Three rounds to run, but McIntyre felt too ill to compete in the Belgian Grand Prix at Spa. Immediately before the race Liberati's Gilera wouldn't start and the team manager, Roberto Persi, decided to give him Bob Brown's bike. Duke, spectating, describes the 'episode' as 'most unpleasant. I was incensed by this unfair action and argued the point with Persi, but to no avail.'

Across a cut and thrust opening lap Liberati led, Surtees overtook him at Malmedy, but an Australian, Keith Campbell (Moto Guzzi), led at Stavelot. Crossing the line Campbell stretched his lead, Surtees signalling to his pit *I'm in trouble*. A holed piston. *Motor Cycling* reported that . . .

With one-third of the race gone Campbell is out on his own – hardly surprising because on the third lap he pushed the lap record to 118.04 mph (189.96 kph) and on the fourth to 118.57 (190.81 kph). Next time round, on the sixth lap (of 15) Liberati appears in second place and then it is Brett ahead of Surtees, who pulls in to his pit, a puff of smoke exploding from his machine as he slows down to retire. There is no holding Campbell. He screams through on the eighth lap, then, as the crowd turns to watch his meteoric progress up the hill, it rises to its feet and a groan goes up as the Guzzi stops by the roadside – out of horses!

Liberati ran smoothly to the end almost a minute in front of Brett. *Motor Cycling* wondered . . .

But has he won? As Liberati walks up, expecting to receive the victor's garland, he is greeted by an announcement from the public address that, as he had taken over Duke's! [author's!] machine without notifying the officials, the legality of his ride has been queried and the International Jury is meeting to discuss the awkward situation which has arisen. Time drags on and the crowd disperses. There is no victory ceremony and no decision is announced until late in the evening, when we are told that Liberati's victory has been quashed. Liberati's race speed of 114.93 mph (184.95 kph) would have constituted a record.

Liberati 14 points, McIntyre 14, Surtees 14 – still.

Liberati *did* win the Ulster Grand Prix; McIntyre forcing himself to second place 38 seconds behind. Contemporary accounts make no mention of the jarring which McIntyre took, nor that he was violently ill after the race. His neck hurt as badly as that. On lap 3 of the race Surtees hammered out 95.69 mph (153.99 kph), an absolute circuit record (beating the time set by Mike Hawthorn in a Jaguar). However, Surtees dropped out – engine. Liberati 22 points, McIntyre 20, Surtees 14 – still.

And they came to Monza, came to the final race, came to the 'disappointment'. McIntyre raced in the 350 event and won it, the pain now so bad he was physically sick on the bike as he went round. Of Monza, McIntyre would write that the circuit 'is perhaps the one for which I have least time. It is three and a half miles long and set in a park. There are, in fact, two circuits, a road circuit and a high-speed banked track. The use of the banked track in car racing Grands Prix has caused outcries from British drivers. Motor cycles do not use the banking, but even so the circuit is nothing but a fast tear-up with only a couple of real bends – the rest are sweeping curves. The surface is notoriously bumpy . . .'

Each bump jarred.

Duke writes in his autobiography that 'during practice, Bob had had several very near squeaks, which I put down to a lack of ability to concentrate resulting from his accident in Holland. In the break between the races, therefore, I took him back to the hotel for a rest. On returning to the track, it was soon evident that he was in no fit state to race.'

I asked Duke to expand on this. 'The hotel was just at the end of the road beside the Gilera factory and I think Gilera had a 50 per cent share in it, a very popular place, superb food (contrast Duke in earlier years, risking only bread rolls). That's where we always stayed. Normally it would only take about 10 minutes from the circuit. I did it to get Bob away. I didn't think he was in any state to race in the 500s but, you know, Bob was a difficult bloke to convince. I could only hope he'd rest and then decide not to race.

'Bob Mac was a very hard man, a very fine rider and a superb engineer as well. He could put a bike together and even design things like springs. Quite honestly he wasn't an absolute natural but he developed a terrific ability; and he had a tenacity, never gave in. Whereas I wanted him to be successful and win the World Championship, at the same time I didn't want him to risk his life in the process and if you are not 100 per cent fit you are doing that. I took him back to the circuit and he went to the doctors, because you have to report to them, and they said in essence "we don't think this is on."'

In his autobiography McIntyre wrote 'I was obviously ill and Mr Gilera packed me off to hospital, refusing to let me ride in the 500cc race. He was right. The doctors found I'd broken a bone in my neck at the Dutch TT and my sickness at Monza had been caused by the jolting it received.'

If Liberati didn't finish he'd have the 22 points – two wins and a second place. If Surtees won he'd have 22 points – two wins and a second place. Presumably it would have gone to minor places and neither had any, an interesting thought. Surtees led the race. *Motor Cycling* reported that . . .

On the second lap Liberati and Duke have passed Masetti and are pressing the MV of Surtees. Milani passes Duke, only to be re-passed by him, but the real battle is now developing at the head of the field. Liberati and Surtees change places on nearly every lap; their struggle has reached an almost terrifying intensity, especially on the corners. On the ninth lap Liberati sets up a new record at 118.11 mph (190.07 kph). From the thirteenth lap he secures, and begins to increase, the lead.

On the final lap, Surtees would remember, the engine went 'flat and suddenly died.' Liberati won from Duke, Milani third, Surtees fourth.

What did Bob Mac think of this? The man who might have told us died in a crash at Oulton Park in 1962, and even if he'd survived that he might not have said much. You may be curious to know that in the book he wrote, *Motor Cycling Today,* he makes no mention of losing the Championship at Monza 1957, simply discussing his injury as just another injury. We do know he never would be close to the Championship again.

That September Gilera announced their withdrawal from Grand Prix racing to, as they said, concentrate on making road bikes. Moto Guzzi were going, too, and Morini. MV said they'd join them. It would create a vacuum, a dangerous thing. Soichiro Honda had already visited the Isle of Man in 1954, and being mildly shocked by how far his company were behind, had vowed to take on the best. If you left a vacuum, any vacuum, the Japanese were eager to fill it, then expand it; but nobody knew that then, nor dimly suspected it.

Postscripts

Motor Cycle News wrote that 'the new World Champion in the 500cc class, Libero Liberati, is 31 years old and has been racing since 1946. He joined the Gilera camp in 1952 and began to hit the headlines two seasons ago.'

From the season Zeller took only eight points on the BMW, making him sixth in the Championship. 'I finished at the end of the 1957 season because my brother Kurt had been ill and died. We owned a little factory, a steel plant, which Kurt ran and now I had to take that over.' No German has won the 500cc Championship.

In his book McIntyre wrote: 'In November 1957, as a last gesture before putting their machines into mothballs, the Gilera company sent me to Monza to do some record breaking. The main object was the world's one hour standing start record which at that time still stood to the credit of Ray Amm who had put away 133 miles in an hour (214 kph) on a 500cc Norton at Montléhry, the French high-speed track, in 1953. We were using the banked circuit. I had been on a banked circuit only once before in my life.

'My practice laps were a bit hair-raising and I felt sure the bike would not last. I feared bits would fly off. I was soon hitting the banking at 155 mph (249 kph). Because of the bumps I had to stand up on the footrests, holding on to the handlebars grimly as though I was riding in a scramble but, with the banking, it was more like riding a fairground wall of death. Then, after 15 minutes, the bike stopped. It was a magneto fault.'

McIntyre felt relieved, and imagined that the attempt was over, at least for the time being. Two hours later, a new magneto fitted, he was to try again. 'Round and round I tore, the throttle wide open, just concentrating on staying on. My legs ached, my arms throbbed from the constant vibration. At the end of the hour they put the flag out for me and I came in. They had very nearly to lift me from the machine. My wrists were swelling and my feet were sore. The instep of one of my boots had been broken by the jarring of the footrest beneath it. I had covered 141 miles (226 km). All records are beatable but I do not think this one is likely to be broken in the near future. It would require a 500cc machine and a smoother-surfaced track than Monza – and I do not know of any suitable circuit.'

Nobody knew in November 1957 that a shy young man who'd just embarked on his career would find a smoother surface, in Florida, and beat the record on a 500cc MV, although not until 1964. Mike Hailwood would say publicly that he didn't want what he had done compared in any way with McIntyre. He regarded McIntyre's feat as superior.

Looking back at the Nations Grand Prix at Monza, 1 September 1957 Duke says: 'Something I've never been able to agree with is race doctors allowing blokes to ride – no matter how important it may be to the individual – if they are not 100 per cent fit. It's something I would never have done myself. Ray Amm once rode with a pinned collar bone and people have ridden with their legs in plaster. I think that's ridiculous. It's not simply that the rider is a danger to himself, he's a danger to other riders. Was it more lax in the 1950s? Well, I don't know. I wonder, really, because you hear of riders riding in the present day in all sorts of disrepair, so maybe it wasn't more lax then.

'In fact the ACU doctor was very keen on that kind of thing, because I remember once I slipped off at Silverstone – I'd just been touring round – and the tank hit me on the head. I suffered concussion, although not very bad concussion. I don't think I would have started the race but the doctor made quite sure I didn't.'

Duke again: 'Liberati was a great rider and he won the Championship in 1957 against a lot of opposition, which speaks for itself. He was a man I didn't know an awful lot about. He didn't speak any English and I virtually spoke no Italian so I suppose between those two situations I didn't have a great deal of contact. I only had one real dice.' As we've seen, that was Monza, 9 September 1956 – the year before Liberati won the Championship.

'Liberati was a very good rider,' Surtees says, 'typical Italian but quite serious; not excitable, or a womanizer. The Gilera was a super bike but if you take the McIntyre-Duke-Liberati trio, the fastest was Liberati.'

1958

Riding the storm

West German Grand Prix, Nürburgring

THE SITUATION IS explained by Tommy Robb, an Ulster rider long steeped in the ways of the sport. 'MV conned everybody. You know that story, don't you? Well, MV conned all the other Italians to withdraw from racing, anyway. As soon as the Count got his new bikes he stayed in and called them private. By doing this he obviously created a situation where MV didn't really have any challengers.'

Brian Wolley emphasizes it in *Directory of Classic Racing Motorcyles*. 'At the end of 1957, labouring under a dreadful recession in sales, Gilera, Moto Guzzi and Morini withdrew from racing. After originally letting it be understood that they, too, would retire, MV changed their mind.'

MV had Surtees and Hartle and . . . really no challengers. Moreover, as Surtees says, 'we got the MV about how we wanted it at the end of 1957 testing for 1958. We'd managed to make a new frame and start getting the bike a lot tidier.' Quickly, quickly, as it seemed, the riders reached the Nürburgring, fourth round, on 20 July.

The very name Nürburgring held a sort of monstrous majesty: 14.17 miles (22.80 km) cut through and laid onto the Eifel mountains, a brooding place of seemingly endless dips and descents, ditches and ravines, curves and crescents and, as someone said . . .

It contained no less than 172 corners of infinite variety, 88 being left-handed and 84 right-handed. The two schleifen (loops) share the same parallel dual strips on a high plateau, containing the grandstands, timing boxes, paddock, pits and other facilities, all loftily overlooked by the Schloss Nürburg (castle) on its own mountain.

Loops? The man meant separate ciruits but joined like Siamese twins, the big one of 14.17 miles (22.80 km) and the shorter 4.8 miles (7.72 km). They were called, respectively, the North and South loops. The bike racers would use the full, raw, unprotected circuit, just as the Formula 1 car racers did.

The Nürburgring dug conflicting emotions. Some tried to conceal their trepidation, some felt naked fear, some loathed the place and loathed the *idea* of a place like that; some adored it as something to measure themselves against, an ultimate gesture of man and machine. Same in the cars . . .

'This was my first time back at The Ring since 1955,' Surtees says, 'and in fact only the second time I'd ridden it. If you had to choose circuits in the world which gave you the most satisfaction to win, the first group would include the TT – obviously – the Nürburgring and the old, full Spa. Although the Nürburgring was very fast in places, the sheer speed of the corners and the precision one needed at Spa was something else. If you got Spa all right it gave immense satisfaction: nowhere apart from the hairpin were you going much less than 100 miles an hour, and at one point 175 even in those days.'

Neither The Ring nor Spa intimidated John Surtees.

To understand the Nürburgring that July day you only had to look at the face of a 20-year-old Southern Rhodesian (as it was called), Gary Hocking: one eye black, nose and cheeks gashed and scarred by a fall in practice the day before. In that practice a Norton rider, Jack Brett, had been quickest, but during th 350 race *Motor Cycling* reported . . .

Fate struck him on the first lap when his front wheel broke away on a tight left-hander and he was thrown, his team-mate, good sportsman Alan Trow, voluntarily abandoning the race in order to stay and look after him.

Surtees won easily enough, and Hocking (Norton) came in sixth. Brett broke his arm, and his team agreed to lend his 500 to Hocking, who hadn't sat on it before. There'd been rain. The track dried, but if the rain came back what might that mean for Hocking? The trees which hemmed the circuit shielded tracts of it from any sunshine. Hocking faced what *Motor Cycling* described as a circuit which 'snakes its way round the wooded Eifel mountains like a demented Wagnerian dragon.' He'd try and cover nine laps, which translated to 127.56 miles (250.28 km), which in turn translated to 1548 corners.

Duke rode a BMW – although the company had withdrawn with the Italians (as we have seen) they 'supported' him and Dale; and privateers ran BMWs, too. At The Ring Duke had a mediocre practice session and Walter Schneider wrecked a BMW engine in the sidecars. As Duke says, no spares were available and since he had nothing to lose – he'd scored points only in the Belgian at Spa – while Schneider nursed a real chance of the sidecar title, Duke let him have his engine. Duke's own bike would be fitted with an 'ordinary' engine.

Surtees faced The Ring with confidence. He'd won all three rounds, the TT by more than five minutes from Bob Anderson (Norton), Assen from Hartle by more than a minute and a half, Spa by 45.9 seconds from Campbell (Norton). The Nortons were no match for Surtees, and Hartle on the other MV was no match for Surtees either. The ratchet: four best finishes from the seven rounds. If Surtees won here he'd have an impregnable maximum.

'Hartle was a very good rider,' journalist Rous says, 'but always in the shadow of Surtees. He seemed an excellent team player but never a winner. He did win a 350 at the TT on the Isle of Man (in 1960) but only because Surtees broke down. Hartle had a strange bone condition which meant that they took a long time to heal so his career went up and down like Tower Bridge because of his various injuries.'

Motor Cycling reported that . . .

The race started with a typical Surtees getaway. Hartle was hard on his trail but it looked as though the MVs would not have everything their own way, and an excited gasp went up when the rather erratic leaderboard showed national idol Ernest Hiller (BMW) out in front after seven miles. However, Surtees and Hartle led the German at the end of the first lap, with Hocking lying fourth ahead of the BMW's of Gerald Klinger and Dickie Dale and Norton-mounted Alan Trow and Bob Brown.

The field was well spread out when Geoff Duke, last of all, struggled in to retire after changing a plug in his Munich twin. Hocking took Hiller on the second lap but seemed to have no chance of catching Hartle who, momentarily, snatched the lead from Surtees as they passed the grandstand. At the start of lap 3 Hocking was nearly half a minute in arrears, but then the storm broke, rain and hail lashing the track with monsoon violence and covering the surface to a depth of inches.

The speeds dropped – the last time they'd raced here, 1955, Duke averaged over 81 mph (130 kph), now it tumbled towards, and then below, 70 mph (112 kph) and that included the two flat out dry laps.

Trow shot unexpectedly into a young lake at the bottom of a hill and came off, fortunately without injury. One after another the sodden riders called it a day, but not so Hocking, nor Surtees, nor Hartle. With Surtees now about 50 yards in front, the youngster thundered after Hartle and had regained all but 11 seconds at the end of lap 5. Then half way round the next lap Hartle, slowed by the rain and confident of his lead, had the surprise of his life when the turquoise-blue Norton 'single' streaked past him, and he had to ride again in grim earnest to catch up. It took him over half a lap on the slippery track and even then his final advantage was only 12 seconds.

Surtees of course continued his splendidly inexorable way to the double [the 350 Championship] but at the end of the race there were only 10 riders other than the duelling couple left of the 32 starters and Hiller, who comfortably headed Dale and Brown over the line, was more than four-and-a-half minutes behind Hocking.

Surtees	1 hour 50 minutes 51.6 seconds.
Hartle	at 44.3 seconds.
Hocking	at 1 minute 31.5 seconds.

Hocking had ridden hard towards the future. Of him, fellow Rhodesian rider Jim Redman says 'Gary was very quiet, Mr nice guy, very intense, wanted to win so much: no drink, no smoke, only poke – he did a lot of that (chuckle).'

Postscripts

The Formula 1 cars came to the Nürburgring two weeks later. Hawthorn (Ferrari) took pole but Tony Brooks (Vanwall) won at an average speed of just over 90 mph (144 kph) in a dry race. On lap 11 Peter Collins, friend of Hawthorn, and also in a Ferrari, went off the circuit at a place called Pflanzgarten $10^1/2$ miles from the start. He was killed. Surtees, Hartle and Hocking had passed this way nine times, six of them in the storm. A twitch, a wobble, a skid . . .

Hawthorn went on to win *that* World Championship, and when he'd done it he'd have a very interesting social chat with Surtees. This chat was one reason why, in time, Surtees rode bikes no more but tried to emulate Hawthorn.

Two months after the chat Hawthorn died in a road crash.

1959

Ends and beginnings

Dutch Grand Prix, Assen

COMING OFF THE podium – a wooden platform – a boyish smile enveloped his face and a vast garland hung round his neck, so vast it reached full down to his waist. He gripped the railings as he came down, the hands as they remain today: extremely large, extremely strong.

A few moments before, Surtees had come round the final right-hander, moved from the tuck position to slightly upright as his MV coursed past the bowl of an open grandstand towards the finishing line. An official in a white shirt leant towards the rim of the track and waved the chequered flag.

Surtees beat Brown (Norton) by 1 minute 52.4 seconds, a very long way. Nobody expressed even mild surprise. The ratchet: the same as 1958. The possibility: the same as 1958, a maximum. Surtees won the first, France at Clermont Ferrand, by one minute 30.8 from his team-mate Remo Venturi; won the TT by more than five minutes from Alistair King (Norton); won the West German at Hockenheim from Venturi by 14.5 seconds. Now, at Assen, Surtees had his third 500cc World Championship but 27 June 1959 assumed importance for this and other reasons. The day began with the 250 race and *Motor Cycle News* reported that . . .

Round the back of the circuit the leaders could be seen in a bunch and as they streaked through the start to complete the first lap it was Ubbiali inches ahead of Mike Hailwood (Mondial), Emilio Mendogni (Morini) and Provini (MV). On the second lap Derek Minter, making his debut on a works Morini, forced his way through to fourth place. On the fourth lap Minter passed Provini, Hailwood and Ubbiali to take the lead! Fifth lap and Hailwood took over . . .

It finished with Provini first from Ubbiali, Minter (with no brakes) third, and Hailwood on his elderly (by works standards) Mondial fourth. Stanley Michael Bailey Hailwood had not yet won a World Championship race and would not do so for two years. When he did he'd win on a gargantuan scale and only two men surpass his total of wins and Championships.

Hailwood would never, as it happened, beat Surtees in a round of the 500cc World Championship, though. The nearest he'd get would be third. Surtees that day at Assen? *Motor Cycle News* reported . . .

From the flag Surtees went into his usual lead. At the end of the first lap he had a hundred yards over Brown who in turn had the same margin over Venturi, Hocking (Norton) and Dale. On the second lap Hocking passed Venturi and set off after Brown. By the end of the third lap, with Surtees three hundred yards clear, Hocking and Brown were hard at it! Venturi was alone in fourth spot and Paddy Driver (a South African) had pulled well ahead of Dale. Kavanagh lay seventh and Minter, after a poor start, was through to eighth place just ahead of Tom Phillis. At the end of the fifteenth lap (of 27) the order was Surtees – well ahead – Brown just in front of Hocking followed by Venturi – half a mile behind the two Norton riders – and then Minter who was gaining seconds a lap on Venturi and just had him in sight on the long straight.

Lap 16 was disaster for the two Nortons. Hocking and Driver both went out with the valves tangled up with the piston. Next Norton to blow was Minter's . . . then on lap 22 Phillis's Norton went off with a bang and the four leaders were well spread out with a mile between each of them. They toured round to finish with Surtees almost lapping Dale.

'I always reckoned to settle myself in, whether at short circuits or Grands Prix,' Surtees says. 'There is a speed you could go where you had a bit more left but it remained vital for your concentration that you got everything really precise. Although you weren't at 101 per cent it still allowed you to maintain concentration and if that gave you a lead of a minute, so it gave you a lead of a minute.

'The way I did this was *mentally* ride the bike at say 96 per cent but *physically* at say 92 per cent, making sure I changed up a little earlier, changed down a little later so I didn't use the engine-braking too much. Frankly it was to ensure reliability. You'll notice the difference in my record of reliability and John Hartle's, for instance. I worked the bike less. Only when you found yourself committed to catching a rider in front did you run yourself and the machine at maximum.'

It's the ability of a master. Your 96 per cent is faster than other riders' 100 per cent.

Postscripts
Surtees went on to win the Belgian at Spa, the Ulster at Dundrod, the Nations at Monza, a maximum maximum if I can phrase it like that.

Hocking, of such rare promise, joined MV and concentrated on the 250s and 350s the following season, though Surtees nursed and schooled him towards where his destiny clearly lay – the 500s. In 1961 he would be ready, and so would Hailwood.

Redman, who finished fifth at Assen – lapped by Surtees – rode a Norton.

His career seemed to be going nowhere in particular, and at season's end he returned to Rhodesia 'without saying a word to anyone. I packed up everything I had in Europe and came home to retire from full-time racing.' He'd change his mind, return to give the career one last chance. He'd find a works ride at Assen because Phillis crashed and injured himself. The team he'd ride for then? They'd come tentatively to the Isle of Man this season of 1959 for the first time to contest the 125cc race and attracted interest, attracted a certain condescending banter. Honda.

Ends and beginnings, ends and beginnings.

Duke rode the 1959 season as a privateer on a Norton, though he didn't compete at Assen. He came third in the Belgian, third at Ulster, third in the Nations. In September Duke entered the 250, 350 and 500 events at the non-Championship Swiss Grand Prix at Locarno. He won the 250 and 350, but at the second last corner in the 500 Hocking, braking late, tried to take him on the outside, Duke being 'totally unaware' of the move.

With no malice aforethought, Duke cut Hocking up, as they say. Duke won. Duke remembers Hocking being 'livid', claiming Duke had done it deliberately, and some of Hocking's 'compatriots' agreed. Even Duke's powers of persuasion (and reason) failed to convince them. Duke felt very sad. He felt tired, too.

He had burns from the exhaust pipe, a blister on a heel, blisters on his hands. Next day, preparing to go to Italy on holiday, he told his wife at Locarno station that was it. The great years had gone, gone safe into memory.

In October 1959 Surtees' phone rang. Reg Parnell, a former driver now with Aston Martin, asked if Surtees would like to have a go on four wheels at Goodwood, the circuit in Sussex. Surtees said he would and wondered if he could bring Hartle to have a go, too? He could.

Ends and beginnings.

1960

Mr Wonderful

West German Grand Prix, Solitude

ON 18 APRIL at Cesenatico during the traditional Italian mini-series which heralded new seasons, John Surtees won a 500 race on an MV. A week later he won at Imola. Three weeks later he retired in the International Trophy at Silverstone with an oil leak on his Lotus 18. I repeat, his Lotus 18.

Across 1960 Surtees attempted a feat so demanding and so unlikely that no man had made the attempt before and only one, Hailwood, would again: challenge the world on bikes and in cars. Count Agusta stipulated that Surtees ride only in the seven rounds of the bike Championship.

'In 1960 Agusta wanted to restrict my riding,' Surtees says. 'I'd done some events on the home circuits with my own bikes and occasionally I'd borrowed MVs. Actually it was rather nice in the sense that people could have said "ah, he won because he was on the MV" but I beat riders who were my main competitors if I rode a Norton as well. In 1960 I asked for MVs and they said no (apart from the Championship). There was nothing in my contract to say I couldn't drive four wheels.'

The calendar acted as its own kind of ratchet. Races in one discipline sometimes coincided with races in the other, obliging Surtees to miss Formula One Grands Prix to honour his MV contract. He couldn't drive in the Belgian because of the TT on the Isle of Man, couldn't drive in the French because the bikes were in Belgium. This still allowed him to do four car Grands Prix and miss no round of the 500s.

On the MV: 22 May, the French bike Grand Prix at Clermont Ferrand. He beat team-mate Venturi by three minutes 01.7 seconds.

In the Lotus: 29 May, the Monaco Grand Prix. He met great drivers here, Moss, Jack Brabham, Hill. He found the contours of Monte Carlo slightly baffling, not like anything he'd encountered before (the bike riders never went, and because Monaco was a street circuit no practice sessions were held outside the Grand Prix weekend). Surtees suffered gear problems, qualified on the second last row of the grid, and retired from the race on lap 18 when his transmission failed.

On the MV: 13-17 June, the TT on the Isle of Man. He won the 500, beating Hartle by two minutes 39 seconds. (This was the year Surtees was slowed by the gearbox in the 350 and Hartle won, although Surtees broke the lap record). 25 June, the Dutch at Assen. He won the 350, setting a new lap record, but crashed in the 500 – after setting a new lap record. 'A plug went and I fell off, threw it up the road.' Venturi won from Brown, then Emilio Mendogni (MV), Driver, Hailwood and Dale. 3 July, the Belgian at Spa. Surtees won, averaging 120.53 mph (193.95 kph) and setting a new lap record, 122.60 mph (197.30 kph). He beat Venturi by 1 minute 23.1 seconds.

In the Lotus: 16 July, the British Grand Prix, Silverstone. He got on the third row of the grid. In the closing stages Hill chased Brabham hard and spun off letting Surtees into second place. How many drivers these days finish as high in only their second Grand Prix? (Michael Schumacher, widely regarded as an outstandingly talented newcomer, drove six times in his first season, 1991, and came no higher than fifth.)

On the MV: 23-24 July, the West German at Solitude. The ratchet: four best finishes from the seven rounds. He had 24 points from three, Venturi 20 from three, Hartle 6 from one. If Surtees won Solitude he'd be impregnable again. Solitude is remembered for that and something else. *Motor Cycling* reported . . .

The meeting produced no great excitement but left everyone with a feeling of great sadness. It took the life of one of the most popular men that Australia, or for that matter any other continent, has given to road racing. Gentle, careful, courageous Bob Brown, who married only last January, died in a Stuttgart hospital on Saturday of head injuries received when he crashed while practising on a Honda that morning.

Redman had returned from Rhodesia and replaced Phillis, injured, at Assen. Redman would write 'for the West German Grand Prix Tom was still sick, so Bob Brown and I were booked to ride the 250s as there was no 125 class here. Tom, Bob and I were wondering who would be dropped when Tom was fit again.' Yes, a feeling of great sadness. *Motor Cycling* reported that . . .

Lightning, thunder and torrents of rain falling from a black sky had kept the spectator content at a lowish level on Saturday. During the sidecar race, as the field throbbed its way up into the wooded highlands on the other side of the circuit, a hush in the buzz of conversation in the Press stand was caused by the passing through of an official communiqué. It confirmed the rumour we had already heard, namely, that that kind and ever-helpful Australian Bob Brown had succumbed in hospital to an injury to the base of his skull sustained during the morning's practice session when his Honda crashed near the 'Sandpit' right-hander.

The magazine described the 500 race on the Sunday as 'featureless as a headless ghost', a haunting choice of words on such a weekend. The MVs (of course) stood across the front row.

On the starting line, mechanics were busy clearing tyres of clogging mud picked up in the waterlogged paddock, but the road surface itself was perfectly dry by now, though dried mud remained a hazard. John Surtees took possession of the race from flag's fall – and did much as he liked with it.

The man was at the height of his powers. At one point he led Venturi by more than a minute and a quarter, Mendogni on the third MV holding station far behind Venturi.

Towards the end Surtees slowed up so as not to make the difference between himself and Venturi quite so obvious.

Surtees won it, slowing, by 18.7 seconds. That represented the 96 per cent in his mind and the 92 per cent he made the bike do. Ample. Mind you, 'Solitude was the sort of circuit where you could pull a little extra out because it was daunting, like a mini-Nürburgring, full of trees and everything else (boulders).' Surtees says. 'One of the problems you encounter is riders and drivers of a certain mentality who believe that they are – shall we say? – immortal. At a more open circuit like Monza they'd throw caution away and go mad. However, you often found at the more daunting circuits that a rider who was more precise and had a very good relationship with his machine could find more speed.'

And still be at the 96 per cent in the mind, the 92 per cent from the bike.

Postscripts
Later that day Surtees drove. *Motor Cycling* reported . . .

Having been officially garlanded, John Surtees put away the motorcycle, changed leathers for linen overalls and took the wheel of Stirling Moss's Formula 2 Porsche for the afternoon's car race. Small wonder the Solitude announcer persisted in calling him 'Mr Wonderful!'

Yes – and no. In that race Surtees missed a gear and put the Porsche into a ditch. Forgive him. Moss wrote in *My Cars, My Career* (PSL) that 'I did not like the Porsche's gear change, which lacked a proper cockpit gate and was rather rubbery and vague.' No doubt in a year or two Surtees would have coped easily enough and very likely won. Surtees understood the impulses and mechanisms of winning on anything and in anything.

Surtees rode in only four more bike races, culminating in victory at the Nations Grand Prix at Monza on 11 September. From this time on he'd be a driver, and that climaxed on the afternoon of 25 October 1964 when he finished second in the Mexican Grand Prix, giving him a total of 40 points, Graham Hill 41 but only 39 counting.

There's a phrase which is always used because it has a neat and nimble cadence about it. John Surtees, the only man to win on two wheels and four.

Duke offers a perceptive evaluation of Surtees. 'A strange man, obviously a very great rider. Most people would feel that he had it on a plate because he always enjoyed very competitive machinery at a time when most other people didn't, and he had his whole family pushing him. In fairness, one must bear in mind that although he rode without too much competition he broke lap records and won races at record speeds. You can't really say he gave himself an easy ride.'

Big John Surtees would never do that.

1961

The haunting of Hocking

Ulster Grand Prix, Dundrod

SOMEHOW TRAGEDY STALKED the quiet, self-contained man. In time it would force him back to the distant continent from whence he came and stalk him there, stalk him from his own country to another on that continent and claim him in a single instant. You can argue that tragedy stalked many riders and still does, but about the firm-jawed, open-faced Southern Rhodesian there lingered, perhaps, a sense of the inevitable.

He ought, in 1961, to have had the world at his mercy. In the 500 Championship only he rode the MV. Surtees – the nursing and schooling of the pupil completed – departed to cars full time. Gary Hocking might reasonably have anticipated inheriting from Surtees the impregnability, manipulating races as he pleased. Beyond doubt he did not lack the ability, the courage and the ambition for it; a potent mix from which he'd already hewn superb races, not least the Nürburgring in the storm, 1958.

'Gary was a very determined rider,' Nobby Clark – himself Rhodesian and subsequently a famous mechanic – says. 'He was very serious about his racing, and once he set his mind to do something he would carry on right to the end. He had good mechanical sense. For example, when he rode the MV Agusta 500 he said the fairings were too wide and bulky, and had new ones made about three inches narrower. If he thought something would make a bike better he'd want to try it for himself to *prove* whether it worked or not. He was a thinking rider who always raced inside his limit, and although quick he didn't crash often. Like quite a few riders I've had dealings with, he showed great impatience, and the more so just before a race. He claimed it wasn't nerves.

'I first met Gary at Bulawayo Technical School. He rode a bicycle from home to there and back and he had the nickname "sox" because he didn't like to wear socks. He had a good ear for music and played the mouth-organ and the piano accordion. He'd enter local competitions and sometimes win. He had a chest expansion of seven inches from playing the mouth-organ. He was also a good swimmer and could stay under water for ages. He'd challenge anyone to see how many lengths of the pool they could go under it against him, and he always won.

'He joined the Rhodesian Railways as an apprentice fitter and turner. On the way to the workshops on his first day he fell off his Jawa in the rain and promptly caught pneumonia! While serving his apprenticeship he really got interested in bike racing and raced on our local dirt track at Umgusa in the novice class. He won first time out. After a couple of meetings he became virtually unbeatable at any circuit in Southern Rhodesia. Gary had a Triumph Tiger 110. He'd take the headlight off plus the tail light and – pronto! – he was ready to race.'

Hocking was certainly ready to win the Championship in 1961, but sometimes ambition cannot be satisfied so easily because others have it and want exactly what you want; the same appetite, the same range of skills. A young man from Oxford reached towards maturity himself – Hailwood. He rode a Norton, in theory no match for an MV. He could do not better than fourth in the opening round – the West German at Hockenheim, Hocking lapping everyone – and second 1 minute 19.7 seconds behind Hocking, in France; but he demonstrated the skills and the appetite on the Isle of Man.

In the 500 race, as Hailwood has explained, 'over breakfast on the morning of the Senior, Stan [Hailwood's dynamic, rich, explosive father] and I talked over the best method to counteract the advantage of Gary Hocking's big MV. We realized that my Norton couldn't hope to match the MV for speed – there was about 10 mph difference. We agreed that the best plan was for me to stay as near as possible to Gary and pick up some extra time by slip-streaming whenever possible.

'The theory was good but in practice it didn't work out like that. When I tried to get near him Gary merely screwed it on a bit and the MV's superior acceleration wafted away any chance I had of hanging on to his tail. Yet, in the end, the plan did work, though not in the way we'd expected. Gary piled on the pressure and paid the penalty for doing it. He vanished up the slip road at Ballacraine when he hit the bend too fast. I dodged in front but not for long.'

Hocking came back 'like the wind'. Hailwood clung and Hocking had trouble, as Hailwood remembered, 'first with the fairing then with plugs, and I picked up some valuable time when he had to pull into the pits for help.' Hocking retired on lap 4, the throttle sticking.

Hailwood won it by almost two minutes from McIntyre, and thereafter hunted Hocking, urging the Norton to whatever it could be made to do.

The Dutch TT, Assen:
Hocking   1 hour 5m 37.2s
Hailwood   at 26.0 seconds

The Belgian Grand Prix, Spa:
Hocking   1 hour 5m 52.3s
Hailwood   at 1m 39.0s

The East German Grand Prix, Sachsenring:
Hocking   1 hour 5m 08.8s
Hailwood   at 2m 08.9 seconds

Hocking 40 points, Hailwood 35. The ratchet: six best finishes from the ten rounds and Hocking had five, Hailwood six. *If* Hocking won the next, Ulster, he'd reach 48 points, and *if* Hailwood came second again he'd reach 38. The ratchet tightened hard. Three rounds to run after Ulster. *If* Hailwood won them all and Hocking scored no points Hailwood could count only two for each (eight for the wins but subtracting six for the second places in France, Assen and Spa). He could total no more than 44.

The Ulster must be seen in scale, a big scale. Jimmy Walker says that 'the Prime Minister and a lot of the cabinet came. If the Ulster Motor Cycle Club wanted something doing, like a bit of road resurfacing, they rang Stormont (seat of the Northern Ireland government) who rang the appropriate department and the guy arrived within hours. The race proved to be a marvellous tourist attraction and the Northern Ireland Tourist Board underwrote the race until 1962: any losses and they wiped them out.'

At Ulster, Hocking won the 350 (Hailwood not in it) but tragedy stalked Dundrod. In practice for the 500 an Australian, Ronald Miles, slid at a corner, was thrown off his bike and crashed fatally. In that 350 race Hocking beat King (Bianchi) – 1 hour 35m 47s against 1 hour 36m 24.6s – but during it *Ireland's Saturday Night* reported that a rider called Roy Ingram (Norton) was . . .

. . . saved serious injury when he came off on the famous Dear's Leap, where bikes are airborne for a split second, and two riders unseated themselves avoiding him on the ground.

Ingram would ride in the 500, on a Norton. Under grey, looming clouds the immense crowd wondered if they'd see the first 100 mph lap. Drizzle fell as mechanics wheeled the 500s out. At the start – against a backdrop of pastures rolling away to trees on the skyline, those scholarly-looking spectators of the early 1960s arranged along the trackside: pullovers and tweed jackets, collars and ties, cheese-cutter caps – Hocking moved fast, Hailwood pushing hard and low against his Norton before he mounted it, Hartle more upright as he straddled his bike.

Further back Anderson and Ellis Boyce, both on Nortons, collided, their bikes falling and splaying across the road, other riders dipping and angling to miss them. Anderson and Boyce were bruised. Both retired.

Hocking crossed the line to complete lap 1 with King and Hartle behind, Hocking's lead already eight seconds. The rain fell harder –

pelting, a contemporary account called it. On lap 2 Hartle overtook King, Hailwood overtook a young Englishman called Phil Read, and Hocking registered 130 mph (209 kph) on the flying kilometre (a nice and very Irish juxtaposition of imperial and metric measurements), increasing his lead over Hartle yard by yard; and Hartle went out – engine. On lap 3 *Ireland's Saturday Night* reported tragedy . . .

The accident involved two riders, Tom Phillis (Norton) and Roy Ingram. Unlucky Ingram and the Australian Phillis collided at Quarry Corner and involved a flag marshal, Edward Walter, in the crash. All three were rushed to the Victoria Hospital, Belfast. There, it was reported that Walter had died, that Phillis is to be detained overnight for observation and Ingram's X-ray will decide whether he be kept in.

The accident occurred when the riders skidded together as they came round the corner at speed. Ingram's pretty young wife, watching the race in the paddock, was told the news as her husband was being rushed to the Royal. She earlier had had the unpleasant shock of hearing about him coming unstuck during the 350cc event – and by split second timing Billy McCosh of Ballymena and George Purvis of Belfast had to throw their machines to the embankment to avoid the sprawling Ingram.

Mr Stanley Russell, a travelling marshal at the race said 'Tom Phillis skidded and Mr Walter gave oncoming riders the yellow (flag) according to rule. The next thing people saw was Ingram's machine going up in the air and Ingram himself thrown with it. The machine struck Walter a severe blow. There is very great regret in the entire motor cycle world over this as Walter was very popular with everyone.'

Deep into the race the rain made even Hocking slow, putting the fabled 100 mph out of reach, although he'd almost touch it with his fastest, 98.37 mph (158.30 kph). Surtees' record set the year before, 99.32 mph (159.83 kph), would last at least until 1962. Hocking maintained 'a substantial lead', however, and after 12 laps (of 20) lapped all bar the first seven. *Ireland's Saturday Night* reported that . . .

Further up the field Tommy Robb was giving a great display in holding down fourth position. Second and third were still King and Hailwood. Hocking was now well out on his own but there was a change in the second position, Hailwood taking over from King. Then came excitement for the Ulster followers when Robb was seen to pull into the pits. After a few minutes during which he cleaned his goggles he was back there in the race but he had lost vital moments and dropped back to seventh position.

The position after 13 laps was Hocking, Hailwood, King, Langston fourth, Chatterton fifth, Thorp sixth, Robb seventh. With four laps to go there was a surprise when King and not Hailwood came through in second place. The young Oxford rider had lost a bit of ground over the back stretches of the course and was now just ahead of Langston.

Meanwhile Hocking, despite the rain which was getting heavier, increased his

*lead and clocked 137 mph (220 kph) over the flying kilo on his sixteenth lap. He
had now lapped everyone except King, Hailwood and Langston. With only two
laps to go it was obvious that Hocking had the race sewn up but instead of easing
he increased his speed and on the seventeenth lap clocked 137 on the flying kilo
again. After Hocking had been seen safely home everyone craned forward to the
right-hand bend approaching the finishing straight to see who the second man
would be. A flash of a red helmet and it was Hailwood just in front of King.*

Gary Hocking looked fresh when he'd done it, a US marine haircut, a
crisp sort of presence, and on the evening of Saturday 12 August 1961 he
did have the world at his mercy.

'I got on very well with him,' Jimmy Walker says, 'although a shy guy;
never really had a lot to say. He used a minimum of words in his
description of any race and described it in a straightforward way. A dull
person to interview compared to say Hailwood – he'd make up something
for you or get in a quip about one of the organizers.

'Hocking would just shrug his shoulders. "Good day out, I've enjoyed
myself, I didn't expect to do this well." He was a bit like the young John
Surtees, sort of shied away from everyone – grinned at you and said
nothing. You'd ask Surtees a question and he'd grin again. Same with
Hocking, answered everything with a grin, a shake of the head.'

Postscripts – one (inevitably) from Jimmy Walker
'Phil Read rang me today [August 1993] out of the blue, must be 20 years
since I'd spoken to him. He's hoping to have two of his sons racing here at
Kirkistown, one of the short circuits, but the interesting thing was that he
said "I'm going to bring them to the Dundrod circuit to show them what
we had to put up with in those days. I'm going to take them round so
they'll see." It was extremely bumpy then, extremely rough . . .'

Read, from Luton, made his Grand Prix debut this season, the Dutch, and
on a Norton finished fourth. 'Not bad for my first race, was it?' There'd be
more, a lot more.

1962

Mike's first

Nations Grand Prix, Monza

THAT EARLY SEPTEMBER afternoon subtle mind games were being played out around the leafy parkland. The three men who might recapture those mind games – their interplay, their nuances, their unstated tensions – are gone now, gone into the great silence and we'll have to make do without them.

We do know that Count Domenico Agusta looked and behaved like an autocrat, genuinely dynamic and a shrewd reader of human beings. We do know that for the Count's own reasons he invited Mike Hailwood to ride 350 and 500 MVs at the Nations Grand Prix that early September afternoon in *1961*. We do not know what Gary Hocking, who three weeks before had won the 500cc Championship for MV at the Ulster, thought of this.

Did Agusta imagine both these riders would co-exist happily and form, with his bikes, an irresistible force in 1962? Did he indulge himself, as he could – and which may have given him pleasure – in pitting one man against the other simply to see what happened? Or did he exercise his curiosity about what Hailwood might achieve on his bikes as an end in itself? Another great silence about that.

At Monza in 1961, Hocking took the 350 *from* Hailwood but, both men playing out the mind games, crashed in the 500 which Hailwood won. The rest is plain enough. Count Agusta decided. Hailwood would remember that 'before I went to Sweden for the last race in the Championship (two weeks after Monza) Count Agusta had watched me after being told all about me by Bill Webster, the MV distributor in England. He said he had enjoyed my riding. And then he didn't ask me to join MV: he told me to. It was as simple as that. I was flabbergasted.'

It may well be that Hocking was flabbergasted, too, but in quite another way. The few sources we have suggest, only suggest, he expressed less than delight.

During the winter of 1961–1962, Hailwood said, 'I don't know whether it went to my head, but I went wild and broke out into a rash of high living. I had a new-found freedom because I was no longer under Stan's direct control. I took a flat with a few other blokes and we lived it up to no mean tune. Too many women, I think, popped into and out of my life with what became almost boring frequency. I drank too much and went to too many all-night parties. I lost a hell of a lot of sleep and with it the vital edge of fitness. That flat was like a madhouse, a death-trap for a man in my profession. The result was I started the 1962 season an extremely tired man. On top of that I was faced with the problem of adapting myself to the intricacies of riding four-cylinder MVs, whereas all my experience on big bikes had been with the uncomplicated singles in the 500 and 350 class.'

The mind games began again very quickly, at the TT on the Isle of Man in June, first Championship round of the season, although they'd be partially lost in a great shadow. During the 350 race Phillis asked to borrow Redman's Honda and Redman, who actively disliked The Island, readily agreed. Redman remembers Phillis saying he'd love to 'sort out' Hocking and Hailwood on the MVs.

Redman and his wife Marlene went to the bottom of Bray Hill to watch. 'There we saw the tingling, awe-inspiring sight of Gary Hocking leading Mike Hailwood and Tom by only a matter of feet. When they came hurtling down at the end of the first lap they were really going some and the Honda, which did not handle as well as the MVs, was bucking and bouncing all over the place. He must have been pulling out all the stops on every part of the circuit.'

On lap 2 Phillis hit the wall at Laurel Bank nine miles from the starting line. Redman remembers 'his name suddenly disappeared from the loudspeaker commentary, which is always a bad sign, as the commentators usually make a point of saying that a man has "retired with engine trouble" or "has crashed, but rider is OK." Nobody seemed to know where he had got to. He was just missing. I waited and waited in agony for some mention of his name but somehow I knew it was no use. Somehow, and I can't explain it, I knew he had been killed.

'Gary had had a few minor troubles and differences of opinion which were making him think hard about his career, and when Tom was killed that was the last straw.'

Stan Hailwood described the race. 'It was perhaps the hardest decision on tactics we have ever had to make. Mike started ten seconds in front of Hocking which is a definite disadvantage. We talked it over secretly and came to the conclusion that if Mike was to go flat out from the very start he would probably blow up, and the chance was that if Gary was trying to catch him he would break down as well. Two blown up MVs would not have pleased Count Agusta.

'We decided to take a gamble. Mike was not to go flat out all the way but to let Hocking catch him on the first lap. We felt this would give Hocking confidence and make him think he had the edge on Mike. The gamble was based on the assumption that both riders were roughly equal but I felt that whereas Mike had ridden in some four hundred short circuit races and Gary in perhaps only a hundred, Mike might have a slight edge on the drop down the Mountain which is a short circuit rider's dream.'

The two bikes plundered a path round the Island as 'though tied with a 10 foot rope' and Hailwood won – just.

Hocking abandoned his career immediately after the 500, where Hailwood had clutch problems and Hocking beat Boyce by nearly 10 minutes. Hocking returned to Rhodesia. Hailwood remembered Hocking as 'inconsolable' – compounded, Redman believes, by the fact that Phillis had been pushing so hard to catch him.

It left the whole 500cc season emptied. Hailwood filled the emptiness, and the ratchet – five best finishes from the eight rounds – didn't matter. He beat Minter (Norton) at Assen by 23.2 seconds, beat Ian Shepherd (Matchless) at Spa by 1 minute 56.2 seconds, beat Shepherd again at the Ulster by 3 minutes 45.2 seconds, beat Shepherd again in East Germany by 1 minute 37.3 seconds. It must be stated: Hailwood was now clearly the best rider in the world, and on the best bike. A strong young man, he'd long shed the excesses of the winter.

He raced against himself, sometimes a difficult discipline to handle because concentration is so easily lost, and at real speed that's dangerous. Real speed? Here are Hailwood's averages: Assen 87.346 mph (140.570 kph), Spa 119.349 mph (192.073 kph), Ulster 96.549 mph (155.380 kph), East Germany 102.098 mph (164.311 kph).

The East German Grand Prix, first run the year before, came to play (as I've hinted earlier) a central role in future Championships and equally became a sociological event, the background as interesting as the foreground. The circuit, on ordinary roads and called the Sachsenring, represented the only place on mother earth where people from both sides of the Cold War met to share mutual pleasure normally.

Germany had been divided into zones after the War, the Soviet Union taking the east and installing what the west regarded as a puppet German government there; and the refugee flow grew to such proportions that the East Germans literally sealed the whole zone. This was the fabled and feared Iron Curtain. The Berlin Wall went up on 13 August 1961, two weeks after Hocking won at the Sachsenring and one day after Hocking won the Ulster.

By 1962 the sealing was increasingly sophisticated, and that year Tommy Robb first journeyed there as a member of the Honda team. Because the Sachsenring will assume such importance I break the flow of the narrative to give you his memories. 'Bob McIntyre and I became friendly – he a Scot, me Irish – and when we joined Honda we weren't the established riders like Jim Redman and Luigi Taveri. We felt a little bit like outsiders, and maybe that made us closer to each other. I had never been behind the Iron Curtain before.

'Bob had an Alfa Romeo which he kept in Germany. I flew over and Bob met me. We got in the car and away we went to the East German border and I can remember it so clearly. On the West German side stood police in nice, what I suppose you'd call turquoise blue uniforms, immaculate hats, immaculate everything else. They saluted you through, bade you farewell and wished you a good journey. We drove across no man's land to tree trunks across the road forming barriers. You had to zig-zag between them. As we did we were halted and a machine gun came through the window. We were asked for our papers and showed what we had. A voice said 'you must have a visa.' To get one we stopped at a railway line and walked over it, grass growing through the sleepers and tracks, walked along the other side to the station, went down steps.

'It was the nearest thing to what you see in espionage films. We came to a door with cobwebs round the edges, went in and faced two long slotted windows. An electric lightbulb swung to and fro, old glasses on a dusty table below it. You handed your passport through a slotted window to get a visa stamped in it – you were only allowed in for so many days. I thought: *Am I in a scene for an espionage film here?* We emerged and Bob said "are you sure we're doing the right thing going to this bloody Grand Prix? Maybe we should go back." We didn't. Mind you, we looked over to the right and saw a watch tower with machine guns or whatever poking out. We drove another half mile, saw another watch tower.

'We stayed at a hotel in the town of Chemnitz (then re-named Karl-Marx-Stadt). There was a night club at the bottom of the hotel and girls would come in and dance. You could get a smile out of them but they didn't have the light-hearted smile of the west, always a strained smile. Chemnitz was grim, grim; even the tram lines would go along and suddenly end. In fact, Luigi Taveri was driving in his Citroën, struck the end of some cut-off tram lines and ripped the whole bloody base out of the car.

'When we got to the Sachsenring they were selling bananas and oranges on stalls by the side of the road, first time they'd been seen since the War. They'd never had them before and this was 1962. If you tried to change your prize money you got a ratio of five to one (East German marks weren't valid in the west and held at an artificial official rate in the east.) I'd go into tool stores and buy bench grinders, vertical drills and things like that to bring out.'

Yes, this is 1962, and after the Sachsenring Hailwood had four wins from the five rounds. Only Shepherd could overhaul him, and then only by a freak of statistics. Shepherd would have to win the last three – the Nations at Monza, Finland at Tampere and Argentina at Buenos Aires – giving him 45 points, but only 34 counting, and have Hailwood score no more than a fifth place in any of the three.

The front row at Monza: Hailwood, Silvio Grassetti (Bianchi), Franktisek Stastny (Jawa), Driver (Norton) and Shepherd. At the flag Stastny led, marginally, Hailwood accelerating on the inside, Read (Norton) surging in the middle of the pack.

Hailwood pulled away, Driver and Bert Schneider (Norton) tracking him. Crossing the line to complete lap 1, Hailwood led by a hundred yards from Venturi and Grassetti, Shepherd panting along in fourth, then Driver,

Schneider and Read. Monza was fast and they strung back behind Hailwood, pushed on and pressed on as best they could. Only Venturi could stay near Hailwood, and at ten laps these two lay far ahead of Grassetti who led Shepherd and Read by quarter of a mile; Driver and Schneider falling away. *Motor Cycling* reported that . . .

As a cool evening breeze swept across Monza Park, the race wore on with no change until, at the end of lap 15, Shepherd pulled into the pits with a dead engine. This seemed to inspire Driver. He put in a spurt and caught Read while Shepherd lost over a lap changing a plug before rejoining the fray.

He also lost the Championship.

Then Venturi began to close the gap that separated him from Hailwood and, to the delight of the crowd, the Italian Champion took the lead on lap 21 (of 35) and held it for four laps. Then Mike fought back and when Venturi went ahead again on lap 28 the pair of them had lapped third man Grassetti!

Who knows if Hailwood played mind-games with Venturi? Who knows if his mischievous sense of humour, his irreverence, led him to make a race of it to entertain the crowd? Did he allow Venturi to go by and tease him simply for the pleasure of it, knowing he could re-take him as his fancy decreed? The evidence, based squarely around the fact that Hailwood was not just the best rider on the best bike but arguably the best rider who ever lived, suggests it. *Motor Cycling* reported that from the lapping of Grassetti . . .

. . . there was never more than yards in it and Venturi must have had hopes of winning as he screamed into the last lap leading by 20 yards, but Mike had other ideas and, leaving it until the last corner, he swept round the Italian to win.

A little theatre on a big Italian stage, the chequered flag representing the final curtain and the play – the great play in many acts – only just beginning. From this moment on Hailwood would move towards joining the dynasty of Duke and Surtees as multiple winners. If you're this good, one is never enough. That might or might not have been apparent on 9 September 1962 as the cool breeze swept Monza, and Hailwood posed with Venturi – Hailwood, leathers unzipped and a tee-shirt underneath, holding a bottle of Coke in one hand, a garland of flowers in the other. Venturi stood almost motionless, a man with short cropped hair, a slightly oval face and a pleasant smile.

Read finished fourth, but so far behind that no time was released. 'I didn't do that many Grands Prix because I'd just got married, but against Mike on the MV you had no chance. You didn't go to win, you went to compete for second place.'

Postscripts
Venturi had won the 500cc Dutch Grand Prix in 1960. He'd never win another, no matter that he'd just been within 0.5 of a second of Hailwood

at Monza. That was surely not apparent on the evening of 9 September 1962.

On 5 March Libero Liberati had ridden a road machine on a road near the town of Terni, where he had a Gilera dealership. He skidded and hit a wall. He died. He was 36. Each year all the way to now, a small society of admirers meet to celebrate his Championship.

Bob McIntyre had crashed at Oulton Park in August and died some days later. He remains one of the greatest riders never to win a World Championship. He, too, would have only a single Grand Prix victory in the 500s – the TT on the Isle of Man in 1957.

Gary Hocking died racing a car in South Africa in December, a Lotus Climax which had been entered for the Natal Grand Prix. Moss ought to have been in it, but he was still recovering from a crash at Goodwood at Easter. Phillis, McIntyre, Hocking, almost Moss. Somehow tragedy stalked them all. Some it released, some it didn't.

Of the death of Hocking, Nobby Clark says 'Gary was not a person who wanted to stay with bikes. The challenge of Formula 1 cars appealed to him. I am sure that, had he lived, he would have reached the top there, too.'

Of the death of Phillis, Hailwood would say 'you live with that narrow margin between life and death all the time, and any additional worry is not going to help the concentration. How much it affects you when somebody is killed depends a lot on how well you know him. If it's a stranger then, obviously, it doesn't mean very much. It's like reading in the paper that someone you've never heard of has been knocked down by a bus. If it's a friend then of course you feel it more; but you can't afford to show it. You simply have to get on with the job or pack it up altogether. It's no good going on racing and thinking all the time that "old so-and-so was killed doing what I'm doing now."'

Redman remembers Hocking spent a lot of time after the death of Phillis 'trying to persuade me to give up racing, too, but I refused because I did not want to run away from things. I knew if I did I would be letting myself down.' That's how Redman coped, Redman who, that September day at Monza in 1962 won the 350 and the 250 and came fourth in the 125, Redman who – four years hence – would try to win the 500 but find himself in a hosptial at Spa instead; and be lucky to be alive.

Some, tragedy released.

1963

End of a dream

Finnish Grand Prix, Tampere

THERE'S A BLACK and white photograph which is so ordinary you can barely believe what it would lead to. Geoff Duke stands beside a Gilera on the grid at Oulton Park. A couple of officials with armbands watch with what seems mild curiosity. The starter holds a Union Jack slack in both hands and gazes down the track. It's late 1962 and the meeting a tribute to Bob McIntyre. Duke, who hadn't raced for three years, said yes when the organizers asked if he could get a racing Gilera vintage 1957 – the year Gilera withdrew, of course – and take it round to entertain the crowd. The presence of Duke on a Gilera would enhance the meeting.

Duke took it round and 'thoroughly enjoyed' doing that, and he began to wonder just how competitive the old bike might *still* be. The next day, as Duke recounts, Avon were at Oulton with 'cling' tyres. Duke tried them on the Gilera and they gave him an astonishing amount of grip. Despite his age and the inescapable fact that he was no longer race-fit he lapped Oulton faster than he'd ever done in his pomp. Duke wondered *harder* just how competitive the old bike might still be, wondered what current riders might do with it against Hailwood on the MV.

A dream began, lovely in its conception, genuinely bold in its ambition and, loveliest of all, simple.

Duke travelled to Italy and spoke to Giuseppe Gilera. He outlined the simplicity. If Gilera lent Duke some 1957 bikes Duke would find the funding. Duke had several interesting reasons for believing MV could be beaten, not least because they'd won the Championship every year since 1958, and the incentive to develop, develop, develop their bikes may have been at a minimum.

Putting MV's record in stark statistics, they beat Norton in the 1958 Makes Championship 48-35; in 1959 beat Norton 56-36; in 1960 beat Norton 54-33; in 1961 beat Norton 64-60; and in this year of 1962 beat Norton 48-35.

Giuseppe Gilera wasn't satisfied with Duke's assurances. He wanted proof. Minter and Hartle travelled to Monza to try the Gileras and the future of the dream rested on how quickly they went. Minter, from Kent and famed for the absolute mastery he exercised over Brands Hatch, was regarded by some as the equal of Hailwood. Hartle, from Chapel-en-le-Frith, we've already met.

They lapped Monza at a steady 117 mph (188 kph) which Minter raised to 118 (189.8 kph) near the end. It compared favourably with the track record held by Surtees, 119.14 (191.73 kph) winning the 1959 Nations Grand Prix. Since Duke would find the sponsorship, Gilera said yes.

The dream team took the name *Scuderia Duke* but internecine strife crept into it. Minter said the suspension of the bikes was too hard and the new regulation fairings for 1963 – called 'Dolphin' – removed a significant amount of downforce. Minter later claimed he was ignored.

Duke experienced such difficulty attracting sponsors that essentially he faced paying for the team himself. It meant allowing Minter and Hartle to race other bikes outside the Grands Prix. They had a living to make, after all.

The return of Gilera created a cameo of thoughts, anticipations and questions and, cumulatively, they stirred the whole sport: Gilera taking on MV and possibly beating them. Who knew? Who could say? The prospect of dogged Minter, a man deeply charged with self-belief, taking on Hailwood posed more questions. Who the better rider? Who knew? Who could say?

Minter and Hartle drew a vast crowd to Silverstone for a spring meeting, which Minter won from Hartle. They ought then to have raced Hailwood and the MV at Brands Hatch, but Hailwood crashed in the 350 race. In the 500 Minter won, Hartle second again. At Oulton, Hailwood still injured, Minter and Hartle both broke the lap record; and at Imola they met Hailwood on the MV, a race of which dreamers dream. Hailwood moved away fast but Minter caught and overtook him, Hartle caught and overtook him and for the first time since 1958 the 500 Championship, to begin at the Isle of Man on 14 June, seemed open not shut.

Hailwood has recounted how MV offered him £1000 (a living annual wage in 1963) to race at Imola and, although his wrist hurt, he fancied the money and fancied a 'go' at the Gileras. 'It was an unwise decision against men like Hartle and Minter. My wrist wasn't fully mended; sore and not very strong.' After leading for 10 laps the wrist 'gave way completely' and The Count, watching as usual on television at home 'must have been embarrassed' seeing MV 'being whacked by his biggest factory rival.'

Next day The Count summoned Hailwood and 'laid into me as hard as he knew how. I yelled back at him just as loudly.' Hailwood departed, but within the hour the Count summoned him from his hotel and apologized.

In May, Minter rode a Norton at Brands Hatch and had what someone has described as a 'lurid and downright terrifying battle' with a rider called Dave Downer. They crashed, Downer killed, Minter's back badly hurt. All else aside, and with due respect to the memory of Downer, the news 'shattered' Duke because he believed Minter could have beaten Hailwood in the World Championship. Duke hired Phil Read. On the Island Hailwood won the 500, Hartle 1 minute 13.4 seconds behind.

'Joining the *Scuderia Duke* was the worst thing I did in my life,' Read says. 'It blew my image of Geoff Duke because obviously I'd followed him. He didn't have the contacts, the wherewithal to make it work. We came to the TT and fantastic, Mike there on the MV, the Gileras back. The bikes looked as if they had been dragged out of a scrapyard. Unbelievable.'

At Assen, the Dutch TT, Hailwood retired (holed piston) and Hartle won from Read. A week later Hailwood reasserted himself in the Belgian Grand Prix at Spa by devastating the Gileras. He averaged 123.987 mph (199.532 kph), this average faster than the previous lap record. Hartle's bike broke down and Read finished second, 1 minute 13 seconds behind. Probably the Championship was decided then.

Certainly the schisms within *Scuderia Duke* grew at Spa. 'In qualifying,' Read says, 'Geoff stood at Malmedy corner, a fourth gear sweeping 180 degrees. My bike didn't handle well, I wasn't happy with it. Afterwards Geoff came up and said "you're bloody useless round there." I replied "OK, you get on it and show me how to do it . . ."'

Minter returned for the Ulster Grand Prix, but Hailwood won it comfortably enough and the speed trap caught him at slightly over 143 mph (230 kph), a good 5 mph faster than the Gileras. Read crashed, damaging the bike. It compounded a delicate situation because Minter had crashed another testing at Monza. While Hailwood won the East German at the Sachsenring from Minter by 55.2 seconds, Hartle crashed and damaged *that* bike.

One remained intact and Hartle took it to the Finnish at Tampere. A contemporary report set the scene. 'Resurfaced and altered from its 1962 layout, the narrow, twisty, tree-lined 2.27-mile (3.65 km) Tampere circuit was felt by many riders to be unfit for a World Championship, and indeed for 1964 the FIM have told Finland they must find another venue.' *Motor Cycling* reported that the spectators . . .

. . . anticipated a battle royal between Hailwood on the MV and John Hartle on the lone Scuderia Duke Gilera flown up from Italy for the meeting.

That would have to wait until after the 350 race where Redman (Honda) led, Hailwood colliding with a Soviet, Nikolai Sevostianov. (Where is he now? What has he been through, if he's survived the thaw of the Cold War? And what monumental Communist bureaucracy did he have to convince to be allowed to go to Finalnd?) They went off – 'both taking to the sand and grass on the trackside' – but Hailwood recovered, sixth. Within four laps he'd passed numbers five, four, three and two, caught Redman and a lap later, slipstreaming, took him and pulled away.

In the 500 Hailwood found himself under real pressure. Crossing the line to complete lap 1 Hartle hung 20 yards behind, but gearbox trouble struck at the Gilera. The dream moved into waking reality then, moved into the chilled light of day.

Hailwood provided his own climax. He hammered the lap record, held by Shepherd at 1 minute 52.1 seconds (72.02 mph/115.90 kph) with 1 minute 40.30 (80.47 mph/129.50 kph). Shepherd himself finished second but a lap behind, the rest scattered even further. Hailwood's race average – 78.73 mph (126.70 kph) – was also an absolute record, beating Shepherd's 68.04 mph (109.49 kph) in 1962. Repeating, Hailwood 78 mph, Shepherd 68 mph. If Duke's thesis held – that MV hadn't been developing their bikes – the 10 mph difference is explicable in only one way: Stanley Michael Bailey Hailwood.

Motor Cycle News reported that . . .

The 500cc race was merely a high speed demonstration for the MV four. With only 27 of the 35 laps run, Hailwood had lapped the entire field, and at the flag the Oxford flyer was a complete lap and 30 seconds in front of second placed man Alan Shepherd. Sven-Olaf Gunnarsson, the fearless Swede, lost his chance of World Championship points when he dropped his Norton on the tricky paddock hairpin when lying fourth behind Mike Duff.

Postscripts

Gilera had three bikes ready for the Nations Grand Prix at Monza two weeks after Tampere. Duke hoped for a 'face-saving finale' and no doubt a result good enough to sustain the team into 1964. Hartle crashed in practice, Read's bike lasted only 10 laps, Minter's 13.

M. Hailwood	1hr 03m 33.3s
J. Finlay (Matchless)	at two laps
F. Stevens (Norton)	at three laps
B. Smith (Norton)	at three laps
L. Richter (Norton)	at four laps
V. Loro (Norton)	at four laps

This represented, as Geoff Duke knew, the end of it. The dream became a memory, part vivid, partly misty, as dreams are.

'At the end of 1963,' Read says, 'I had a telegram from Yamaha asking if I'd race their 250 bike in the first Japanese Grand Prix. I led until the last lap when the bike cut to one cylinder and I finished third.'

J. Redman (Honda)	1hr 01m 34.3s
F. Ito (Yamaha)	1hr 01m 34.4s
P. Read (Yamaha)	1hr 01m 52.5s

This represented, although Read did not know it, the beginning of a dream. 'Yamaha asked me to contract with them for the following year, which I did. In the 500 Championship only MV mattered and you couldn't get one. They had Mike Hailwood and didn't need anyone else – didn't hire anyone else until Giacomo Agostini. I rode for Yamaha until they pulled out in 1968.' Read's dream which did come true: three World 250 Championships and two second places, both behind Hailwood.

1964

Straight five

West German Grand Prix, Solitude

'IN 1964 A REVOLUTION hit motor cycle racing. It was the year when the spotlight and the spectator excitement switched from the glamour of the big 500cc machines and fell on the smaller, sleeker 250s. The race promoters realized, and soon afterwards began to run the 250 races as the last event of the day because they knew the lightweight machines were providing the most thrilling spectacles. I suppose people were getting fed up with watching the endless trail of Mike Hailwood wins on his unchallenged machinery.' Well, yes. The words come from Jim Redman and he is right. Redman and Read (Yamaha) battled and slogged the whole 250 season, Read winning from Redman's Honda by four points.

An endless trail of wins in the 500? Well, yes.

United States GP, Daytona, 2 February:
1. M. Hailwood (MV)   1hr 16m 09.00s
2. P. Read (Matchless)   at two laps
3. J. Hartle (Norton)   at two laps

Tourist Trophy, Isle of Man, 12 June:
1. M. Hailwood (MV)   2hr 14m 33.80s
2. D. Minter (Norton)   at 03m 22.80s
3. F. Stevens (Matchless) at 06m 20.80s

Dutch TT, Assen, 27 June:
1. M. Hailwood (MV)   1hr 03m 35.40s
2. R. Venturi (Bianchi)   at 03m 34.20s
3. P. Driver (Matchless)   at 04m 42.80s

Belgian GP, Spa, 5 July:
1. M. Hailwood (MV)   1hr 04m 23.50s
2. P. Read (Matchless)   at 04m 30.30s
3. P. Driver (Matchless)   at 04m 34.10s

Hailwood broke open the ratchet of five best finishes from the nine rounds. He came to Solitude contemplating a formality. Read cheekily took the lead but, as *Motor Cycling* reported . . .

. . . with Hailwood content to sit on his tail. By the end of the first lap Mike was well on his way to another effortless win.

Late on, Jack Ahearn (Norton) forced his way past Read to take second place but 2 minutes 38.3 seconds behind Hailwood, who by then had dismounted and hung around patiently for the rest to come along. *Motor Cycling* added . . .

The man of the race was Marsovsky. Riding superbly, and lapping as fast as Ahearn and Read, he cut through the field to finish fourth, unlapped by Hailwood despite a crash with Roy Robinson (Norton) at the start.

To be unlapped by Hailwood had become a yardstick, almost the stuff of headlines.

Postscripts
Motor Cycling reported that in the 250 race . . .

From the start Giacomo Agostini (Morini) shot away, his single-cylinder machine out-accelerating all the multis, but by the end of the first lap Redman was just ahead with Read and Agostini in his slipstream.

Morini were a small Italian company founded long ago (1924) and in the 250cc Championship Agostini finished twelfth with six points (against Read's 50, 46 counting, and Redman's 58, 42 counting.) Agostini? Ah, handsome, sun-kissed, a flower of youth. Ah, Agostini, of wealthy stock who'd begun at 17 riding Morinis in small-time Italian events and hill climbs. Who could know that evening of 19 July at Solitude as Hailwood prepared to celebrate enormously (the way he did, win, lose or draw), that within a year Agostini would challenge him for the 500 Championship, that Agostini would inherit the dynasty and pass on into a seemingly endless sequence of wins?

Count Agusta attended the Nations Grand Prix, Monza, 13 September 1964, and witnessed this in the 250 race:

1. P. Read (Yamaha)   41m 24.20s
2. M. Duff (Yamaha)   at 10.00s
3. J. Redman (Honda)   at 10.30s
4. G. Agostini (Morini) at 23.60s

Count Agusta pondered it and when he felt ready – nobody could hurry him – made one of his decisions.

1965

Lessons from the Master

East German Grand Prix, Sachsenring

'THE TROUBLE WITH the Count was that he was unpredictable. One just did not know what he was going to do next. Now whether this was the result of his Latin temperament or that he was such a busy man I don't know. Busy he undoubtedly was, working well into every night running his large business. Racing was just a hobby to him and he was apt to overlook the rider's point of view.

'For instance, when Alan Shepherd wanted a talk with the Count he sat in the outer office for well over a day, actually it might have been two days. Mike once sat for over six hours and then went again the following morning. All the top riders suffered from this sort of thing – Surtees, Hocking, Hartle and Taveri.

'Then there were the difficulties in getting machines for British races in which Mike always likes to ride. I can quite see Count Agusta's point of view. Why should he pay a rider good money and then send machines over to Britain with the chance of the rider falling off and injuring himself, perhaps when a World Championship is at stake? But in Mike's case he had the right to use his own machines so the risk remained.

'To be quite frank about the whole matter, I think the real reason for all this trouble was that at long last the Count felt he had a man from his own nation capable of taking a World Championship – Giacomo Agostini. The Italians are very nationalistic indeed. One has only to go to Monza to see this, either at car or motor cycle meetings. The minute the Ferraris drop out and Jim Clark is leading in a British car the crowds lose interest. If a Norton was winning there would be a general exodus.

'My sympathies are with the Italians. They produce wonderful machines but have not produced a 500 World Champion since Libero Liberati in 1957. Naturally they want one of their own countrymen to take the honours once again. If the positions were reversed surely we in Britain would want a British rider on a British machine to do the same. In Agostini they have this chance. He is a brilliant and daring rider and one of the nicest guys to know. Mike and he are the biggest of pals, no unfriendliness, just a natural spirit of keen rivalry as team-mates.'

Thus spoke Stan Hailwood, exploring the currents and undercurrent which flowed through 1965. The currents surfaced early, in a handful of races in Italy.

Hailwood had been riding at Snetterton and, as Stan wrote, 'we chartered a plane and Mike took off from the circuit for Italy. He got to Imola where the organizers refused to let him have a practice lap because they said he was late. My own opinion is that they wanted an Italian rider to win and Mike was shoved on the back row not even knowing if the gear ratios or the carburation were OK.

'Grimly determined to keep the Union Jack flying, the result was never in doubt – Mike won! But after this weekend he was well and truly browned off. Mike did not mind playing second fiddle to Agostini and letting him win two races to secure the Italian Championship (the traditional early-season races) but at San Remo we got really angry when they tried to persuade Mike to lose there as well. In the end it did not matter because, with the race in his pocket, Mike's MV developed a mysterious ailment and Agostini won.'

Hailwood remembered that 'the Count asked me to let Agostini win at Riccione and San Remo; he told me to take second place. I was annoyed because I reckoned Agostini should have to beat me on his own merits and not be given anything if he was to prove himself. I had far more to lose than he did and I was certainly going to give nothing away. I had to try really hard to get the better of him. I was surprised to find that he was so good. As it turned out he did win both races so all my anger at being told to back down was wasted. It was my resolve, however, that if Agostini was going to achieve World Championship status, even if we were in the same team, he would have to beat me to do it.'

In fact, as Ted Macauley – journalist and friend of Hailwood – explains, 'for tactical reasons Mike concentrated on the 500 with Agostini supporting him, and the other way round in the 350. You have to remember that the 350 was a very big and important class in those days, and of course you had Jim Redman on the Honda in it. Maybe MV did favour Agostini towards the end. Agostini spent a lot of time with the Count's son Rokki on his yacht at Porto Fino and so on, they were friends and that, I think, is how Agostini got so deep into MV. And he was good, anyway.'

The 350 went full to Suzuka, Japan in October.

Hailwood stormed and swamped the 500, winning Daytona from an American, Bruce Parriott, by one minute 36 seconds, winning West Germany from Agostini by 1 minute 39 seconds, winning the TT on the Isle of Man from Joe Dunphy by 2 minutes 19.8 seconds, winning Assen from Agostini by 52.8 seconds, winning Spa from Agostini by 1 minute 30.8 seconds. How far does a racing bike go in a minute? At Spa, averaging 120 mph (193 kph), Hailwood covered two miles. He beat Agostini by *a mile and a half.*

Thence the visas, the formalities, the watch towers and dog runs, the wall which had to be penetrated to gain East Germany and the Sachsenring. The circuit – roads, as we've seen – measured 5.4 miles (8.6 km). The start was cut into a hillside with a curious control tower (like something from an airport) to one side and stands to the other. The riders went through right and left sweepers, rising to the village of Hohenstein-Ernstthal: cobbled streets where solid old houses, their pastel-facades flaking, loomed. The riders passed the village green, climbed and turned hard, hard left at a crossroads, climbed again out of the village past a church which peered from the trees.

At the top of the hill a panorama of undulating countryside spread. The road twisted and ran for perhaps two miles alongside an autobahn, twisted again sharp through 90 degrees onto another road, this one slightly broader; skimmed down a long uncoiling left – a descent – with, now, trees on both sides, the occasional red-brick house locked into decay and passing as a glimpse. A hospital nestled in the trees; another glimpse. The road dipped and rose sharply to a 90 degree left, and there was the start-finish line.

Motor Cycling covered the whole race in a single paragraph . . .

For the first five laps Mike led Agostini until Agostini took the lead himself. Then 'the master' took over and showed his pupil, riding very much more safely than he had the previous day, how it should be done.

This was a direct reference to the 350 where *Motor Cycling* reported that . . .

As the riders lined up on the grid Hailwood, the hero of the Sachsenring crowd from his exploits on the circuit in previous years, got a thunderous welcome. But the cheers changed to groans when Mike's MV failed to start. Twice he had to pull the MV back on compression before it would fire – and then it was slow to pick up. Mike had lost a full half-minute before his engine finally burst into life and he rocketed away.

Meanwhile Redman had been first off the grid but after only a mile Agostini, riding aboslutely on the limit – and at times seemingly well over it! – passed him. By the end of the first lap the Italian was fifty yards ahead of the Honda – the MV snaking viciously as he powered it out of the rising left-hander into the start-finish area. On the second lap Agostini gained another fifty yards and Mike had thrust his way through to an incredible fifth position. But as he completed the lap he coasted into his pit and retired. He reported that the engine, which had been partially seized when he had to start it, had gone 'zonk'.

Towards the end the light drizzle really increased, wetting the circuit and Agostini's lead increased even more quickly. Then, with only three laps to go, came disaster for the MV camp. Agostini's three 'lost' one cylinder – a broken valve suspected – and he was out of the race.

In the 500 the master showed the pupil. The master beat Agostini by 58.2 seconds. It was Hailwood's fourth consecutive 500cc Championship and no man had done that before. A thought to make you wonder: no man *except* the pupil would win it again until the late afternoon of 21 July *1973*. Nobby Clark says crisply that 'I think Ago had the talent but needed Mike to show him how to use it. I also think Ago was lucky to have Mike in the same team. Who could want for a better tutor?'

Postscripts, punctuated by question marks

'Mike's main ambition that year, 1965, was to win every 500cc Grand Prix, but a few days after the Finnish GP we opened *Motor Cycle News* to find that Agostini had been sent there and won both the 350 and 500 races. Mike had not been told anything about it!' The words are those of Stan Hailwood, and a trifle ingenuous, particularly since he was a sharp man seeing all the angles. If Hailwood wanted to win every round did he not enquire about going to Finland (Imatra, incidentally, not Tampere)? If he did not, why not? If he did, what did MV say to him? Were MV playing mind games with Hailwood? Did they uniquely want Agostini? How did the Count rationalize it?

You can hear the silences, so many of them.

Towards the end of 1965 Redman told Honda that they needed Hailwood. Redman constructed a theory on the most pragmatic of grounds; if you have Hailwood you don't have to beat him.

For the final meeting of the season, at Suzuka, Hailwood rode a 250 Honda and won. In the 350, however, as Hailwood wrote, 'Agostini stood a good chance of winning the Championship. I was put in the unenviable position of holding off Jim Redman to let Agostini get ahead to win the race and the Championship. It was particularly unenviable because I had just agreed to join Honda and this was to be my last ride for MV, but my loyalty to MV and Agostini had to take first place and I know that Jim realized my spoiling tactics couldn't be avoided. As it turned out Agostini broke down when he was leading. I moved into first place and Jim was second.' To Redman, the Championship.

Honda had not so far contested the 500 Championship, but if you sense a vacuum you fill it and if you need the best rider, hire him. Redman didn't see it exactly like that, but he wouldn't, would he? Fasten your seat belts. Hold on to the handlebars. Don't close your eyes unless you have to. You might have to . . .

1966

Hailwood – exhausted

Nations Grand Prix, Monza

'IT WASN'T JUST the usual matter of trying to win, it was trying to stay on the thing. It really was the most frightening experience. To try anything at all on the 500 I felt I was risking my life. I had no confidence in the bike. I had to concentrate all the time on keeping it stable. I had trouble with it at almost every point of a circuit: into corners and out of them, on the straights, winding it on over the bumpy bits. It whipped like mad and bent in the middle. Then it wobbled all over the road.'

Mike Hailwood was not a man given to overstatment and that lends a particular weight, almost a ferocity, to his description of the Honda 500, a bike of genuinely awesome power but which has passed into legend for another reason – unrideability. Three other men tried: John Cooper who, when it wobbled, went from footrest to footrest clinging on like a passenger; Taveri who, having a comparatively gentle test run at Zandvoort, couldn't make it go in a straight line and felt his heart beating very hard indeed; and Redman, long accustomed to the vagaries of Honda handling.

Nobby Clark, by now a Honda mechanic, charts this. 'Honda challenged Europe and MV and thought they could win easily with a bike which had a lot of power – fast down the straights but slow round the corners and bends.' Clark charts a broader context, too. 'The Japanese factory teams withdrew in the 1970s and when they came back and challenged a second time everything was different, suspension, frames, brakes all much better and compared to MV they spent vast sums of money, worked day and night and the results had to come; and as their technology advanced so did the tyres, chains and lubricants – but that simply wasn't the case in 1966.'

On this relatively unsophisticated bike Hailwood faced Agostini and the obedient MV. At least Honda had 250 and 300 bikes which behaved well in comparison to the 500.

The legend, too, embraces dark tales of political intrigue at Honda, something which surfaced publicly during the season's opening round, the West German Grand Prix at Hockenheim, fed by rumours that Honda had produced only one 500cc bike and Redman, not Hailwood, would have it.

Redman explains that he'd discussed this with Hailwood and they'd reached an amicable agreement. Hailwood, in Redman's words, had won 'plenty of 500 titles but not the 350,' Redman had won 'plenty of 350s but not the 500.' Redman would therefore concentrate on the 500, Hailwood the 350 and both tackle the 250.

Macauley feels, however, that Honda accepted the agreement in recognition of what Redman had done for them since 1960, and that Hailwood was 'not entirely pleased'. Repeating that Hailwood rarely overstated anything, these words, too, have weight.

The situation compounded immediately. Honda did have two 500 bikes but in practice at Hockenheim Redman broke the gearbox of one, eliminating it. Worse, someone calculated that if Redman and Hailwood competed in the 250, 350 and 500 they'd cover 319 miles (513 km) in a single day, nine more than the stipulated FIM maximum. Reportedly Honda asked for an exception to be made, but the organizers said no. Redman and Hailwood had to drop a race each.

Peter Carrick (in *The Story of Honda*) suggests that 'the combined power of Mike and Jim was needed in the 250 race to counter the ultra-fast Yamahas. They both agreed on that. The wily Redman suggested that Hailwood was better equipped to ride against Agostini in the 350 event, where the Italian would obviously be a greater threat than in the 500cc class. Hailwood, though forced to acknowledge the strategy of Redman's suggestion, felt out-manoeuvred.'

In the 500 Redman beat Agostini by 26.1 seconds, Redman estimating that he reached more than 165 mph (265 kph) on parts of the circuit. Hailwood won the 250 from Redman (and indeed had won the first 250 of the season at Barcelona two weeks before; no 500 race there).

MV now worked frantically, as Carrick says, 'on an enlarged three-cylinder machine with a capacity of around 420cc' and had it ready for Assen only five weeks after Hockenheim.

Redman led Agostini, but Agostini came 'whistling by and I thought to myself "hey, my bike's supposed to be quicker than his."' Hailwood's Honda wouldn't fire at the start. When it did he caught and overtook Redman and Agostini, missed a gear, locked the front wheel and went down. Redman won by 2.2 seconds.

A week later in a wet Belgian Grand Prix at Spa Redman crashed heavily. Hailwood would say that 'I had to do well in Belgium to make it five titles in a row. I must say I felt reasonably confident. Things went according to plan to start with and I built up a long lead but then down came the rain, as it only can at Spa, and I literally could not see where I was going. Conditions were appalling, the circuit swamped.

'Jim fell off and broke his arm and I thought "this is ridiculous, we're not racing any more, just hanging on for survival" so despite my lead (and

I think I could probably have won the race by pushing the bike home) and despite my eagerness to win the 500 Championship for the fifth time I cruised into the pits and called it quits. I don't think I have ever felt so relieved.'

Agostini won from Stuart Graham, son of Les, on a private Matchless. Redman was out, as it seemed, for the rest of the season, leaving Hailwood alone against Agostini in the 500 and 350, and alone against Read in the 250.

Honda (at Redman's suggestion) hired Graham to help Hailwood in the 350, a decision Graham – a 500 man – still thinks strange. In the round after Spa, the East German, Hailwood's Honda broke down 'under Agostini's relentless pressure, (Carrick) after only five laps but Agostini crashed towards the end. Graham, new to it, had driven there straight from Spa and arrived late at night. 'I was keen to have a look at the circuit and, you know, sometimes doing that at night is good because you haven't got all the scenery to distract you. You can identify specific points. It was a fairly daunting place, a real full deal place and for men, not boys.'

The ratchet: five best finishes from the nine rounds. Four rounds gone and Agostini had 20 points, Redman 16, Hailwood none. Hailwood responded, beating Agostini by 1 minute 16.6 seconds in Czechoslovakia; Agostini responded to that, beating Hailwood by 40.7 seconds in Finland. Agostini 34 points, Redman 16, Hailwood 14.

If Redman could ride he held a theoretical chance himself. Agostini, the ratchet tightening, already had five finishes, the lowest of them second places. Every time he won he'd have to drop a second place, rationing the value of the win to two points. Redman and Hailwood had only two finishes and could fully harvest whatever they reaped.

Redman, at home in Southern Africa, cabled Honda and asked if they'd give him a bike for the Ulster Grand Prix. He flew from Johannesburg via Paris and London to Belfast, but when he rode the bike his arm stiffened. Gazing back, Redman estimates that 'if I could have come third in the Ulster, won the TT on the Isle of Man – delayed that year by a dock strike – and the Nations at Monza I could have won the Championship. I had a special thin plaster bandage which I wore under my leathers so nobody knew I had it, but when I took it off the wrist swelled so much that that was it.' A career ended, the 500 Championship gone forever.

In Ulster Hailwood beat Agostini by 1 minute 29.4 seconds – second places useless to Agostini now. Agostini 34, Hailwood 22. Hailwood won the TT (on 2 September the dock strike concluded) from Agostini by 2 minutes 37.8 seconds and if this was not Hailwood's greatest ride it's certainly among them. The Honda wobbled so visibly that other riders, watching, could barely believe Hailwood covered lap 2 on the Island at 107.07 mph (172.30 kph), could barely believe Hailwood covered every lap faster than Agostini. The final average speeds demonstrated that, Hailwood at 103.11 mph (165.93 kph), Agostini 101.09 (162.68 kph). Agostini 34 points, Hailwood 30.

Robb says that 'we had had Italians before Agostini and a lot were good but they tended to reach a point where they tried to stretch themselves beyond their limits. Agostini never did that. I don't think he did even against Mike. In fact I think Mike had to stretch himself beyond *his* limit to stay with Agostini because that Honda really was such a fearsome brute.'

Hailwood had to win the Nations. *If* he came second he lifted his total to 36 – enough, but only assuming Agostini finished behind him. It meant *somebody else* winning the Nations, a ridiculous notion.

At Brno, Hailwood and Agostini had lapped the entire field, and at Imatra, and in the Ulster. You could not of course lap people on The Island because $37^1/2$ miles is too long, but Hailwood and Agostini both finished an astonishing distance ahead of the third man, Chris Conn (Norton), Hailwood by more than 10 minutes, Agostini by more than eight minutes. So: Hailwood had to win the Nations, holding Agostini to the 34 points he'd been on for so long.

Monza would be hot, 100 degrees. Charlie Rous in *Motor Cycle News* reported that . . .

Everyone had come to see the 500s – just two of them really. This was the big decider. The fury of Agostini and Hailwood was a sight to see, the biggest battle for the title since 1957 when, coincidentally, Italian Liberati (Gilera) won. From the start Mike Hailwood was lightning itself, Agostini nowhere near so brisk, but this was no great worry because he was right behind the Honda at the end of the opening lap and closer still after two.

On lap 3 Agostini took the lead. Rous, and everyone else, wondered if Hailwood . . .

. . . deliberately dropped back to play a waiting game.

The race stretched 35 laps, 125 miles (201 km). A waiting game? Rous wrote . . .

. . . this is difficult to imagine lapping at 123 mph (197 kph).

There's a photograph which captures it: Agostini cranking the MV far, far over at the mouth of a right-hander, Hailwood perhaps the length of two bikes behind poised like a predator. Monza, broad and fast, had always welcomed slipstreaming, one rider (or driver) tracking and tracking another, selecting his moment, content to let the leader make the running, knowing he can nip out and take the lead himself. On lap 6 Hailwood increased the tempo and hammered the lap record – 1 minute 44 seconds, 123.67 mph (199.02 kph). Both riders lapped and lapped two seconds inside the old record. Rous wrote . . .

But the Honda could not stand the pace. A rush of smoke from its exhausts marked the end as one or several of its 16 exhaust valves fell into the motor. Agostini was then 500cc World Champion with 28 laps of the race still to be run.

There was a standing ovation as Hailwood pushed the bike into the pits, and the first to shake his hand in sympathy was Count Agusta who, although pleased that Agostini and MV finally won, would undoubtedly have preferred to have seen the race go through to the end.

Agostini lapped the rest of the field twice.

'I remember particularly 1966,' he says, 'when I won my first title at Monza in front of my fans. After the race all the crowd came onto the track. An invasion? Yes, an invasion. I have a picture where they are holding me up, very nice.'

There he is, smiling politely, still in control of himself, the dark hair impossibly in place. He might have been out for a stroll and in a certain sense had, although he averaged 118.970 mph (191.464 kph). Agostini reduced the pace towards the end, and Hailwood's overall record speed – 119.15 mph (191.74 kph) set in 1964 – remained unbroken.

Postscripts

Hailwood insisted that 'I have no regrets whatsoever about my decision that day at Spa' although it altered everything.

'Mike used to say he was more Italian than Agostini because he lost his temper more often!' Macauley remembers, and it's a topic Robb expands. 'Ago was a fantastic man, a gentleman, a thinker and outwardly not at all typical Italian, not temperamental. You couldn't ruffle him, couldn't make him flap. He dedicated himself to what he did. He kept himself to himself but merely because in those days he didn't speak any English and through that felt a little embarrassed.

'I get embarrassed because I don't always hear everything people say – my hearing – and I back out of conversations: I don't want to participate, so I understand Ago's problem. But, to be perfectly honest, there could not have been two nicer and better people racing motor cycles at the same time than Mike and Ago. That would have been impossible.'

1967

Oh no, not again!

Nations Grand Prix, Monza

THE CHANTING AND cheering rose like a clamour, just the way it had the year before. It deepened from a swell to a roar as the fans, the *tifosi*, saw their Chosen Son ascend the podium. Agostini had just beaten Hailwood by 13.2 seconds. If only it had been that: another race, another win, another title.

Hailwood, a man to accept whatever fate brought with equanimity, at first refused to go to the podium. His friend Bill Ivy chipped away at him saying that he should, that he had to, and eventually Hailwood did. When he reached that podium the chant echoed *Ago-stini! Ago-stini! Ago-stini!* At that moment Agostini insisted Hailwood join him on the top rung, a genuine gesture born of friendship and respect – and something equally profound, a need to recognize natural justice.

No rider pitted himself against a season as Hailwood had done. If you glance at the results you might assume 1967 resembled 1966, but that's false. In 1966 he'd contested the 250, 350 and 500 with *help*. In 1967 he contested the 250, 350 and 500 virtually alone. The weight of it bowed him and made him act completely out of character at pressure points, as here at Monza.

The weight of '67: to beat Read and Ivy on Yamahas in the 250, Agostini (MV of course) in the 350, Agostini again in the 500. Moreover, the fearsome 500 Honda still had the frame which wobbled, and Hailwood described it as a 'nightmare'. Many are the witnesses who experienced fear as Hailwood wrestled and arm-locked it. Macauley wrote that Hailwood felt he 'risked his neck every time he rode it. I have seen him reduced to near collapse, shaking and jumpy after races all over Europe. Once I saw a young woman, sick with fright, ask her husband to drive her back to their hotel after she had just seen Mike skilfully tame a particularly fearsome wobble.'

The 500 Championship alone comprised ten rounds, the ratchet tightening to a rider's best six finishes, and it stretched from Hockenheim in May to Canada in September – including the Isle of Man where Hailwood would have to average well over 100 mph again. The 250 comprised 13 rounds, from Barcelona in April to Japan in October, the 350 eight rounds from Hockenheim to Japan.

In a desperate attempt to improve the 500's handling Hailwood hired a brake expert, Colin Lyster, and they went to a welder in Italy to have a new frame made. Hailwood tested it at Modena and, though it didn't feel 'quite right', he sensed they'd found the direction to go. Hailwood raced it at Rimini as the Grand Prix season neared. The press reported that and Honda were 'furious'. They'd much prefer Hailwood to ride a Honda made by Honda than a Honda made by other people, thank you.

For the West German Grand Prix at Hockenheim, Hailwood rode Honda's Honda and took a comfortable lead, but the crankshaft broke. Agostini 8, Hailwood 0. At the TT on the Isle of Man, an epic race huge in its concentration of move and counter move, Agostini led, Hailwood rode with a twist grip loose and Agostini broke down when the MV's chain let go. Agostini 8, Hailwood 8.

Hailwood described the 250 race there. 'I started ten seconds in front of Read, and coming over the Mountain on the first lap I could look back and see him. He must have been really flying but I think he frightened himself so much that he slowed down a bit.' You don't really need a repetition of what Hailwood felt on the 500 Honda . . .

At Assen Hailwood won the 250, 350 and 500, a physical feat of such intensity that for an instant he seemed poised to fall from the 500 when he'd crossed the line 5.3 seconds in front of Agostini. This podium ceremony had to be delayed until he recovered. Agostini 14, Hailwood 16.

At Spa during the Belgian Grand Prix he couldn't tame the 500 enough to catch Agostini, who won by 1 minute 02.6 seconds. Agostini 22, Hailwood 22. At the Sachsenring Hailwood's engine dipped to three cylinders shortly after the start and the gearbox failed. Agostini 30, Hailwood 22.

This mid-season, the 250 Championship stood at Read 34, Ivy 28, Hailwood 26, although the 350 proved no trouble. Hailwood won Hockenheim, the TT, Holland, and East Germany and cumulatively it brought him to the threshold of that particular title. He took it at the next race, Czechoslovakia, and beat Agostini by 15.8 seconds in the 500. Agostini 36, Hailwood 30. Incidentally Hailwood destroyed the Brno lap record with 103.77 mph (166.99 kph). Think about that on a bike that wobbled through the villages of Brno, protection minimal.

At Imatra Hailwood crashed heavily, just missing some trees. Agostini 44, Hailwood 30, but the ratchet now held Agostini: he had six finishes and from here he'd drop points just like 1966, a win worth only two. Hailwood had only four finishes, an aid and a comfort.

In the Ulster Agostini's clutch burned shortly after the start, leaving Hailwood to average 102.88 mph (165.56 kph) and beat Hartle (Matchless) by 2 minutes 24.4 seconds, with Agostini nowhere. Agostini

44, Hailwood 38. Hailwood took the 250 from Ralph Bryans (also Honda) – neither Read nor Ivy got a point.

And he came back to Monza in September, came back to the Nations Grand Prix. The numerals and statistics need a closer examination. Agostini had the 44 points but even *if* he won here and won the final race, the Canadian Grand Prix, could only increase his total by four. Hailwood had the 38 points but from five finishes. He'd keep whatever he got in the Nations but faced the ratchet in Canada. Simply put, Hailwood needed to win the Nations because a second place was useless to Agostini. It would have left Agostini still on 44, Hailwood now 46. *If* Agostini beat Hailwood he'd gain two points, giving Agostini 46, Hailwood 44 and making Canada very, very difficult for Hailwood; arguably impossible.

And he came back to Monza, came back to the emotion of that immense place. Hailwood swept past Read and Ivy to lead the 250 race, held that for a couple of laps and a con-rod broke. Read beat Ivy by 0.6 of a second. Read 50, Ivy 50 but only 46 counting, Hailwood 44.

Bryans remembers 'after Mike broke down I had a fantastic race with Read and Ivy, very close all the time and I led them into the final corner, but they both came past,' or as *Motor Cycle News* reported . . .

Read and Ivy were content to sit behind and wait until the last dash for the line when they simply swooped ahead as they pleased.

The emotion – a noisy, turbulent, unrestrained thing, the *tifosi* eager and vocal and partisan – now rose towards the 500. *Motor Cycle News* reported that . . .

From a superb start Hailwood went straight ahead and was on his own. Nobody, and that includes Agostini, had a chance against him as he put on the pressure and shattered the lap record every time he came round.

He powered clean through his own 1966 lap record of 123.67 mph (199.02 kph). The emotion all around, he did 126.77 (204.01 kph). By only lap 9 of the 35 he'd lapped everyone except Agostini who 'while still capably close was over 10 seconds behind.' Reporter Charlie Rous sensed with perfect clarity the seeming contradiction of what unfolded. Hailwood, he knew, was almost cruising home, albeit at an average speed higher than the old lap record.

Three laps remained and Hailwood led Agostini by 17 seconds. Without warning the crankshaft buckled, the Honda trapped in top gear. Agostini convulsed Monza by overtaking Hailwood as they passed the vast, teeming grandstands – a moment of contradictions, the Italians abandoning themselves, crying with the joy of it, Hailwood a sad and angry prisoner of the bike.

Agostini says that 'Mike slowed, I didn't know why, I only really knew a lap later when I got a pit signal "Hailwood out of contention". I said to myself "OK, easy now" because, you know, it was never easy when Mike was in a race . . .'

Agostini won; Hailwood hobbling along 13.2 seconds later.

Honda mechanic Katsumasa Suzuki says that 'Mike was locked in fourth or fifth gear and the drum wouldn't open. Mike was trying so hard to stay in front but there was no way he could win the race. Agostini passed him, there was a huge crowd and they were all cheering Agostini. Mike did not stop, he continued, finished and just after he crossed the line he stopped his machine and got off. We expected and understood that he didn't want to talk to anybody. However, when we saw him walking towards us he didn't show any upset and disappointments. His face was just like before, always smiling.'

That was typical, Hailwood not a man to show anything else to people who had worked so hard for him. Privately he told Macauley 'I was about three minutes from winning that race. Three minutes, that's all, and a stupid thing like that had to go wrong. I could have cried. It was the last of the European classics and I needed to win there to have a chance of taking the Championship in Canada. If there'd been a river near enough I'd have thrown the Honda in, I was that sick of it. There was all hell to pay for the mechanic who had prepared the bike.'

That's when Ivy had to persuade him onto the podium, that's when Agostini insisted on sharing the top rung.

Postscripts

'Mike could get in a mood, a black mood,' Bryans says, 'but he'd come out of it quickly enough. We had a big party that night, as we generally did, at a hotel near Monza. I can't remember the name but I do remember it had fountains and its own grounds. Quite a party, actually, and yes Mike had got over it, back to his normal self. Agostini, incidentally, was the most un-Italian rider I ever knew. Normally you expected Italians to go flat out, crash in a heap, get up and go flat out, crash in a heap. He was controlled, very consistent, didn't make many mistakes.'

Hailwood won the Canadian Grand Prix, beating Agostini by 37.7 seconds, a result adequate for Agostini's purposes. Agostini 58 but 46 counting, Hailwood 52 but 46 counting. Both had won five races so the Championship turned on the most second places, and Agostini won that by three to Hailwood's two.

Hailwood also won the 250 in Canada but he and Read didn't finish in the finale at Fisco/Fuji in Japan. Hailwood 54 points but 50 counting, Read 56 but 50 counting. This tie-break decided on wins in Hailwood's favour by five to four.

In February 1968 Honda withdrew from racing. Mike Hailwood never rode in another motor cycle Grand Prix.

1968

The Ago era
(Part One)

East German Grand Prix, Sachsenring

THE MAN HIMSELF can't remember one race from another in the sequence, and who can blame him? They've melted and merged into a communal memory because their characteristics were so similar: same place, as near as dammit the same day of the same month year after year, same result.

Jack Findlay, a pleasant Australian, rode all through this. 'We didn't race against Agostini, we had our own race. He'd clear off into the distance and the objective of the other riders – apart from beating each other – was to finish on the same lap as Agostini. Sometimes we did, you know. You didn't think of beating him, that wasn't in your thoughts at all. Mind you, he didn't play the superstar, he was more one of the lads and I got on well with him.'

The statistics are slightly stunning and to appreciate them we need to look beyond 1968. This chapter is not just the story of a season but an exploration of several situations. First, the statistics.

In 1968 Agostini won all 10 races, forcing the ratchet so wide open it had no meaning. In West Germany he lapped everyone, in Spain everyone bar Findlay, he took the TT by more than eight minutes, Holland by more than a minute from Findlay, Belgium lapping everyone but Findlay, East Germany lapping everyone, Czechoslovakia by more than five minutes, Finland lapping everyone, Ulster by more than three minutes, the Nations lapping everyone except Renzo Pasolini.

In 1969 he won all 10 of the 12 rounds he contested, Spain by 37.6 seconds, West Germany lapping everyone bar two, France lapping everyone, the TT by more than eight minutes, Holland lapping everyone bar two, Belgium lapping everyone bar one, East Germany lapping everyone, Czechoslovakia by more than four minutes, Finland lapping everyone, Ulster lapping everyone bar one.

In 1970 he won all 10 of the 11 rounds he contested, West Germany by nearly three minutes, France by 48.2 seconds, Yugoslavia lapping everyone, the TT by more than five minutes, Holland by nearly two minutes, Belgium by more than three minutes, East Germany lapping everyone except John Dodds, Finland by more than a minute-and-a-half, Ulster by nearly two minutes, the Nations by 43.7 seconds, everyone else two laps and more behind.

In 1971 he won all eight of the 11 rounds he contested, Austria by 36.4 seconds, West Germany by 13.2 seconds, the TT by more than five-and-a-half minutes, Holland by nearly a minute, Belgium by more than a minute and a half, East Germany lapping everyone bar one, Sweden lapping everyone bar two, Finland lapping everyone bar two.

We'll come to 1972 in due course, but you get the idea.

Iain Mackay, who now works for Honda, says 'Ago had two great years against Mike Hailwood but then Honda went and Ago just paralysed everything: incredibly boring in one way but in another everybody had something to shoot at, something to measure themselves against. You did it by how far you finished behind him. Simple as that. Ago did what he had to do.'

True, in 1968 the MV was the best bike by a distance – or a lap, if you prefer – and only Agostini had it. 'The MV represented 65 to 70 horsepower where we had 45,' Findlay says. 'There's not much you can do about that.' Findlay had a Norton, a couple of others had Matchlesses, the rest Lintos and Seeleys and Patons and Benellis and Metisses and Vostoks and Triumphs and CZs. No chance.

Another rider, the Australian Dodds, reinforces this. 'Between the point where Mike Hailwood stopped and Jarno Saarinen began, Ago had no opposition. In those years there were two races – him against himself and then the rest of us. You'd be lapped twice even if you were running second or third. You'd only actually see Agostini when he lapped you.

'Nobody was making any money, we were just having a good time. There were no works rides anywhere in sight because the Japanese had stopped racing. If you go back to the early 1960s, every privateer rode to make a name for himself to get a works ride. When the Japanese stopped, you were looking at a horde of private riders on old bikes. The last Nortons and Matchlesses had been built in 1962 so the bikes were 10 years old, 12 years old and constantly repaired – but not modified. The tyres we used you only had to change once a season, and that was at the Dutch Grand Prix. We didn't know Ago had special tyres from Dunlop! The good part about it was that one change of tyres didn't cost much.

'There were a lot of good private riders, some super good and you might put them on a par with Agostini; John Cooper, Derek Minter, John Hartle, Guyla Marsovsky from Switzerland, Jack Findlay. That's not to detract from Ago because he was a really keen go-er. You never approached a race thinking about being lapped twice, no use even thinking about it because you were in another race to Agostini, it was completely uninteresting to consider things like that. There wasn't any private rider in the paddock that ever thought about Agostini because it was as if he wasn't there. The only thing to hold your interest was being second. How could you contemplate racing the bloke? He'd have to lose a wheel or something. I don't know what you could compare the horsepower difference with. I suppose a 125 and a 500.

'Ago won and won. It must have been boring for him, although, when you're winning, races are never exactly boring. He's one of the best riders I've ever seen, but I don't think as good as Mike Hailwood because in my time Hailwood – with Saarinen – were the best.'

Glancing from 1968 to 1970, Kawasaki, Yamaha and Suzuki began to work their way into the 500 Championship, and in 1971 Agostini's winning margins were at least held to sane proportions.

Agostini himself is naturally protective of his own career and sensitive to suggestions that his stature as a rider is being diminished because he did win easily, did paralyse races against riders not as good or, at least, struggling on inferior machinery.

Question: Was it difficult?

'What do you mean, difficult?'

Because you won, won, won and people expected that.

'Yes, but I was good. Yes, yes, sometimes in my career when I finished second people said Agostini's nothing. In their eyes I had to win. I don't know why. In my career I raced with and I beat many, many riders, Mike Hailwood, Phil Read, John Cooper, Kenny Roberts, Johnny Cecotto, Barry Sheene, Jarno Saarinen, Marco Lucchinelli and he was World Champion. So I raced with all these people and I beat all these people.'

Question: Which of these races – '68, '69, '70, '71 – can you remember? They were all at the Sachsenring.

'First, it was a very difficult circuit but good to go there because the people were so nice. East Germany was communist, of course, and they didn't have many events, so when we raced there it was an occasion. About 150,000 spectators came, but the circuit: difficult and dangerous, because it was normal roads . . . normal East German roads.'

Question: How did you celebrate in East Germany?

'We have always a big party because you couldn't take the money out of the country, you must spend it. Otherwise what could we do with the money? Nothing.'

But which of these four races can you remember?

'I don't remember exactly. I'd have to read my own book to refresh my memory.'

That's the merging and the melting; and forgive him for it. The races are uncannily similar and scarcely memorable in terms of racing, incidents, drama or anything except the neat, handsome man of medium height ticking them off.

Mackay says that 'Ago immersed himself in the whole thing and behaved very professionally. He didn't just turn up, ride, win and walk away. He went testing, he went to bench testing, he noted all the engines, where they delivered power. He knew what he wanted, he asked for it and he was a great asset to a team. It wasn't just a case of "oh we've got the fastest bike, we'll turn up at the weekend and win" – no, it was actually development and development and development of what they had. He made a huge input into that side of it.

'The crowds didn't take it very well when he was winning the 500 Championship with five races to spare, six races to spare, but he was a good, good rider. He'd done it when it counted. His career didn't begin when there was no opposition. He'd raced against people like Mike and held his own for several years, particularly with the 350. He earned and received respect because he had pedigree. If he'd arrived from nowhere, taken the fastest bike and run away with everything he would have been greatly resented.'

The 350? From 1968 onwards Agostini won that, too, and would win it consecutively until 1974.

As we've seen, the Sachsenring represented a window on the world, that world East Germans could no longer visit, hence the 150,000 spectators. What was it like then? 'You drove to meetings in a van,' Dodds says. 'There weren't many people with caravans. Most of the guys had a Ford Thames. The Ford Transit had just come out, and only people with money had one (chuckle). I slept in the back of the van or in a tent, but since most of us were single that wasn't a bad thing.

'At the Sachsenring all that interested us was getting the birds into the paddock. We'd go out with the vans, pick up these tootsies and bring them in, and about an hour later the Stasi (the feared secret police which actively monitored the whole population) came and removed them. Then everyone would go out with the vans and bring them back in again. You didn't have to work on the bikes. After a race, for example, you'd check the timing, put the bike in the van and clear off, and all you'd be thinking about for the next week was birds and booze.'

On a more sober note, Dodds adds that 'I've always been of the opinion there should be a way to find the fastest rider, not the rider with the most guts. One of the best things which has happened to motor cycle racing is that these days the circuits are so much safer. Riders can now fall off and they've got to be really unlucky to hurt themselves. In those days at places like the Sachsenring and Czecho, if you were to survive you learnt not to fall off. You raced at a speed where you never fell.

'The Sachsenring was a fantastic place because I've never seen so many enthusiastic spectators. There wasn't anything else for East Germans to do – well, that's not strictly right but very, very little else. I remember the first time I went there in 1967 and about 200,000 people showed up on the Thursday, the day before racing even started!

'After a couple of years the authorities stopped the restaurants and pubs selling beer because they became worried. People might have got out of control. Those days in those countries nobody opened their mouths too wide or they were picked up and taken off. As riders, you could only enter East Germany with an invitation. You were more or less invited to come to the East German Grand Prix and you had to have this invitation to get a visa. They'd keep us for four or five hours at the border, no reason, and we'd sit there and bugger around. They'd change the Border Guards' shift and then let us go.'

Motor Cycle News covered the decisive race of 1968 in a few paragraphs . . .

Giacomo Agostini clinched his third 500cc World Championship with an absolute lap record of 109.79 mph (176.68 kph) at sizzling Sachsenring during Sunday's East German Grand Prix.

True to form, and well on his way to becoming the first Italian to win both 350 and 500cc titles, Agostini played a brilliant power game winning both classes on his fabulous MV-threes.

All except Derek Woodman got away to a clean start. He pushed his Seeley the whole length of the pit area before it fired. After six hard working laps he gave up a hopeless job. By then, after the initial thunder had died down, the race pattern emerged. As expected, Agostini went faster and faster, breaking the lap record and doing even better next time round. Though not fitted with the disc brakes he tried in practice, his MV-3 ran faultlessly under the watchful eye of the best racing mechanics in the world.

Agostini covered the 107 miles (172 km) in 1 hour 39.4 seconds and lapped everyone. Findlay, Dodds and the rest can scarcely have been surprised – or bothered.

Postscripts
The riders held a meeting at the Sachsenring and announced they intended to form a Grand Prix Riders' Association – confined to riders with two or three years' experience – to negotiate proper starting money, 'flat rates' from £125 to £200. John Cooper, for example, received only £25 to race at the Sachsenring and that included getting there.

In the 125cc race Ivy, friend and kindred spirit of Hailwood, became the first man at that class to lap the Sachsenring at over 100 mph. Perhaps he liked the place.

1969

The Ago era (Part Two)

East German Grand Prix, Sachsenring

'THE SPECULATION AND excitement surrounding the anticipated battle between Ivy and Agostini began to grow, even before practice started. Many thousands of fans swarmed to the circuit, braving the wet, dismal conditions just to watch the training sessions.' This is how Alan Peck describes the build-up to the 350 race in *No Time To Lose*.

Agostini had 60 points, Ivy (Jawa) 24, but the Jawa was temperamental – although when it went, it went and Ivy could handle it. He'd even overtaken Agostini at Assen, something stretching credulity. Hence the 'anticipated battle'.

During the Saturday morning practice the Jawa went 'erratically' and, approaching the village of Hohenstein-Ernstthal, Ivy fell. The engine had seized. As Ivy skittered across the road his helmet came off and he received fatal injuries when he struck a wooden fence. *Motor Cycle News* reported that . . .

A crowd of 130,000 braved the bad weather on race day and they observed a minute's silence after a floral tribute was placed on the spot Ivy and his Jawa would have occupied on the grid. It was a moving scene but the show went on and Agostini worked off some of the emotion he felt over the loss of the only rival who could seriously have challenged his superiority.

Agostini won from Rod Gould by nearly a minute, and in the 500 . . .

. . . cleared off with typical dash.

Karl Auer, an Austrian and noted performer in the wet, clung to a distant second place although Agostini moved imperiously past even him on the last lap. And that was World 500 Championship number four.

Postscripts
A week later Agostini won the 350 in Czechoslovakia and that was World 350 Championship number two.

The scoring in the 500s had been changed. From 1950 to 1968 the sequence went 8, 6, 4, 3, 2, 1. That now became 15, 12, 10, 8, 6, 5, 4, 3, 2, 1 and stayed like that until 1988. Truth to tell, it didn't matter how you arranged or altered this scoring in the Ago Era. If you win all the races you win all the Championships and no system can stop you.

1970

The Ago era (Part Three)

East German Grand Prix, Sachsenring

ON 3 MAY at the Nürburgring a West German, Ernst Hiller, finished eighth in the West German 500cc Grand Prix behind a Finn, Martii Pesonen. Hiller rode a Kawasaki, Pesonen a Yamaha. They did not of course trouble Agostini – Pesonen 5 minutes 55.8 seconds behind him, Hiller 6 minutes 20.1 seconds – but from this moment on the power balance began to shift. This did not happen immediately, but it began here.

Ginger Molloy, who'd finished fifth on a Bultaco at The Ring, moved to Kawasaki and in the next round, the French at Le Mans, came second to Agostini, 48.2 seconds behind. This represented a close finish in the Ago Era, almost a photo finish. The ratchet? Forget it.

Molloy couldn't sustain this (nor could anyone else) so that on 12 July Agostini found himself back on the familiar autobahn towards Karl-Marx-Stadt and facing the familiar scenario; win, go to the party to get rid of the winnings, go home.

Robb, riding a Seeley, describes the start. 'Pole position was on the left-hand side beside the conning tower. No green light in those days but a starter with a flag – the national flag of whatever country you were in. The starter positioned himself on an elevated rostrum further down the road on the left and raised the flag. An official stood behind him holding a stop watch so that the starter didn't have to bother about that.

'The official tapped him to indicate he'd begun the count-down and sometimes whispered into the starter's ear. You knew then it would go 10, 9, 8, 7, 6. You watched that official – not the starter – because he'd tap again when the count down reached 5. If you saw the official's coat move, if you saw a muscle in his body move you knew 5 seconds to go, now 4 and you were gone at 3, pushing at 2, bumping the engine at 1. Somehow I still had *lazy* starts.

'If you did make a better start than Agostini at a place like the Sachsenring you could lead him through the section to the village. In his sensible way he wouldn't do anything to overtake you there because he knew he would disappear when he reached the country. As soon as he got round the corner in the village the performance of the MV compared to its weight ratio started to come into its own. From then on you'd only see him close when he lapped you.

'On the first lap at the long right-hander on the downhill you might catch sight of him already turning left into the start-finish but you wouldn't catch sight of him again until he did lap you. You don't really see the speed difference in terms of him pulling away at the start. It comes when you are totally frustrated because there is nothing you can do about it; his bike comes alongside you and if the rider is of equal or better ability and if his bike goes 10 mph faster than yours – and the MV must have been that – you're helpless.

'You break down the 10 mph to feet per second and consider what that difference is, and then multiply it by a race lasting more than an hour. Actually I don't remember him lapping me. I think I spent some time in the pits that race because I finished tenth and usually I'd be higher than that.' *Motor Cycle News* reported that . . .

Hopes of a 500cc challenge from Pasolini fizzled out when his big Benelli seized while chasing Agostini. The chase lasted eight laps. The Italian rivals were four seconds apart when they parted company, leaving Dodds a minute behind the champion. Though bothered by cramp in his legs, the small Australian could not believe his Linto had lasted 21 laps, the whole race.

Dodds commented at the time 'it's not the best it has ever gone but it is certainly the longest.' Dodds began his final lap just as Agostini crossed the line to win. Dodds had done it; stayed unlapped.

And that was World 500cc Championship number five.

Postscripts

'I had a Ford Transit van with three bikes in it and a caravan which I towed behind the van,' Robb says. 'We got about three or four miles away from Karl-Marx-Stadt and crunch, the gearbox main shaft breaks on the van. I freewheeled and luckily came to a lay-by. I had my wife and daughter with me. I thought *that's great. I'll never get spare parts in East Germany and every other rider had already left except Godfrey Nash.* He had a big converted ambulance and I knew he was still in the paddock when I'd driven out of it. I said to my daughter "go and stand at the edge of the autobahn and if you see him wave him down." Sure enough along came Godfrey, my daughter – who must have been all of 11 – flagged him and we hitched my van and caravan to the back of his ambulance and he towed us out.'

This postscript is not as innocent as it sounds. Britain did not recognize East Germany. A British citizen in trouble had no diplomatic representation and who knew what might happen if you were lost behind the Iron Curtain?

Everybody remembers Agostini but what about some of the others in that race? What about McDonald and Trabalzini, Julos and Ravel? Melted, and not even into memory.

In August 1993 I interviewed John Dodds about the race. Like Agostini himself, there's been a melting. 'You say I was the only one on the same lap at the end? (chuckle) I can't believe that. It was about the only Grand Prix I finished on that bike. Everything broke on it from the back spokes to the front spokes, more or less. In reality it ruined me financially. By the time I'd finished with it you couldn't sell it because nobody wanted it. I was lucky to get the loan of a 250 Yamaha . . .'

1971

The Ago era (Part Four)

East German Grand Prix, Sachsenring

McDONALD AND TRABALZINI, Julos and Ravel? We won't be meeting them again, but at the Sachsenring we meet riders who won't be merging and melting. In the 125cc race a chirpy Cockney on a Suzuki finished behind a master, Angel Nieto (Derbi), but running hard at him. His name: Barry Sheene. In the 250cc race a West German, Dieter Braun (Yamaha) won, Read (Yamaha) third, the Finn Saarinen (Yamaha) fifth. And a statistical oddity in the 350 race; Gould (Yamaha) actually led Agostini for two laps until his carburettor broke. Agostini won, of course.

The ratchet in the 500? Forget it. Agostini had pole, of course. He'd done 2 minutes 58.7 seconds, Dodds 3:08.3, Turner 3:09.7, Offenstadt 3:10.0, Bron 3:12.5, Carlsson 3:12.8. *Motor Cycle News* evaluated the race itself (correctly, surely) by devoting but one paragraph to it . . .

Agostini has no problems in an event that slumped to a nine-machine field at the end of its overlong 21-lap distance.

Only Keith Turner, a New Zealander, finished on the same lap – just.
What else is there to say?

Postscripts

Michael Scott writes in *A Will to Win* (1984) that Sheene 'disliked East Germany' and 'criticised it for being colourless and stifling the pleasure of living. On the journey back near Karl-Marx-Stadt, Sheene and others espied a big flan in a shop window and, hungry, offered to buy it – a good way to shed the non-convertible East marks. The woman wouldn't sell, but they heaped so much money on the counter that eventually she did. Soviet soldiers had gathered and Sheene started throwing them bits.' Barry Sheene would be intimidated by no circuit, no bike, no situation and certainly not Soviet soldiers.

Braun, a West German don't forget, won the 250cc race. 'Around the start-finish line alone there must have been 200,000 people at every vantage point, even in the trees,' Dodds says. 'Nobody expected Braun to win this race and, of course, they had to play the West German national anthem. I've never seen a more moving moment in all my life. Everybody got up and sang and all the East Germans knew the words.

'You could see the police, really nervous, they had machine guns in their hands and people didn't know what they were going to do. It was at the point where it might have got out of control. Incidentally, they never had sidecar races at the Sachsenring because the West Germans dominated the event . . .'

You must see it, this Iron Curtain which followed ancient boundaries and divided one village in the west from another perhaps a hundred yards away in the east; divided, in Berlin, one side of a street from another; and on both sides were Germans, the same Germans, a mother here unable to visit a son there, a father there unable to visit a daughter here. East Germans singing the West German national anthem was a way of saying – no matter how many million Soviet soldiers occupied East Germany – we are a people, we are one people.

It's touching that so many bike riders sensed and saw this and went back year after year when they'd have been better off in many significant ways (like financially) simply staying at home. In racing terms in this book, of necessity, we pass quickly across Agostini's races at the Sachsenring because so little happened in them. In the big world beyond sport a great deal happened.

Oh – World 500cc Championship number six.

1972

The Ago era (Part Five)

Belgian Grand Prix, Spa

GIACOMO AGOSTINI DID not win World 500cc Championship number seven at the Sachsenring for two reasons: the number of races had been increased from 11 to 13 and the ratchet altered accordingly. A rider could count his seven best finishes. Agostini won six of the first seven races and locked away the Championship a race before the Sachsenring.

Included among these victories was the TT at the Isle of Man, but there Agostini's friend Gilberto Culotti crashed fatally in the 125 race. Agostini vowed not to return, and never did.

A harder season, the MVs not completely reliable. In the 350 Championship Saarinen (Yamaha) took the first two rounds, but MV produced a new bike and on it Agostini won and won and won. Alberto Pagani partnered him in the 500, a straight fight between MV and Yamaha, but Yamaha was not yet strong enough. Nor was Pagani strong enough to withstand Agostini.

A curious thing happened in the 350 race during the French Grand Prix at Clermont Ferrand (second round of the 500 Championship). Read, riding a Yamaha, went well. 'After the race I said to Pino Allievi of the Italian paper *Gazzetta dello Sport* "if you want to call Count Agusta, tell him I'm available to help Ago." A cheeky remark, but Pino did it. Next day I rang my secretary and she said "oh, we've had a call from a Mr Agusta. Can you ring him?"' That was May. Read had found another dimension to his career. 'I rode the 350 to support Ago because (at that stage) the bikes weren't competitive.'

The ratchet in the 500? Forget it. *Motor Cycle News* reported that . . .

The seemingly endless stream of problems that are following the MV team around this season struck again in Belgium and almost relegated Pagani to the non-starters' list. During Saturday morning's closing practice session his 500 shed part of its exhaust system and developed front brake failure. He didn't have time to make a machine swop so he was left with four wet laps on Friday and two more slowish affairs in Saturday's damp conditions. This put him in 22nd place and well below the official qualifying speed.

But Pagani was in luck. There were a lot of other riders with slow wet speeds so the stewards lowered the qualifying times. If they hadn't, the grid would have contained just about six riders who took advantage of the only dry session on Thursday. Even Giacomo Agostini could only manage a 4 minutes 57.6 seconds lap to make him twelfth fastest, the result of arriving a day late.

It put Agostini on an 'unheard of' third row. He took the lead within a quarter of a mile, Pagani 'hustling' up to fourth at the end of lap 1. Pagani kept hustling, was second at the end of lap 2 and catching Agostini. Imperious Spa, a panorama of a circuit with a great and classical descent from the hairpin to the twist and climb of Eau Rouge, bubbled at the sight of it. Pagani passed Agostini after five laps and Agostini tracked him for another three.

Would it happen, could it happen? Could Agostini be beaten?

Without warning Pagani's exhaust pipe began to fail, the power ebbing from the bike. He slogged forward, milked the machine for what it could still give and came home 32 seconds behind Agostini.

And that was World 500cc Championship number seven.

Postscripts

The Ago Era would continue, but only after an interruption. Before we reach that, a word from Geoff Duke. 'Agostini didn't get the credit he deserved because it happened that most of the time the competition wasn't there. To get a really accurate view of Agostini's ability you have to go back to the TT in 1967 where he had a big dice with Mike Hailwood and led him, very nearly beat him. Quite honestly, anyone who could do that on the TT course had to be extremely good.'

Read sees it a different way. 'It's unfair Agostini won 15 Championships, ten of which were in five years with no competition. To my mind, that's not winning by your own ability and courage and daring. You've the fastest bike and you simply open it up on the last lap.'

At a meeting at Silverstone during 1972 MV gave Read a 500, and he lapped a couple of seconds quicker than Agostini. 'MV thought "ah, he can ride a 500." I got a full contract for 1973.'

Interesting. Very interesting.

1973

Read and the bitter season

Swedish Grand Prix, Anderstorp

SOME OF THE facts are clear. Early in 1973 Jarno Saarinen travelled to Japan, mounted a new and highly secret Yamaha and lapped their test track a full second quicker than anybody else had ever done. A whole season began to unfold then, drawn into a single, sharp dimension. Yamaha would take on, and beat, the unbeatable: Agostini and MV.

Count Agusta had Agostini and Read on the 500s. Yamaha hired Hideo Kanaya – who Macauley describes as 'a young and hitherto unknown Japanese with a ready grin and an easy manner' – to help Saarinen.

Saarinen stirred everything by winning the Daytona 200, the first European to do that, and at the Imola 200 took the lead early, cantering home by a distance. It brought them to the bleached circuit of Paul Ricard in the South of France for the first Grand Prix, 22 April.

We need not dwell on the 250, which Saarinen won by 27.6 seconds from Kanaya (no MVs) or the 350 which Agostini won (no Yamahas). The 500 was *the* race, the point of departure where everything would be explored, perhaps proved. In the background MV, sensing the depth of this direct challenge, worked urgently on a new and faster four-cylinder.

Saarinen set fastest time in both practices, and before the race Agostini seemed pensive, taciturn, and Saarinen was withdrawn into absolute concentration. Read grasped the lead with an enormous start, the mid-field runners still leaving the grid as he'd pulled 30, 40 yards clear. Saarinen caught and overtook him, bending the Yamaha to Ricard's curves, smoothing it down the immense straight. Read tracked but Agostini, pushing and squeezing – he'd rattle over the kerbing at corners under the enforced urgency of his entry speed – made a mistake among tail-enders and fell. He walked slowly, hesitantly to an ambulance, shaken; almost bemused.

Saarinen beat Read by 16 seconds, with Kanaya 2.1 seconds behind Read.

At the Salzburgring, wet, Read led again, Saarinen took him after two laps and they duelled: breathless, breathtaking combat round the majestic, mighty sweeps. They touched and that stirred a bitter argument afterwards. Read retired with mechanical troubles. Agostini never figured and Saarinen took it from Kanaya by 25.4 seconds. At Hockenheim MV gave the new bike to Read, not Agostini, and Read led again. Saarinen hounded him but Read withstood and towards the end Saarinen's chain broke.

At Monza a week after that Saarinen contested the 250 prior to the 500. Pasolini (Harley Davidson) led, but at the Curva Granda hit oil left by a rider in the previous 350 race. Pasolini lost control and was thrown. Saarinen, close, struck Pasolini's bike and the pack, travelling at perhaps 120mph (190 kph), engulfed them. The pack disintegrated as if a bomb had burst, men and machinery ramming, falling, spinning.

Neither Pasolini nor Saarinen survived.

The 500 race was cancelled and, on the day of Saarinen's funeral, Yamaha announced their withdrawal from the rest of the season. Nobby Clark, now with Yamaha, says 'Yamaha were devastated when they lost Jarno. They had made their plans for years to come and then suddenly he was gone, leaving them in a vacuum.'

It left the Championship and the whole sport diminished at several levels, not least that Saarinen had touched authentic greatness, and many sound judges aver he'd achieved it. Motor sport will always produce such: men with a great brilliance which illuminates and remains awkward to quantify, and the darkness they leave becomes precious as a flame, almost mystical; the more because all the great questions – what would Saarinen have done in the years to come? Where would the brilliance have taken him? – can never be answered.

Read and Agostini filled the vacuum because they could do nothing else. They did not co-exist comfortably. Macauley writes 'it became clear the bitterness that had eroded the Read-Agostini partnership, fired by the apparent preferential treatment of Read by Rokki Agusta, the MV boss's playboy son, had alienated Agostini beyond the point of no return. Why this should have happened (apart from Rokki's recognition of Read's great skill) is not clear. But people close to the centre of activities at MV have suggested that Rokki did not take too kindly to having all attention focused away from him and on to Agostini whenever the Italian group gathered in the usual haunts of the jet-setters.'

These many years later Read comments on that statement, 'No, no, not true because Rokki was a name in his own right, the son and heir and a multi-millionaire. He'd done all the jet-set scene before. What was it between MV and Agostini? I don't think it was bitterness, I think they just felt he was dragging the lead, wasn't putting himself out to overcome the deficiencies of the machine to win the World Championship. The bitterness may have been only that he resented me coming into the team. He'd had it easy for so long, and I lapped faster. You've been cruising round at eight-tenths and now you've to ride at ten-tenths, on the limit. He didn't like it. The competition was becoming quite intense, too.'

Moreover, Kim Newcombe, a New Zealander on a Konig, came into the equation, winning Yugoslavia and finishing second to Read at Assen before Agostini reasserted himself by taking Spa and Brno: Read second both times. Read 66 points, Newcombe 51, Agostini 30, three rounds to run. The ratchet: six best finishes from the eleven rounds and Read had five, Newcombe five, Agostini only two. No matter. *If* Read came second to anybody in the next race, Sweden, he had the Championship.

Typically he said he'd do it by winning, and you can keep your second places. Retrospectively, Read adds 'I approached the race with great concern, in a way worry. I couldn't afford to fall off. I wanted to beat Agostini fair and square but not get into a situation where I made a fool of myself. Those are your fears beforehand; when it comes to it you'll make a mistake and people will say *that Read, he can't hack it*. No team orders, either. Years before when Bill Ivy and I were on 250 Yamahas I said to Bill *if you want to win the Championship you're going to have to race me*. So we raced. Same thing now with Agostini.'

Agostini qualified badly and made a bad start, Newcombe leading Read who pressed immediately. *Motor Cycle News* reported that . . .

Agostini was struggling to get away and failed to show in the first 12 as the pack swooped round the left-hander on the approach to the pits area, well over half a mile from the start. The speed of the Konig certainly seemed to be a match for the MVs and even when Read smashed the record on the fourth lap he still failed to get by.

In the right-hand south curve on lap 5 Newcombe missed a gear and Read was not the rider to miss the chance. He sliced past but . . . Agostini, recovering hard, caught Newcombe and floated through on the straight a couple of laps later.

And then there were two.

Agostini spread his splendour over the entire circuit. He destroyed the lap record three times. Agostini, as *Motor Cycle News* reported . . .

. . . moved in behind Read and after trailing him for three laps eased in front on the main straight at half distance. The two rushed round at times side by side but with Ago usually a fraction in the lead.

Read battled against brake problems, too, had to pump them on the straight to build up pressure for the hairpin at the end of it. Some background to that: 'I'd brought disc brakes to MV. The old drum brakes were a bit antiquated. You had to pump the discs because they weren't perfect. Sometimes on a bumpy surface at the end of a straight the bumps would knock the pads back and you'd grab a handful of brake and find nothing there. So you pumped them.'

On the second last lap Read matched Agostini down the straight and dived by into the hairpin. They grappled again and Read's bike 'cut to two cylinders, cut back on to three. I went for it on the last lap, left my braking to the latest on the final right-hander because the object of my exercise was to beat him, not just finish second.' Read resisted, resisted to the line. He won by a fifth of a second.

'It was nerve wracking,' Read said at the time. 'Ago got by me and although I desperately wanted to get the Championship with a victory I didn't want to risk blowing up my machine in a high-speed battle. When the bike went onto two cylinders I thought *my luck's really out,* but I managed to hold on. I was determined to finish ahead of Agostini.'

Newcombe came third, although 58 seconds from Read. He'd be fourth in the race after Sweden – Finland, in which Agostini won from Read. Two weeks later he was killed at Silverstone. People do not speak of him as they speak of Saarinen, although posthumously he occupied second place in the 1973 World Championship, 69 points and 63 counting against Read's 108 and 84 counting. What might Kim Newcombe have done in the years to come?

Postscript

'Saarinen was the most dynamic rider,' Read says. 'I'd raced him before the 1973 season and he'd certainly matured when he rode the 500 Yamaha. He'd ride the wheels off that bike, ride it across the grass, ride it with the whole bike sliding around. Unbelievable. But somehow he had the skill or the luck to survive until, you know, his luck did run out.'

Some, tragedy did not release.

1974

Read and the better season

Finnish Grand Prix, Imatra

IT WAS DONE with such elaborate secrecy that about the only thing they didn't use was code-names. Yamaha wanted to return and wanted to win the Championship but who to ride the bike? They knew, everybody knew, of Agostini's unhappiness at MV, and they knew his contract had expired.

At first Yamaha rejected the notion of signing him because, as arguably the best rider in the world, he'd be winning the races in the public's perception, not he and they. Rumours suggested Honda prepared to come back and might or might not reason the way Yamaha did.

Yamaha moved. 'Towards the end of 1973,' Clark says, 'I'd go to the races not just to watch but deliver letters from Yamaha to Ago and vice-versa. No-one suspected anything was going on.' After frequent flights between Italy and Yamaha in Amstelveen, their European HQ, Agostini signed: an enormous news story but also enormous in its implications. He'd face Read and Sheene. The ratchet: six best finishes from the 10 rounds. The battle lines:

MV: Read, Gianfranco Bonera
Yamaha: Agostini, Tepi Lansivuori
Suzuki: Sheene, Findlay

Macauley writes that 'the two protagonists (Read and Agostini) grew further apart as the season drew on, frequently giving vent to public displays of slanging, insults and jibes. When they lined up against each other at the Italian meetings held early on in, so vital for the (Italian) National Championship and the prestige that went with it, the Englishman was delighted to hear the home crowd booing and jeering their former hero for leaving MV. It may have upset Agostini but he was experienced enough not to show it.'

Read softens this impression. 'It wasn't strictly true because Ago wasn't the kind to start a slanging match with you. We'd tease each other or psyche each other but really we kept apart. Face to face in hotels or restaurants we'd probably have a bit of a dig but we respected each other, too.

'I won at Misano (one of the early Italian meetings) and he had difficulty getting out of the circuit. People were hammering on his car, booing and jeering and what have you.' At Imola a couple of weeks later, and with 50,000 watching, Read overtook Agostini at the end, a vignette of the season to come. 'The crowd erupted,' Read says. 'I had three of my sons with me and I had to lift them over a fence to the transporter to save them being crushed because the crowd had erupted to that extent. Perhaps in a way I was shy and I should have milked it for everything it was worth, laps of honour and so on.'

Iain Mackay says that Agostini adapted to Yamaha quickly because he constructed onto his natural talent an analytical mind and a precise memory. He wanted to work, wanted to test, wanted to watch the mechanics strip an engine; wanted to delve deep into that engine. He wanted to understand the suspension, what it did, why it did that. 'He left nothing to chance,' Mackay concludes.

Clark confirms it. 'When Ago came to Yamaha he brought a lot of know-how with him. For instance, before this we never changed gearbox ratios, only the normal gearing but he liked about six different first, second, third, fourth, fifth and sixth ratios! I think the other Japanese factories took pictures of this and followed. Ago always kept a record of the specs of the bikes he raced, jet sizes, tyre compounds, gearing.

'He wasn't a rider who could nurse a sick bike to the flag. The bike had to be perfect but, given that, he could show you just how good it was. Like all gifted riders he learnt circuits quickly and this in turn helped the mechanics to get on with the gearbox ratios and suspension settings. Ago had had quite a few easy Championships with MV but when he arrived at Yamaha he had to work for it. Yamaha did not have a huge power advantage over anyone. The 500 was the same as Jarno Saarinen had ridden. After Jarno's death no development work had been done.'

At the first round, the staccato circuit of Clermont-Ferrand – where the riders went past rockfaces – Agostini led, shattered the lap record but broke down on lap 9, leaving Read to win by five seconds from Sheene.

The riders boycotted the West German Prix at the Nürburgring, the old long circuit considered too dangerous now. Armco had been installed round it, invaluable for preventing racing cars from plunging into the scenery but potentially lethal for riders who want to shed their machines and roll to safety. Jim Redman, ruminating down the years, says 'it's amazing that people don't realize what armco can do to a rider. Armco is about the last thing you want.'

In Austria, extremely wet, Read broke down – he toured, an arm raised to warn those behind – and Agostini won from Bonera, with Sheene third.

At Imola, Macauley wrote that Agostini was 'anxious to please his supporters and re-awaken lost affection. The race distance was increased by two laps to meet the FIM's minimum time for a race. With no time to get bigger tanks set up Yamaha were forced to take a risk and hope that the bike would hold out with the petrol it had aboard, but the pace was so quick – much faster than Agostini had anticipated – that Yamaha's bluff was called. As it swept across the line for the start of the last lap, well in the lead but still hotly chased, Agostini's brave 500 spluttered to a halt.'

So quick? Agostini set fastest lap with 96.43 mph (155.19 kph) and that's really travelling at Imola with its nagging corners clawing you back. Read, who had 'flu, toiled in third behind Bonera and Lansivuori. Bonera 37 points, Read 25, Lansivuori 20, Agostini 15. Agostini dominated Assen but made a wrong bike decision at Spa, selecting a new lightweight version which proved slow. Read beat him by 1 minute 12.20 seconds. Read 50, Agostini 42, Bonera 44, Lansivuori 32 and three rounds to run, Sweden, Finland and Czechoslovakia.

Sweden detonated. Michael Scott wrote that Sheene and Agostini 'flew into the catch fencing at around 130 mph (210 kph) and it was said that if there had been armco at that point neither would have had much chance of surviving. The injured Agostini gave Sheene a fair roasting in the Italian press for causing the smash.'

Sheene made his reply in an interview with Rous of *Motor Cycle Weekly* . . .

When I went down Phil Read was right behind with Jack Findlay and they reacted instinctively by keeping on line and passing inside as I slid out. Ago was behind and picked up his bike to go round the outside where there wasn't sufficient room. He must have realized this too late and grabbed a handful of front brake. The wheel locked and he was off. At no time did we collide. I certainly didn't crash at 130 mph to knock him out and help Phil retain his title. If the position was reversed I would not blame him. Situations like this are all part of racing.

Scott adds 'true enough, and since a seized water pump caused Sheene to fall and not his own error he was justified in feeling aggrieved.'

Lansivuori won from Read. Read 62 points, Bonera 54, Lansivuori 47. Moreover, Agostini hadn't recovered enough to ride at the Finnish Grand Prix, which ought to have made the Championship straightforward for Read. It was anything but that, although Imatra – only five miles from the Russian border – did offer compensations. 'We stayed at a beautiful hotel, like a castle,' Read says, 'and I remember I had a superb room which was completely round.'

Motor Cycle News reported that . . .

Read had a couple of anxious moments in practice. Finn Penti Korhonen crashed on the railway station bends when oil from the gearbox of his Yamaha twin found its way onto the back tyre. The Englishman managed to stay on line and avoid the falling rider. Later in the afternoon during the second outing and on the race machine Read was confronted by a dog that found its way onto the circuit. Luckily for him, and itself, the canine headed rapidly for the grass verge.

'I remember that dog,' Read says, 'and although Imatra was out in the country it wasn't a rabbit or anything like a rabbit. It was a proper dog!'

There was another moment for Read when he went into a slide on the final bends before the start area. As he successfully battled to keep things on an even keel team-mate Gianfranco Bonera got the pit team in a sweat as he came through on an expectedly close inside line after taking a right-hand detour to keep clear of Read.

Before the start of this qualifying a little girl ran across to Read and gave him a sprig of heather for luck. Read thanked her by taking four seconds off the track record and decided to tuck the sprig into his overalls for the race for more luck. He'd need that. He returned after practice and gave instructions to leave the bike alone. 'It was set up as well as it could be and I did not want any changes made.'

Read started slowly – ninth – but urged the MV to its maximum in a great surge, and at the first corner steamed past Lansivuori for the lead. 'The MV had more power, didn't it? The track was a bit damp as well, I whistled up the inside of them. Lansivuori had crashed in the 350 race and I thought he might be injured from that.' *Motor Cycle News* reported that . . .

Bonera set his sights on the Yamaha rider (Lansivuori) and on the fifth lap took second place with a high speed inside line over the jump near the main paddock entrance. Bonera was then five and a half seconds behind Read who was rattling off the laps at around the 2 minutes 19 second mark, some four seconds higher than the previous lap record, but that did not deter Bonera.

It didn't. Half way through the 20 laps he'd drawn up to within four seconds and drawn eight seconds from Lansivuori. On lap 12 Read did 2 minutes 18.1 seconds but even that didn't break the 'determined' Bonera, and on lap 15 – five to go – he forced and cajoled himself to no more than one second behind. *Motor Cycle News* reported that . . .

Gianfranco then lowered the lap time to two minutes 17.8 seconds and on the next lap the MVs were side by side and Lansivuori, back in the groove, was actually closing the gap on both of them. In two laps he knocked almost four seconds off the MV advantage.

'We had no team orders,' Read says, 'but actually we weren't racing against each other, we wanted to stay ahead of Lansivuori. I wanted to win but equally I didn't want to risk anything. We imagined we'd pulled out enough, then Lansivuori started pegging that back and Bonera was seeing pit signals *minus four seconds, minus three seconds, minus two seconds.* I'd been easing off and he really went for it, broke the lap record – which dispels the notion that his injuries left him uncompetitive.'

As they rushed into the last lap Lansivuori was only four seconds in arrears of Bonera who was just a fraction behind Read. To crown it all an unwanted neutral gear on the very last bend of the race almost robbed Read. Bonera, right on his tail, slipped into the lead as Read fumbled for transmission – 'I missed a gear, you see, and naturally the rider behind goes past' *– and then the Italian almost fell in front of the Englishman as he found himself off line and on the grass. Read sorted himself out just in time to get across the line one fifth of a second ahead of his team-mate.*

'It was,' Read concluded, 'a close call.'

Lansivuori, friend of Saarinen, cruised up to Read as they slowed and offered his congratulations. 'If only I'd got going a bit earlier it might have been different,' he'd say.

The story of a lot of races in a lot of places.

Postscripts

Read said, the dust of battle settling around him: 'At last the pressure is off. It has been a really hard time for all concerned in the 500 Championship this year and for me no race was tougher than the Finnish. I had to win to settle the Championship and I felt really up-tight before the race. Tepi Lansivuori was riding quickly and I knew I could not make a mistake during the opening laps. I found myself hanging on to the bars with a vice-like grip. I certainly wasn't relaxed enough. That neutral on the last bend was a real headache.'

Everybody's fallible, even twice World Champions. I assume that Phil Read awoke the following morning still with the headache, but this one caused entirely by a hangover. One way and another, he'd earned a drink.

At the prizegiving in the hotel, Lansivuori was summoned to receive his award for finishing third in the 500 race. 'Naturally he was a hero, he'd had the crash on the 350 and nearly won the 500,' Read says. 'The ovation was tremendous and I turned and said "well done." Tepi was a brilliant rider but unlucky. He would fall off. My team-mate Bonera? He hadn't had an easy start with MV because we tested at Modena – at the airfield – and going round a long curve he hit a straw bale and broke his leg. He was a very easy-going man but perhaps without dedicated ambition.'

The story of a lot of racers. Surprising, but true.

1975

The Ago era (continued)

Czech Grand Prix, Brno

CURIOUS AFTER SUCH an immense amount of it, but Giacomo Agostini felt 'so nervous I didn't want to speak to anyone.' As the minutes ticked, he locked himself in the Yamaha motorhome and prepared himself, composed himself. In something over an hour a turbulent, virulent season would be decided. Agostini needed seventh, no more, and it's not a place you can calculate to finish in. His Yamaha must last 115 miles (185 km) and who can guarantee any highly-stressed machine – however much it has been made with loving care, honed and tested – will do that? No man, no mechanic and no machine which makes machines. The battle-lines which brought Agostini to this:

Yamaha: Agostini, Kanaya
MV: Read, Bonera
Suzuki: Sheene, Lansivuori

Early on, practising for the Daytona 200, Sheene crashed, battering his body mightily. He missed the opening Championship round at Paul Ricard where, in practice, Read fell, hurting a finger on his braking hand. Agostini won from Kanaya, and Read was third.

Sheene arrived at the Salzburgring for the Austrian Grand Prix and, as Michael Scott writes, 'demonstrated to officials that he could push-start the bike, but on race morning they finally decided he wasn't fit. He made a rude sign and left in a rage.' Agostini set fastest lap but broke down. Kanaya winning from Lansivuori, with Read third again.

Agostini beat Read after a torrid struggle in the West German Grand Prix at Hockenheim by 3.90 seconds, and beat Read by the more comfortable 1 minute 00.80 seconds at the Nations at Imola. Sheene stormed Assen, Agostini second, Read third; Read won Spa; a puncture stopped Agostini in Sweden, Sheene winning. Read 69 points, Agostini 56. The ratchet: six best finishes from the 10 rounds, and Read's quota filled, Agostini only four. Read would have to start dropping third places – 10 points – and a win became worth only 5, a second place only 2.

Michael Scott explores the background to Sweden, third last race. 'During 1975 Sheene and Phil Read fell out in a big way. Read said "we had been good friends, and for various reasons we became un-friends." Sheene later blamed much of the disagreement on a matter which has yet to be resolved. It concerned a request from Read that Sheene could help him win the 500 World Championship from Agostini by giving way to him in a race. The two men's accounts of the incident are very different. Even the place is not the same.

'Sheene says that Read asked before the Swedish Grand Prix if during the race Sheene would let him (Read) through, assuming such a position arose. He was deeply offended, went out determind to win the race and did so. Read strongly denies that version of events and places the incident at the following Finnish Grand Prix. "I reckoned it would be better for Sheene and Suzuki if a British rider on an Italian machine won the Championship, rather than Agostini's Yamaha. I asked him as a mate – and it was only if the position arose in the race. We both retired anyway. I felt I had helped Sheene all those years, and the first time I asked him to do anything for me he wouldn't. I don't know whether the MV team might have offered him money. I didn't."'

These many years later Read confirms 'that's absolutely true, it happened at Imatra and Alberto Pagani is witness to it. Barry and I had spent a lot of time together, he'd been at my home often and I'd helped him on his way up. I'd be on the MV, he'd be on an uncompetitive bike and I'd set up races so we diced – in actual fact I helped him a lot.'

Sheene won Sweden from Read, but Agostini won Finland from Lansivuori. Read led, but his magneto failed at mid-distance. Read might have hoped that Bonera would beat Agostini, but Bonera fell. 'I was leading, Ago way back, Barry way back five or six seconds. Bonera was with me and the bike failed. I thought *it's not so bad because Bonera can win to help in the Championship*. When Bonera came past the pits they gave him a pit signal telling him *first* and he got so excited he fell off.' Agostini 72 points from four finishes, Read 71 and facing the dropping, facing the dropping.

So: seventh at Brno, final round, and Agostini had it. And he stayed quietly in the motorhome preparing, keeping his own counsel. Maybe he wondered what Sheene might do. Maybe he sensed, as a reader of human beings, that Sheene would race Read and race Read hard, no quarter.

'It's absolutely frustrating,' Read says, 'because it's out of your hands. In fact I approached it as Agostini did: to secure a finish. At the end of a season, you see, all people see in print is the name of the rider who won the Championship, not how he did it. I hoped the Suzukis would finish in front of Agostini.' *Motor Cycle News* reported that . . .

Read made a rapid start in company with Sheene but the eager Phillipe Coulon

(Swiss, Yamaha) and Korhonen (Yamaha) were the first into the first left-hander on their Yamahas. At the end of lap 1 Read was two-and-a-half seconds in front of Sheene, and Agostini, losing some of his pre-race jitters, found himself in third place. Lansivuori moved round fourth closing on the leading trio.

Order: Read, Sheene, Agostini, Lansivuori.

On lap 2 Sheene took Read and they duelled, but on the third lap Sheene's Suzuki began to vibrate alarmingly and he retired; Read alone, isolated, leading Agostini by seven seconds, Lansivuori pressing hard on Agostini. Early moves, a long way – 17 laps – stretching. *Motor Cycle News* reported that . . .

The Suzuki rider (Lansivuori) rushed past Ago going by the pits on lap four and in one lap came to within three-and-a-half seconds of the leader. The expected happened and they were racing side-by-side a lap later, but when Tepi ripped a visor from his helmet that let Read slip by at the start line on lap seven.

Under the impetus of the race Lansivuori re-took Read and drew away drawing Read with him. Agostini, third, made a calm decision. He pitted for more fuel, 11 litres of it, unconcerned that he remained stationary for *seven* seconds. He rejoined without losing third place 'happy where I was.'

Lansivuori and Read grappled but on the second last lap Lansivuori's clutch failed; Read alone, isolated, travelling safely to the end 1 minute 0.40 seconds before Agostini. No consolation.

'I feel so relieved,' Agostini would say. 'I know I only had to finish seventh but it was a long race and anything could have happened to the machine.' Yes. Who can be sure? No man. Never had been, never could be. It's one of the themes of this book and it nags, inescapable and yet also part of the fascination.

Postscript

Sheene departed Finland with sixth place in the Championship but already deep on his journey to a quasi-pop quasi-hip cultish figure, a Cockney cadaver vibrating with cheeky charm which moved across all class barriers; not to mention his bravery. The season of 1976 wouldn't begin for another eight months but he'd be ready for it. Know what I mean?

1976

Sheene's life saver

Swedish Grand Prix, Anderstorp

'TWO BLOKES WERE just standing there looking. I undid the strap of his helmet that had pulled up tight under his chin. I took out a load of dirt that had got into his mouth and pulled his tongue out of his throat so he could breathe properly.' Irony is an easy word to conjure, pathos is invariably more apt, particularly in motor sport. Mortality rests a milli-second in front of you, and you never know which milli-second. On 24 July, during a practice session for the Swedish Grand Prix, pathos laid itself hard, as a man lay on a track.

In a long left-hander the Suzuki of John Williams 'stepped out', as they say, and threw him. Sheene swerved, stopped, dismounted and sprinted back. Sheene, incisive because he'd seen and felt accidents before, knew the drill. Undo the strap, cleanse the mouth, use your fingers to free the tongue (common sense, not first aid) and do it, think about it later – a racer's reaction. Sheene saved Williams, irony as well as pathos.

All season long the 'team-mates' at Texaco Heron Suzuki feuded over equal treatment, itself an easy word to use but one which regularly drives wedges. We know what it means, but how do you prove you're getting it or not? Sometimes that's more difficult than you might think; sometimes it's easy.

'Perhaps,' Scott writes, 'the greatest problem was a difference in understanding of the team's formation. Barry and the Japanese had one idea: that he was the No.1 rider, and that he alone was entitled to the very latest machinery from the factory, while his team-mates rode last year's bikes. Merv Wright (Team Manager) and the other two Suzuki riders (Williams and John Newbold) viewed it differently; they believed that everybody in the team should be treated as an equal. It was a rather naïve view, especially considering the fact that Sheene had already received a very unequal fee for signing with the team, far larger than the other riders.

'Then perhaps Barry Sheene pushed it a bit too far the other way. When the new machinery did arrive from Japan, determination and good timing by Barry secured for himself all three of the more powerful and lighter 1976 bikes – one for Grands Prix, one for Britain and one for his "international" bike. No wonder John Williams on his year-old bike was jealous.'

Any team carries tensions within it. The tensions are intrinsic, sewn into the seams. Each member wants to win and that can only be at the expense of the others. How you reconcile this often remains beyond the powers of very wise men. If the competitors don't have the egos, the self-belief, the all-consuming self-wish for it, the brashness and the brassiness and ultimately the ability for it, they'll be losers, anyway.

Around this point (you can never define the point precisely) Sheene had moved further along his journey to a pop-cult hero who proved Britain was a meritocracy – anyone can make it. And here he was, medium-sized, lean and nearly slight, bristling with street cred but brighter than that; a proper hero because of what he was, where he'd come from and what he'd made himself.

He stroked his Rolls round London town, became familiar with the interior of *Tramps,* and to a hungry media fed a rich diet of instant printable quotes (or quips), genuinely witty, controversial; insights from the East End where they know what life is and what life is not. *Innit?* The boy had charisma and perhaps worked it. He was too shrewd to ignore that he could. If he'd talked a good race that would scarcely have mattered. He rode good races, great races, too.

He'd have a clutch of Suzukis against him, Lansivuori, Pat Hennen, Lucchinelli, Williams, Newbold, Venezuelan Johnny Cecotto – reigning 350 Champion – on a Yamaha, Agostini back on the MV. Sheene tore the season apart. He beat Cecotto by 3.84 seconds in France; beat Lucchinelli by 13.40 seconds in Austria; beat Read (now Suzuki) in a fling to the line at the Nations at Mugello by 0.10 of a second.

Sheene said 'I headed Read as we approached the final corner, where braking tactics had to be called for. I braked a little early to let Read through on the inside, an opening he accepted, but it left him four feet further over than he should have been. That was perfect. So I went out and took a wide swoop in and a tight swoop out. I was under the screen going flat out while he was still cornering. I have to say this about Phil: of all riders in all classes I have faced he's always been the most difficult to beat. He never would give up.'

Read has another perspective. 'I made a terrible start and pulled up through the field to catch Ago and Sheene. I sat behind Sheene and he started to go away so I went with him. Ago dropped back and retired, for whatever reason. I passed Sheene and we diced throughout the race. On the last lap I pulled out a second on him. In the fast right-hander he lost it. I went "under" him (inside) and went for the line. He beat me to it by half a wheel. I was the hero of the meeting and he didn't like it. Madelaine (Read's wife) and Stephanie (Sheene's girlfriend) had a bit of a fight in the hotel afterwards. Stephanie was so bloody rude because I'd taken the limelight from Barry.'

The top riders did not contest the TT on the Isle of Man, a place considered too dangerous. Sheene hammered Hennen by 45.60 seconds at Assen, but Williams beat him at Spa by 7.40 seconds. Read didn't finish in the points. 'I had domestic pressures, sponsor problems and I wasn't very happy with the bike. I decided to call it a day.' Thus a career, begun in 1961, ended: an astonishing span.

Scott writes that 'the Belgian Grand Prix was unusual because Sheene came second, not first. It was his uneasy team-mate John Williams who won. He hadn't expected to – he'd hoped to lead the race, then concede it to Barry on the line to show he was better but he was riding to team orders.'

Someone said 'Belgium proved that Barry did have something to fear from John, because he was such a good rider and he was determined to win or kill himself. That's quite a formidable attitude.'

Of Cecotto, Macauley writes that 'he bought himself a £10,000 Ferrari and burnt the clutch out the first day he drove it. Soon he was asking £7000 appearance money and at times getting it, but by the middle of the season his winning streak had faded. It seemed he just could not handle the 500cc Yamaha. Too often he was left sprawling in the road while Barry Sheene, the man he was desperately trying to catch, disappeared into the distance.

'He became pompous; a prima donna who seemed to bear no resemblance to the happy-go-lucky character he had been only 12 months before. His organization was chaotic. Often he would turn up for a Grand Prix without bothering to confirm entries; he would be allowed in only because of his status, without hotel bookings or arrangements for paddock parking space.

'In mid-season, just before the Dutch Grand Prix, Cecotto's mentor, Andrew Ippolito, who had guided him on his way to his 350cc world title, withdrew him from the 500cc Championship series. Ippolito, a Yamaha importer in Caracas and the power behind Venemotos (Cecotto's team), felt that the £250,000-a-year youngster was putting himself too much at risk and had crashed his machine too often.'

The ratchet: six best finishes from the 10 rounds. Sheene opened the ratchet, 72 points from only five, Lansivuori 24 from three, Hennen 21 from three and Lucchinelli 22 from two. Four races remained, the next Sweden, and Sheene fully intended to win the race as well as the title. It's how he judged it should be done, and that tells you about the man, the mood and the moment.

And it was in that Saturday practice that Williams crashed – evidently his slick tyres hadn't warmed enough – and they took him to hospital concussed. Sheene would say that the 'incident brought home the importance to me of knowing what to do to help an injured rider. When I

Right *The very first medal. This is what Les Graham got in 1949. It's the size of a lapel badge* (Stuart Graham).

Below *Les Graham on the AJS* (Stuart Graham).

Bottom *The start of the Dutch TT, 1949, where Graham finished second to Nello Pagani* (Stuart Graham).

Showdown on camera

ran back he was lying choking with two guys just standing there. I could help straight away and the only reason was that I had been shown by Dr Claudio Costa in Italy a couple of years ago exactly what to do to ensure free breathing and not to cause further injury to a fallen rider. I really think that every rider, whether racer, moto cross or just the ordinary guy on the road should be aware of what action to take. Just think it could be your life that is being saved.'

In the race Alex George (Suzuki) took a swift lead but was penalized a minute for jumping the start. A New Zealander, Stuart Avant (Suzuki), led and stayed there until lap 8 (of 28) when Lansivuori took him.

Sheene said that 'I didn't get a very good start. I wanted to make sure I gave the machine a real push to be certain it started. When I got going I was well down, but then I started picking them off. Once I got up in front behind Tepi I reckoned it was time to have a rest and knocked it off a bit. I decided I would sit behind him until three laps from the end.

'Then I planned to pass him on the left-hander before the pits straight and, if that failed, on the penultimate right-hander on the last lap. I did pass him once to test out my plans and it was then that I realized he was in trouble. He pointed to his rear tyre. I went alongside to see if there was any oil about. I couldn't see any so I gave him the thumbs up but of course things turned out to be even worse.'

Lansivuori, *Motor Cycle News* reported . . .

. . . *had a swinging arm fixing bolt come loose and it turned his Suzuki-4 into an almost unmanageable monster.*

Sheene beat Findlay (Suzuki) by 34.18 seconds and said, crisp as you like, 'I set out to win this one because I wanted to clear it all up without any doubts and look like a proper champion by standing on the winner's rostrum.'

Postscript

Scott writes that 'John Williams today cannot speak for himself. He died in 1978 after crashing in the Ulster Grand Prix. Back in '76 he ended the year with some bitter quotes in the Christmas issue of *Motor Cycle Weekly*. "I'll not race in the same team as Sheene." He accused him of snatching back the 54X54 engine he had finally acquired, even of deliberately colliding with John Newbold to stop him winning a race, and concluded "when I signed with Suzuki the deal was for equal opportunities that never came my way."

'The season tailed off in triumph and acrimony. Matters came to a head in the British round of the Formula 750 class, the so-called British Grand Prix. The paddock atmosphere was almost unbearable. John Williams was convinced that Barry was hiding engine parts from him; Merv Wright was chipping in; and the ladies, Wright's secretary, Katrina, and Stephanie had a huge domestic row in the motor home. Rex White, still a friend of the team, was on the fringe. "Barry came storming out of the caravan in a rage, and said it's either Merv Wright or me. One of us will have to go.'"

Wright went, Sheene stayed.

1977

Only when I larf

Finnish Grand Prix, Imatra

AND THEN THERE were the Americans.

'I remember talking to Baker about prospects for the 1977 Grand Prix season on one of his many transatlantic trips from his home in Washington. "I haven't ridden a 500cc too much," he admitted blithely, "but I guess it won't be too big a step to switch from the 750 to the 500." The fact that he would be drawn up against Barry Sheene did not seem to trouble him overmuch. "Barry's got more experience than me, sure, and he's raced and won on tracks I haven't even seen but he doesn't worry me. I'm a quick learner – maybe it's because I put everything I've got into concentrating on the job."' This is how Macauley describes the entrance of Steve Baker to Yamaha and Grand Prix racing.

Hennen had already ridden in 1976, finishing third in the Championship on a Suzuki; now Baker came, and soon enough a puzzling paradox arose. The Americans flew over in numbers and gripped the 500s hard, so hard that between 1978 and 1993 only three non-Americans won it. The paradox? These Americans became vastly famous all over Europe, but were virtually unknown at home.

Hennen, Sheene's team-mate (with Steve Parrish), carried a reputation for being fast but wild, a likely candidate for a major crash. Scott writes that 'Pat didn't say all that much. Not in public. That was left to his brother, Chip. He made up for it. Not for nothing did the Sheene camp call him Motormouth Hennen. Maybe it was just Chip's way of helping Pat be competitive but he didn't much help.'

Agostini, meanwhile, rejoined Yamaha.

Sheene started nicely enough, beating Baker by 3.30 seconds in Venezuela, with Hennen third, and Cecotto – partnering Baker – fourth. Austria proved bitter. A single paragraph in *Marlboro's Grand Prix Guide* distils it . . .

The 500cc race was boycotted by several top riders who thought the safety measures insufficient after the accident in the 350cc class, where on the seventh lap, a bike from the leading group fell and bounced on the track, sweeping the next bikes. H. Stadelmann (Swi) was killed while J. Cecotto (Ven), D. Braun (W Ger), F. Uncini (Ita) and P. Fernandez (Fra) were badly injured.

Uncini went down and, as others fell, Hans Stadelmann ploughed helplessly into the wreckage. The race continued, enraging Sheene so much he sprang on his mini bike, rode to race control and said 'for Christ's sake stop it.' Even then the race continued for another eight laps.

Scott writes that 'a recent addition to the travelling Grand Prix circus was the AGV mobile hospital, manned by experienced emergency staff, fully equipped with the latest resuscitation equipment. It could not be used. *It is illegal for foreign doctors to practise medicine in Austria.* The 125cc riders staged a sit-down on the grid. Then the leading 500cc riders walked out. In spite of an offer of double start money Sheene, with the other stars solidly behind him, would not ride.'

The 'race' became a curiosity for record books. Findlay (Suzuki) won, his first since 1973 and his last, followed by:

2. M Wiener (Suzuki)   at 15.40 seconds
3. A. George (Suzuki)   at 15.91 seconds
4. H. Kassner (Suzuki)   at 25.36 seconds
5. F. Heller (Suzuki)   at one lap
6. M. Schmid (Suzuki)   at three laps
    Number of finishers: 6

The TT had gone from the Grand Prix calendar forever. Sheene won West Germany at Hockenheim from Hennen by 9.60 seconds – enough, but not absolute domination – Baker third. Sheene, Scott writes, 'had trouble coming to terms with just how fast Pat did go and just how competitive he was. There were no team orders and Pat was doing his best to beat him. And they were riding identical machines. Sheene had obtained no mechanical advantage this year.'

Sheene won the Nations at Imola, Baker coming fifth and Hennen nowhere; won France at Paul Ricard from Agostini, something deceptive. Macauley writes that '1977 was the year in which Agostini's star finally faded. By the end of the season he found himself on top of the unwanted pile. Even his mechanics had lost confidence in him: when he was bad, they said, he blamed the machine; when he was good, which was not too often in those two years from 1975, it was all down to him. Perhaps the fight of the hungry man had left him; perhaps the edge that would take him right to the brink in a tussle for victory had been dulled by the knowledge that he did not really have to do it – he had more than enough money in the bank and 15 world titles to show for his glorious past.'

Nobby Clark remembers that 'in Ago's last season he was riding for the Italian Yamaha importer. It was not a very successful year and I got blamed for all the bad results. I guess someone had to be blamed. Ago was obviously on his way downhill. At the Dutch TT it started to rain during the 500cc race, and Ago pulled in and said he could not ride in the wet. The Japanese team manager told me Ago could have won but did not have the drive or determination any more and would not get Yamahas the following year. Many times I was told things in Japanese in front of people and, because they could not understand [Clark had learnt the language while working for Honda in Japan] it did not go any further than myself . . .'

Wil Hartog (Suzuki) beat Sheene at Assen; Sheene won Belgium at Spa from Baker and Hennen; Sheene won Sweden at Anderstorp from Cecotto (now recovered from Austria), and Baker was third.

The ratchet: all eleven rounds counted. Sheene had 102 points, Baker 68, Hennen 43. Three rounds remained – Finland, Czechoslovakia and Great Britain. *If* Sheene finished anywhere in front of Baker at Imatra he couldn't be caught.

Sheene decided that, in contrast to 1976, he wouldn't set out to win the Finnish Grand Prix 'unless it was going to be essential to clinch the title' – if Baker led, Sheene would try to overtake him.

Practice proved 'a disaster, to say the least, and it was only the very last lap of the day that I managed to get in the time for pole position. I had been bothered by over-heating and water problems and I left the machine by the side of the road to let the waterlogged gearbox dry out before making the last-minute effort to get in a good time.'

The race proved the nagging fascination of what machines prepared with loving care may do and may not do. In the authentic sense it was scarcely a race.

Sheene: 'I got a good start but before the end of the first lap the temperature gauge was up to around 105 degrees. I slowed down at once and decided to hang on until Steve Baker came along. If he beat me I couldn't win the Championship here. When he arrived I thought I'd have to sit on his tail and hope the bike would keep going. That did not seem very likely because by then it was gurgling and bubbling merrily. Then – luck for me. Steve had just gone by when I heard his machine go on to three cylinders. *Well, now we are both in trouble,* I thought to myself. *I'll press on and hope for the best.* Four laps later the temperature gauge reading was right off the clock.'

Baker: 'I'd just taken sixth place from Barry when my machine went onto three cylinders as I accelerated out of the hairpin. It was a new engine that I had run in during the final practice on Saturday but not as fast down the straight as a 250.'

That happened on lap 2, Baker limping the remaining 20 laps towards twelfth place.

Cecotto took the lead on lap 4 and established complete command, so complete he gave Yamaha their first 500cc win of the season. *Motor Cycle News* reported that . . .

He blew the opposition apart and even Sheene admitted he would have been hard to beat as the Venezuelan shattered the lap record in fragments. On lap 4 Lucchinelli in second place was under pressure from Sheene, and Giacomo Agostini, riding at his best this season, inched ahead of Pat Hennen to take fourth place but Ago was out of luck again.

Agostini: 'I'd just overtaken Hennen for the second time when the machine started to slow and it got slower and slower.'
    Motor Cycle News reported that . . .

With Ago out, Hennen started to close on Sheene and at half distance, the eleventh lap, went into third place with Gianfranco Bonera close behind. Bonera, suffering from clutch trouble himself, passed Sheene on the railway bridge between the start and the roundabout on the sixteenth lap. Sheene dropped to fifth when Frenchman Michel Rougerie nipped ahead to the forward wave of the Englishman.

Sheene: 'I waved lots of riders by, even my team-mate "Stavros" Parrish [Sheene's nickname for him] on the last lap because I had to go slow to keep the machine going and I didn't want to get in anyone's way.'
    Parrish: 'I had no brakes and oil was coming from the gearbox. I was cruising round and came on Barry who was cruising even slower and when I realized it would not bother him I decided to go ahead for a couple of extra points.'
    Sheene finished sixth.

Postscripts

Sheene reflected that 'Johnny Cecotto went by me on the second lap and I quickly decided that to try to race with him would lead to an immediate engine blow-up so I resisted the temptation. A good job that Johnny was no threat to my title hopes. Mind you, I said at the start of the season and still believe it would have been a different story if he had done a full season and had not been sidelined with his Austrian injury.'

Cecotto won the Finnish Grand Prix, 31 July 1977, from Lucchinelli by 43.00 seconds. He'd win Brno – to which Sheene didn't go; Iron Curtain country and no thanks. Cecotto, rich in promise, would only win one more 500cc race in his career.

Hennen took the final round, Silverstone, from Baker, and Agostini was ninth.

Macauley writes that 'the final blow to Agostini's chances of being retained by any manufacturer must have come at the British Grand Prix. He was down the field on what was probably the fastest machine in the 500cc race and struggling to fight off Kevin Wretton, a virtual novice, who was after his ninth place on a 350. There was a lot of headshaking that day as the most famous rider in motor cycling plodded up the pit straight. He was, quite cruelly, devaluing his own fine reputation.'

That reputation: 54 350cc wins, 68 500cc wins, the 15 Championships. There would be no more.

'At the end of the season,' Clark says, ' I was on the Yamaha stand at the Milan motor cycle show. I met a Japanese journalist who I knew from the races and he said he was happy he'd be seeing me in Japan soon. I expressed surprise. He said it had nothing to do with Yamaha. Intrigued, I asked another journalist friend and he asked Ago if Ago intended to go to Japan (taking Clark along as his mechanic).

'Ago said no but added that next month he'd make a Press statement and it would be an earthquake in the motor cycle racing world. We did find out that Ago was going to Japan but (for secrecy) took a really funny route with a lot of stops along the way plus all different airlines: Rome to Athens, Athens to Beirut, Beirut to Bombay, Bombay to Calcutta and so on until he reached Tokyo. What's interesting is that there never was a Press statement or an earthquake. We all think Ago went to Honda and tried the NR500, the infamous never-ready bike. When he discovered that it was not fast enough to win on he gave up the idea of racing again.'

Only when I larf? I've poached that from the thriller writer Len Deighton who entitled one of his books thus. I've poached it because it, too, involved a cockney hero and it seems very apt. The derivation, of course, is *It only hurts when I laugh*. That applied directly to Sheene, famous for his crashes and the number of metal bolts put in him and – in spite of that – his sense of humour.

1978

Roberts runs rings

West German Grand Prix, Nürburgring

QUESTIONS AND ANSWERS, questions and answers.

Kenny Roberts: 'I had to be within three places of Sheene, I think, to win the Championship so all I really wanted to do was stay in front of him.'

Presumably you had never seen the Nürburgring before?

'No, I hadn't.'

This is the old Nürburgring we're talking about, the full 14.18 miles (22.83 km)?

'Right.'

Did that frighten you?

'It frightened me and it also frightened Sheene. He had never raced on it, either. He'd won his Championships before he actually got to the last race and he didn't go. Yeah, it's frightening, it isn't very safe and at that time particularly bad. I could *tell* it also frightened Sheene as well, yeah, yep. Sheene wasn't riding to a hundred per cent, no way.'

It's impossible to make that distance safe?

'All it would take is one little flip on a 500 . . .'

Kenny Roberts remembers the Ring in August 1978 for that and for much else. The whole season is hard to forget. One perceptive contemporary view is that 'Roberts has always shown the same qualities whether he is out on the race track or behind the pit wall: fierce intelligence, total commitment and a burning determination to be best. Credited with bringing the awesome technique of "rear wheel steering" to Grand Prix racing from his native US dirt tracks, Roberts established the Americans as the dominant force in world racing.'

The man from Modesto, California began racing at 13 in the Laguna Seca Classic and in the early 1970s won the US Grand National Championship twice. In 1977 he said publicly that the World 500cc Championship could be no such thing without American racers in it. That year he rode briefly on *our* side of the Atlantic and said 'I guess I'm getting the hang of this European road racing. I figure it might be a good plan to get over there among them and bring something home.'

Roberts joined Cecotto on Yamahas. Nobby Clark insists 'Kenny Roberts was a great rider, a hard rider who faced up to challenges squarely. He'd work day and night if he thought it would help him to win. He always gave us maximum effort and encouragement. I am sure he is the one credited with starting the American invasion of Europe. I also think that the American influence has done a great deal of good, especially turning the image of dirty, smelly bikes and grease-covered mechanics into a clean and well turned-out spectacle. He helped Yamaha a lot in their development. He knew what he wanted and when he got it he'd use it, not bellyache all the time.'

In Venezuela, the first round, Roberts's bike seized after two laps, opening the way for Sheene to win easily from Hennen – but in Venezuela Sheene contracted Bornholm's Disease, a chest complaint which leads to breathlessness and exhaustion. Hennen won the Spanish Grand Prix at Jarama from Roberts (by 7.30 seconds), with Cecotto fourth and Sheene fifth – the Press implied that Sheene suffered from 'Hennenitis' – and Roberts led before a sticking throttle slowed him.

'Kenny only had one 500cc bike,' Clark says, 'and it was not the same as the factory bikes of Cecotto. We got the same engine set-up after the first few Grands Prix. Kenny was faster than Cecotto most of the time, and Sheene was another who didn't like Kenny coming along and blowing him off. The big excuse used was that Kenny had Goodyear tyres – their first venture into Grand Prix bike racing. People didn't realize Kenny did tyre testing *and* had to learn the circuits, *and* had to set the bike up for those circuits.'

Roberts put together a strong run, winning Austria from Cecotto, Sheene coming third and Hennen running well until his Suzuki blew up. 'At the Austrian,' Clark says, 'Sheene said that the Goodyear tyres were worth at least two seconds a lap, but what he failed to mention was that Hennen, his team-mate, was only two-tenths of a second slower than Kenny using the same tyres as Sheene!'

A bizarre weekend at Salzburg.

Scott writes that 'by the time they got to Austria the atmosphere between Pat and Barry was tense, Pat no longer in any way No. 2 rider. They ended up parking apart in the paddock and having furious rows about wheels. The wheels, from Campagnolo in Italy, had a selection of rim sizes to enable the riders to experiment with their tyres. Some had been ordered by the team, some had been ordered privately by Barry.

'The unfortunate part was that Campagnolo delivered the whole batch to Barry's awning. They immediately all became Barry's wheels, and Don [Mackay, Sheene's mechanic] remembers shuffling them out of sight in among a pile of tyres.' Equal treatment is one of those delicate things . . .

Roberts won France from Hennen, with Sheene third again and more than 19 seconds behind Hennen. Roberts won the Nations at Mugello from

Hennen, and Sheene was fifth. Roberts 57 points, Hennen 51, Sheene 47. The ratchet: all 11 rounds counting.

Neither Sheene nor Roberts ventured near the Isle of Man – non championship racing continued – but Hennen did and, in the Senior 500, *Motor Cycle News Yearbook* reported that . . .

Hennen, who made a desperate bid for victory before he crashed on the last lap, hoisted the lap record to 113.83 mph (183.18 kph) and became the first to officially break the 20 minute barrier. Hennen, who had already broken the magic figure in practice, was the only seeded rider on intermediate slicks. After Tom Herron caught him the American star was a comfortable second but he tried to get away. Herron attempted to restrain him by going ahead but Hennen lost control when he clipped a kerb at Bishopcourt at around 160 mph (294 kph), suffering head injuries which kept him unconscious for over three months.

Irony and pathos. This year Mike Hailwood made an emotional and amazing comeback on The Island more than a decade after his competitive career ended. Clutch problems hampered him in the Senior on a Yamaha, but he won the Formula 1 race on a Ducati.

Irony and pathos. Before the Dutch Grand Prix at Assen, Sheene, spending time on a yacht, 'suddenly woke up one morning and felt fine. I knew at once that I was better.' Cecotto won Assen from Roberts, Sheene coming third after a tight struggle. Hartog, replacing Hennen, came fifth, and although the intention had been to give Hartog only this ride he kept it for Belgium – and won, Roberts placed second and Sheene third. Roberts 81, Sheene 67.

'One strange story from Spa,' Clark says. 'We were having a real hard time with the engine on Kenny's bike when suddenly practice time was running out. Kenny had still not qualified and Johnny wasn't getting any good times. Yamaha gave us Johnny's spare bike, we changed the fairing and off Kenny went – the first time he'd ridden on Michelins. He went really well, front row of the grid. It was decided that Kenny would have the use of Johnny's spare engine. (This was also decided in some secrecy. Cecotto didn't know).

'Late that night a Yamaha truck left the paddock followed by a BMW car with myself and another chap, Greg Hansford, in it. We followed at a safe distance and headed into a nearby forest – a pretty dense forest – lights off. Eventually the truck stopped. We had a good look round to make sure nobody had followed us. The van was opened and the engine, carbs and exhaust pipes were transferred to the boot of the BMW. Nobody said anything. We were just about to set off back to the paddock when, no more than 15 feet away, we saw a cigarette glow in the darkness. We still did not say anything and neither did the person smoking. Who the smoker was or where he came from or where he was headed remains a mystery. The next day Kenny finished second, thanks to Johnny Cecotto who didn't know he had done us a favour . . .'

In Sweden Roberts fell in practice and could only finish seventh, Sheene winning from Hartog by 0.05 seconds. Roberts 85, Sheene 82. At Imatra Sheene broke down and gave the mechanics full vent of his anger. Roberts suffered an ignition fault and he didn't finish either. Hartog won and now had 65 points, the Championship not beyond him with two rounds – Silverstone and the Nürburgring – to run. Would Hartog support Sheene?

Silverstone proved amazing: wet, though it started dry. Scott writes that . . .

The race had barely begun when the heavens opened, a downpour such as only an English summer's day can produce. In retrospect, the organizers should simply have stopped the race but they had no precedent since slick tyres were relatively new and their total incapacity on wet tracks a new problem. They let the race run and it degenerated into a farce.

Riders had to decide for themselves whether to pit for tyres – something else quite new. Roberts's crew managed it in two-and-a-half minutes, Sheene's took seven-and-a-half minutes. Sheene unlapped himself twice in a ferocious onslaught, but as the farce degenerated into outright chaos a question loomed. Who'd won? The Public Address announced *Roberts,* with a Briton – Steve Manship – second on a Suzuki, and Sheene third at 1 minute 06.76 seconds from Roberts.

Andy Marriott, a journalist and friend of Sheene, remembers 'it was extraordinary. When the PA announcement was made riders stood there saying "no, no, I won." At least three felt they had – and this while the official first three were on the victory lorry. I wouldn't say they were shouting it in anger but a sort of semi-banter. Personally I'm still not sure who did win.' Sheene had ridden a genuinely staggering race, gaining four *minutes* on Roberts, and the race lasted only 56 minutes. Roberts 100, Sheene 92.

They came to the Nürburgring just two years after Niki Lauda's searing crash in a Ferrari there – Lauda almost burned to death. The Formula 1 car people hadn't been back and would never go back to the old Ring.

'Sheene and I both spent a lot of time going round it on road bikes, which told you where you had to go. I had a pretty good memory for race tracks, anyway,' Roberts says. 'I learnt race tracks very quickly because that year I'd had to do it at almost all of them – so for me it was another normal exercise; for him it was tougher. I got on fine with Sheene. He was more winning races in the Press, I was more winning them on the race track and that is where we differed.'

On Sunday 20 August Kenny Roberts 'never felt so nervous. I got butterflies in the motorhome before going out for the start and I got butterflies on the grid.' He faced 'only' six laps but that translated to 85.13 miles (137.01 km).

An Italian, Virginio Ferrari, had been called in by Suzuki to support Sheene. Ferrari knew the Ring (he'd taken pole on a Suzuki there two years earlier). *Moto Cycle News* reported that . . .

The idea behind bringing in Ferrari was to try to force Roberts down the finishing list as far as possible through sheer volume of riders.

Hartog crashed on the first lap, Ferrari took the lead from Cecotto, then Roberts, then Sheene. 'The only mistake I made,' Roberts says, 'was that I had a board in front of the pits to tell me where the guys in front were, how the race was, what I was doing. After the pits you went round a loop where I had another board telling me Sheene's position.

'First time round I hunted for that second board and as I did I went past my braking point. I had the thing hopping off the ground trying to stop and I had to go wide. I messed up a bit of time there but I kept it on two wheels, that was the main thing. I kept saying to myself *look, just race this bike, forget about if Sheene goes by you, just race this bike and don't lose control of it because you are thinking about something else.* It's very hard. I raced with Ferrari and Cecotto for a little while but they had a pretty good speed advantage on me. For some reason Suzuki's rotary valves ran real well on that long straight and we had a little bit of trouble.'

Crossing the line to complete lap 1 Ferrari still led, Cecotto and Roberts almost level, and Sheene behind. Crossing the line to complete lap 2 Cecotto and Roberts closed on Ferrari; then Roberts dropped back deliberately.

'Every lap I knew where Sheene was, I knew he was right behind me and had he passed me it was still OK, I'd still have won the Championship. I ran the race like that. I didn't care where Ferrari and Cecotto went at all. It was a question of riding around. I wanted to ride at 80 per cent and that it was I did. It's correct that it's easier to hold your concentration if you're dicing with somebody than if you're doing a percentage race. You know what I always found helped me? To ride a bike 10 per cent off what I normally rode it at – but still actually *ride* the bike. *[see Surtees. Nothing important changes!]* The hard part: I kept thinking all the time, kept reminding myself all the time *don't think about it, ride the bike, race the bike, race the bike through this corner . . .'*

Roberts would win the Championship by thinking he musn't think about it, the ultimate self-control and not really a contradiction. Sheene travelled with equal prudence. 'I detest the Nürburgring,' he'd say. 'It is a very, very dangerous place. What did I stand to gain by ending up in the armco? If I'd played the hero I might have won. Even then Kenny would have had to be fifth place or below. The best I could do was finish in the first four and hope Kenny broke down.'

On that lap 3 Cecotto battered the lap record (doing 8 minutes 33.3 seconds) and led from Ferrari. Roberts beat that (8 minutes 31.5) and Ferrari beat *that* (8 minutes 29.5). On lap 5 Ferrari forged past Cecotto, Roberts safe in third, but Takazumi Katayama (Yamaha) forged past Sheene. Sheene struck back and retook fourth. On the last lap Roberts slackened the pace. Sheene drew up to within three seconds of him as the flag fell.

Afterwards Roberts said 'my main worry was that the machine would last the distance. I knew my practice time put the title well within my reach if I could finish. I'd been a little bit worried about the machine because it went slightly off tune on the final lap of training on Saturday and we didn't have much time to run it again before the race and check things out. But it did the job. I rode like an old woman on the last lap, I didn't want anything stupid to take the title from me.'

Sheene, the mechanical failure in Finland still bubbling in his mind, contented himself with this: 'It was at Imatra, not the Nürburgring that I lost my Championship.'

1979

100 per cent Kenny

French Grand Prix, Le Mans

KEL CARRUTHERS, FORMER rider and Roberts's mentor, sets out the background dispassionately. 'In the second year I think we brought racing up to the standard it had required for years: to the same sort of organized level that Formula 1 cars had, with all the proper backing and support. We learned a lot from our first year and I was determined to put it to good use for 1979; even as the factory Japanese looked after Johnny Cecotto, with all the parts in boxes out of the back of a truck and with a cook doing his stuff on a two-burner stove in the middle of the paddock, we got ourselves into a pretty tight-knit and well-organized situation.

'We set up camp properly. We were still financed from America, but, I suspect, it was with money routed from Japan, and we were able to get down to it in the way I knew was necessary. So I had an extension built onto my motor home, we had a big Mercedes full of shelving and places for everything. We worked under cover in a full-sized annexe and in far greater comfort than anybody else.'

The image of racing began to change, but an earthiness remained.

'Kenny could play practical jokes on all of us,' Nobby Clark says. 'Once he got to know you there were no limits. We tested the 500s at Laguna Seca for 1979. He went out, did 10 laps, returned to the pits and asked me to check the bike over. I said OK but only after I'd finished work on his other bike. That gave him time to fix his ploy.

'He said one thing worried him. The back end slid around more than normal. He had tyres of the same compound on both bikes so it couldn't be that. I had a look for any signs of oil or water leaks but I couldn't find anything wrong. He told me to have another look – *look under the seat*. I bent over to do that, mainly to satisfy him, and there neatly gum-taped to the underside of the seat was a plastic pussy looking straight into my face! I asked "the brain" [Roberts's nickname] what the hell was going on but when I stood up – shrieks of laughter all around me, cameras clicking everywhere . . .'

Not all preparations for the defence proved so innocent or amusing. Roberts also tested in Japan and crashed, breaking an ankle, rupturing his spleen and breaking vertebrae. He'd be in a hospital bed when the season opened in Venezuela on 18 March.

Sheene tested in Japan, too, but at Suzuki's circuit with Hartog and Ferrari. The 'fiery' Italian had done enough at the Nürburgring to secure a place in the team.

'The new team-mates,' Scott writes, 'disagreed at the earliest opportunity.' Suzuki had two new bikes and Hartog and Ferrari liked one, Sheene the other. Suzuki accepted the verdict of the former and Sheene did not enjoy being virtually ignored. Sheene said '"Well, OK, give them that bike and let me have this one" but they said I must have the same as Hartog and Ferrari. After Hartog had fallen off about 15 times and Ferrari said it was a camel they sent the frame that I had chosen originally.'

Sheene won Venezuela from Ferrari by 18.60 seconds. Roberts returned for Austria at the Salzburgring five weeks after and won from Ferrari and Hartog, Sheene being hobbled by front brake problems. From here on the pressure mounted on Sheene, Hartog winning West Germany at Hockenheim from Roberts and Ferrari (Sheene out, big end bearing). Roberts won the Nations at Imola from Ferrari, with Sheene fourth.

Approaching Assen, seventh of the twelve rounds, the points told a straightforward tale: Roberts 72, Ferrari 68, Hartog 45, Sheene . . . 23. At Assen Roberts struggled and Sheene rode to team orders (for the first and last time in his life), letting Ferrari win by 0.10 of a second; Hartog third.

The riders boycotted Spa, claiming the re-surfaced track posed too much danger. In Sweden Sheene won and Roberts was fourth; Ferrari going out on lap 1 when a crank broke. A week later in Finland *Motor Cycle News* reported that . . .

Ferrari's team got the carburation wrong and he never climbed into a points scoring position.

Sheene finished third, and Roberts sixth, but Roberts won the British at Silverstone by 0.03 of a second after a glorious slogging match with Sheene. Hartog was third and Ferrari was a distant fourth. Only the French Grand Prix at Le Mans remained: Roberts 103 points, Ferrari 89. The ratchet: all eleven rounds to count. In that crisp, penetrating way Americans have, Roberts says 'I had to get into the points if Ferrari won, if Ferrari didn't win I didn't have to finish.' The race – 29 laps, 76 miles (122 km) – would be run at two levels, Ferrari flinging his Suzuki at the circuit, Roberts playing safe.

At Assen, a 19-year-old fellow Californian had made his debut on a Suzuki. In Finland he'd come second. He was called Randy Mamola. He had the Suzuki again for Le Mans and he represented a spoiler. What might he do against Roberts? Anything. What might he do against Ferrari? Anything. And Sheene felt a strong compulsion to prove he could still compete, dominate, win.

A tight start – Hartog, Sheene and Ferrari together, with Roberts fourth. Ferrari took the lead from Hartog on lap 4, Sheene moved up and took the lead from Ferrari on lap 9. Ferrari didn't like that. *Motor Cycle News* reported . . .

There were some hair-raising manoeuvres in the process (of Sheene taking Ferrari) with their machines colliding on a number of occasions.

Ferrari showed aggression, perhaps unacceptable aggression but certainly understandable. 'He banged fairings with me about 15 times,' Sheene said. 'I don't like people who ride like that.'

On lap 11 Ferrari, moving furiously . . .

. . . overshot a corner on braking and frustratedly rejoined the fray.

Roberts says 'I rode around in fourth place just keeping him in sight.'

Ferrari came upon Cecotto, and Roberts witnessed that. 'Ferrari went to the outside, made a huge mistake, got into the corner too *hot* and fell off. He was trying pretty hard and I think it was the angle in which he attempted to get round the guy. He misjudged it. At the moment when I saw him tumbling through the grass I had just won the World Championship.'

Sheene said that Ferrari tried the same thing with Cecotto that he'd 'tried with me, and Johnny wouldn't give way.' Ferrari fell heavily, breaking his right elbow and suffering abdominal injuries. Roberts decided to enjoy himself (no disrepect, he had no idea how badly Ferrari was hurt). 'I went up into the lead.' *Motor Cycle News* reported that . . .

Roberts, Sheene and the sensational American teenager Randy Mamola sent the crowd into a frenzy with their superb three-way scrap. Sheene repassed Roberts but as they began their final lap it was Roberts going for a glorious end to his second title year. Missing from the action now was Hartog whose works Suzuki broke a main bearing with seven laps remaining, so it was Sheene, Roberts and Mamola who set off in sight of the chequered flag.

Roberts says 'on the last lap coming down to the hairpin I was lapping a slower rider and he fell off in front of me. I had to go wide and I got stuck in the fencing. I thought about what I would have been thinking if Ferrari was winning the race . . .'

Roberts found himself among the bales of straw. 'The hairpin wasn't very fast and I hit his bike, it just knocked me. I couldn't get my tyre from underneath the catch fencing. By the time I did, Sheene and Mamola had already long moved on.' This let Sheene and Mamola break loose, Sheene grasping it by 2.40 seconds. Roberts remounted and finished third, 13.89 seconds behind Sheene.

Postscript

Question: They do say, particularly racing car drivers, that they dislike such races because if you start messing around with permutations you can get them terribly wrong, whereas if you know you have to win it simplifies itself. And you?

Roberts: 'I didn't feel Ferrari was capable of beating me outright and, I think, you're much more in control of a motor cycle a lot of the time than a car. A lot of things happen with cars. The bike does what you want it to do even at a slower pace. I can do exactly what I want to do with the bike. I knew the bike wasn't going to break because they don't break. I knew the tyres were OK. It became simply a matter of riding it around at 80 per cent and it's probably easier to ride a motor cycle at that than to drive a car.

'I'd never actually had any problems riding off my pace because the motor cycles take a lot more concentration than a car, anyway. If you mess up on a motor cycle you learn real quick that it hurts. I have driven cars, and the level of concentration is nothing compared to motor cycles, so if you have to back off it doesn't really matter. You are already concentrating 110 per cent so it's only a matter of concentrating 100 per cent . . .

Or 80 per cent if you prefer. Either way, if you're Kenny Roberts it's enough.

1980

100 per cent science

West German Grand Prix, Nürburgring

THOUGHTS AND PHILOSOPHIES, thoughts and philosophies.

Kenny Roberts in *The Art and Science of Motor Cycle Road Racing* by Peter Clifford . . .

I'm sure that motor cycle racing is one hundred per cent science. For me art is something that you just do: there it is, you've done it, and you needn't know how. If that was the case with motor cycle racing I wouldn't have to spend days before a race testing, practising. I could just fly in, race the bike and go home.

Kenny Roberts on the 1980 season . . .

Last year was so bad even for the FIM that things had really reached boiling point, a very bad year for everybody. All the little things had built into a big mushroom and the future looked very grim. This year the whole atmosphere was much better with everyone knowing what they were getting paid, everybody much calmer and more relaxed, organizers and officials so much more helpful and not working against us.

Kenny Roberts on 24 August 1980:

I consider the Nürburgring to be without doubt the most dangerous track on which I have raced and I would not be racing here if it were not vital for the World Championship.

Memory drifts back to the launch of the Clifford book, a discreet and chic little restaurant in London. Roberts was the guest of honour: a small, chunky, neat, self-contained man, trim but not prim, an aura about him. He did seem a philosopher, happy to talk about this and that, explain the danger and how you overcame it. If you needed a man to rationalize what seemed wrong with Grand Prix racing and put it right, here he sat.

At Silverstone in 1979 rumours began that the riders were unhappy about their status quo and, with Roberts a leading player, prepared to launch their own World Series, which would have destroyed the World

Championship. This is no place to rake over the particular politics of that, but the attempt proved enough to make the FIM and organizers and officials begin to treat the riders in quite a different way. Roberts brought, and still brings, much to motor cycling, but this may have been his finest hour.

During 1980 Roberts applied the science of winning on the tracks, taking the Nations at Mugello from Uncini (Suzuki) – Sheene had departed them and begun his own team using Yamahas, although not works bikes. On them he'd barely figure – but Mamola would and he'd be on a Suzuki. So would a newcomer, the versatile New Zealander Graeme Crosby.

Roberts won the second round, Spain at Jarama, and the third, France at Paul Ricard: Roberts 45 points, Lucchinelli (Suzuki) and Mamola 22. The ratchet: all eight rounds of a truncated Championship to count (no Venezuela after a military coup, no Austria after three feet of snow). Roberts found himself in a strong position very early, the evening of 25 May after the French.

At Assen, he suffered a slow puncture to the front tyre, slid around with that, pitted to have it changed, found the new tyre no better and, as one report puts it, 'was signalled by his pit to be over two minutes behind, pulled a gigantic wheelie and retired.' Jack Middelburg (Holland, Yamaha) won, while Uncini was third, Mamola fifth, and Lucchinelli nowhere.

Mamola won Belgium from Lucchinelli and Roberts, Hartog won Finland from Roberts and Uncini, with Mamola fourth. Roberts 67, Mamola 51, Uncini 41, Lucchinelli 34. Easy does it, in one of those seasons when the leader finds himself solidly competitive and the opposition claw among themselves – no major challenger emerging. Mamola's career emerged, but too late for 1980. Roberts applied his science to the British at Silverstone, finishing 11.15 seconds behind Mamola. Roberts 79, Mamola 66. Even if Mamola won the final round, the West German, Roberts need only finish eighth.

A loop had returned from 1978, a circle had closed on the Nürburgring.

A Press Release appeared attributed to Roberts . . .

My opinion about the Nürburgring hasn't changed during the last two years, I wasn't here. It's nicer to drive here, than on any other track. It's a challenge for the driver and the material. I enjoy it.

You do not need to be a linguist to see that either it was a shocking translation or that no English-speaking person could possibly have used such an arrangement of words and punctuation. When Roberts espied it he exploded and may have used genuine Anglo-Saxon to describe it. Roberts issued his own Press Release . . .

I consider the Nürburgring to be without doubt the most dangerous track on which I have ever raced and I would not be racing here if it were not vital for the

World Championship. In two years since I last raced here the surface has deteriorated and the motor cycles have become faster. This represents a combination which has already increased the danger of what was already an incredibly dangerous track.

As long ago as May the leading riders sent a letter to the FIM asking in the strongest possible terms that we should not have to race at the Nürburgring. In the time since then I have not changed my opinion and neither have any of the other riders who originally signed the letter.

This statement of Kenny Roberts's opinion on the circuit is issued to resolve a mis-understanding which resulted in incorrect statements being attributed to Mr Roberts in the Press Release previously issued by the organizers.

These words struck deep. Geoff Duke is extensively quoted in the *Motocourse* annual. He began 'it was and still is the most beautiful circuit in the world. To me there is no danger, but it must be treated with respect. I drove round the circuit this morning and thought that the safety precautions for the riders were first class and also the condition of the track excellent.' The opinion of Duke must be treated with respect, albeit with a caveat. He discussed (perhaps unconsciously) the ethos of another age; a quite different mentality.

The Formula 1 car drivers had been through the same thing, safety coming reluctantly and largely because Jackie Stewart, after a wild and shocking crash at Spa where minimal First-Aid facilities were in place, began a campaign to change all that; and old-timers called Stewart a coward for doing it. Stewart won the campaign. As we've seen, no Formula 1 cars raced the old, full Nürburgring after 1976 and Lauda's crash.

That the riders reached a concensus later rather than sooner scarcely matters. They were there now, or nearly there. Some spoke openly of a strike, some voiced extreme misgivings. Certainly Roberts and Mamola insisted they'd withdraw if the race threatened to be, or became, wet.

In qualifying, Mamola took pole (8 minutes 29.41) from Roberts (8 minutes 27.20). In the race Mamola took the lead followed by Lucchinelli, Crosby, Hartog and Roberts. *Motor Cycle News* reported that . . .

Mamola streaked away with fellow Suzuki rider Lucchinelli, who had earlier been threatened with dismissal by the Olio Nava Fiat team for not wanting to race at the Nürburgring. He and Mamola exchanged the lead every lap and left the rest of the field struggling to match their pace.

Roberts says 'Randy, Lucchinelli and Crosby were going real fast and I could hang with Hartog (fourth). I kept Mamola and Lucchinelli and Crosby in sight. They had a big speed advantage on me down the straight but I could do that and it's really all I did. Randy or Lucchinelli would win the race.' *Motor Cycle News* reported that . . .

As Mamola and Lucchinelli fought it out a clear 20 seconds ahead of their challengers, the fight for third really hotted up. Roberts had made a steady start but was getting to grips with Crosby and Hartog, thanks to some slick signalling from Kel Carruthers darting from the start and finish straight to the trackside at the back of the pits [remember the Ring, 1978] *giving Roberts all the information he needed. Crosby held third until the end of lap 4 and then Hartog took up the running with Roberts following past the New Zealander. By the end of lap 5 Crosby had repassed the Dutchman as Mamola began to fade.*

Roberts says 'Randy's main bearing seal broke and started puking oil out of the exhaust pipe. He came straight back and kept on going back past me, he just didn't have the power. At that point I shut off and followed Hartog around, and cruised in.'

Lucchinelli won it from Crosby, with Hartog third, Roberts fourth and Mamola fifth a couple of seconds adrift.

Postscripts, then and now

Then: Roberts did not disguise his concern about the Nürburgring even when he'd taken this third consecutive Championship. 'I sure hope the organizers get the new track built before 1982' – the next scheduled race there. The new track? Its design would be supervised by Lauda, computer planned, short in the way of modern circuits and as safe as you can make them.

Now (1993): What was it like winning a World Championship? 'It is a good question to answer. It doesn't really seep in, I suppose. I don't know. I never [pause] . . . it's just winning, for me you know it was just winning and that's something else. When I raced motor cycles I wanted to be the best motor cycle racer in the world. I wanted to beat everybody else. I had honed my talents to do that, to keep beating people, beat them mentally, beat them physically.'

When you say mentally, what do you mean by that? 'There are a lot of mental games being played. Sheene used to be very good at it. If you can beat them mentally then physically it's not so big an effort and that was always the big thing for me – that is what I kept focusing on: riding my motor cycle better than anybody else could ride it, no matter what the problems were that particular year. You always go through years where there are particular problems and I'd still try to do it better than everybody else. That's what I wanted to be remembered as, or my career remembered as: that I could get on it and ride it, anyway.' The other riders would know precisely that, and know your hunger for the winning. Those mental games.

Thoughts and philosophies, thoughts and philosophies.

Not that, on 24 August 1980 at the Nürburgring, the career of Kenny Roberts was finished.

1981

Lucchinelli's luck

Swedish Grand Prix, Anderstorp

THE JOURNEY BEGAN in 1974, and began, as it seems, badly. Marco Lucchinelli contested the first event of his life, a hill climb at a place called Saline-Volterra, on a 250cc Aermacchi and came last. Never read too much into that.

By 1976 he rode for Suzuki and finished fourth in the World 500cc Championship; by 1980 he might have challenged for the Championship itself if his bike hadn't kept letting him down. In 1981, at the age of 27, he'd become widely popular under the nickname Lucky.

The battle lines:

On Yamahas: Roberts, Sheene
On Suzukis: Mamola, Lucchinelli, Crosby, Uncini

At the Salzburgring – the first round – Mamola nursed an injured wrist, but it 'wasn't hurting too bad so I pressed on and got past Marco. He was riding 100 per cent, maybe over the top.' Almost a third of the way through they came on a back marker and, as Mamola says, 'I shot past with an extra burst of speed down to the corner. I guess Marco was expecting me to brake but I went in deeper. He still tried to come past and got into the turn too fast. He ran wide and that was it.' Lucky fell, fell out of the Austrian Grand Prix.

He would not make such mistakes again, although 10 rounds remained and twice among them – the Nations at Monza and the San Marino at Imola – he'd need to master the compression, the claustrophobia and the tumult of an Italian crowd. He knew Imola intimately because he lived in the town, but that could only increase the compression, not diminish it.

At the West German Grand Prix – Hockenheim – he demonstrated he could run with the fast men. On the last lap Roberts led, Lucchinelli behind and Mamola urging his Suzuki to catch up. At the first chicane Mamola 'overdid it', recovered and urged again all round nearly four miles. He knew that the entrance to the 'complex' must decide the race. Once in the 'complex' you followed-my-leader and the finishing line lay too close to the exit to overhaul any rider who exited before you.

The 'complex' at Hockenheim (sometimes called the stadium section) is delicate and potentially fraught. Approached at high speed, a rider twists hard right, spurts, angles round a sharp left-loop, darts through a kink, spurts, angles round a right then another right to the straight and the line. These corners rear and snap.

Mamola found Lucchinelli 'in the wrong place' at the entrance and, although Mamola hustled past, the act of hustling cost him a fraction, cost him any chance to hustle Roberts, who did exit first and did win; Mamola at 0.44 of a second and Lucchinelli at 0.69 of a second.

The compression of Monza had aspects beyond the obvious. Since the deaths of Saarinen and Pasolini in 1973 the riders stayed away, and now Monza had been clad in armco. Pausing here, let's allow John Surtees to ruminate on the past. 'When I went to Grand Prix Drivers' Association meetings you had a little group forcing you to believe that the beginning and end of safety was armco railings. I tried to point out about the circuits used by cars and bikes, and frankly it would have been far better to follow another direction: a bit of space for run-off areas, sand traps in appropriate places, catch fences – but no, it was armco imposed on the organizers and circuit owners.

'Common sense has now prevailed, nothing like a decent bit of soft sand although to some degree catch fences have been discredited. I absolutely objected to running through tunnels of guard rails. This was not what I thought racing should be all about.'

Now in 1981 Uncini, representing the Grans Prix Riders' Association, cast a knowing eye over the circuit several times and pronounced it safe enough. Chicanes had been built at the insistence of the car drivers to cut speed, and their fastest lap in 1975 – 138.88 (223.50 kph) – became 128.08 mph (206.12 kph) a year later; but speeds rose and by 1981 the cars would be doing 133.03 mph (214.09 kph). Roberts set fastest lap in the bike race at 101.88 mph (163.96 kph).

Safe? A Japanese rider, Sadeo Asami on a Yamaha, crashed in a corner during unofficial practice and the marshal there had no fire extinguisher. Asami watched helpless but from a safe distance as his bike burnt. The race, mercifully, passed without trauma, Roberts winning from Crosby, and Sheene third. Mamola retired (engine) and Lucchinelli, whose engine functioned most of the race on only three cylinders, came fifth.

At the French Grand Prix – Ricard – all the fast men struggled except Lucchinelli, who beat Mamola by 4.91 seconds. Mamola 39 points, Roberts 36, Crosby 34, Sheene and Lucchinelli 31. At the Yugoslavian Grand Prix – Rijeka – Mamola struck what might have been a decisive blow, beating Lucchinelli by 0.90 of a second, and Roberts third. Mamola 54, Roberts 46, Lucchinelli 43.

Lucchinelli now put an imperious run together, winning the Dutch at

Assen and the Belgian at Spa. Imola followed a week later and, just like Monza, the Formula 1 drivers had had chicanes built. The riders didn't like them and, typically, Mamola expressed this with some vehemence. 'It stinks. They're not a test of skill at all. A good guy can't really make up any time there.' *Motocourse* reported that . . .

No-one could have staged a more dramatic start to the 500cc race. Black skies and the distant rumble of thunder had everyone guessing as to whether it might rain or not. Kenny Roberts's non-appearance on the grid finally answered questions that had been asked all day concerning his fitness [he had food poisoning]. *Marco Lucchinelli arrived on the grid late and then realized that his team manager, Roberto Gallina, had fitted a hand-cut front slick. In a scene of typical Italian chaos, Lucchinelli decided at the last minute to change this tyre for a slick and left his fellow competitors on the line wondering when the race would be started.*

The organizers hesitated to start the event without the Italian hero fearing, quite reasonably, that the crowd would riot. Finally the pack was sent away for a warm-up lap without Lucchinelli. Barry Sheene completed the lap just as Lucchinelli departed. The tension was incredible as the field push-started and swept away round the left-hand corner to start the 27 lap race. Crosby led by a fraction from Sheene and Lucchinelli.

Everyone agrees that during the next 42 minutes 19.98 seconds – the time it took Lucchinelli to win – he grew in stature, in composure, in maturity. Sheene took Crosby and so did Lucchinelli – and Lucchinelli then tracked Sheene, taking him and the lead on lap 14. In spotting rain Mamola slowed with a tyre vibration and chugged: fourth. Lucchinelli 88 points, Mamola 72, Roberts 58, Sheene 57, Crosby 56; and Crosby crashed at Silverstone in the British Grand Prix, altering the whole Championship.

Roberts and Mamola weren't involved but Sheene was. Scott writes that 'on only the third lap Crosby blew it. At the fast Stowe corner he applied a bit too much power too soon and found himself slithering along the track. Roberts managed to get by the sliding bike and its erstwhile partner. Sheene, just behind him, braked hard: the front wheel slid away and he, too, went tumbling into the catch fencing. Lucchinelli followed, still on his bike, but unable to avoid the fallen Sheene, who was lucky indeed to walk away.'

Lucchinelli remounted and kept on, the fairing badly damaged. He didn't reach the top 10. Middleburg won from Roberts and Mamola. Lucchinelli 88 points, Mamola 82, Roberts 70 and, 15 for each victory, who knew what Roberts might do? Two rounds to run – Finland at Imatra on 9 August, Sweden at Anderstorp on 16 August. The ratchet: all eleven rounds to count. *Motocourse* reported Lucchinelli as 'the model of controlled determination' in Finland . . .

Over a second faster than his nearest rival, Jack Middleburg, in practice, the Italian could only hope that no incident beyond his control like the crash at

Silverstone would prevent his victory. As a light-hearted gesture, his mechanics fitted a tiny rear light unit from a bicycle to the tail fairing of his works Suzuki. 'It's just to show that I am there so that no-one will ram me from behind.' Although he kept his cool on the circuit, the fiery Italian temperament bubbled over on several occasions during the evening and on more than one occasion Marco was the centre of a furore that could have landed him in gaol.

Lucchinelli stormed the race, and Mamola, grappling with an engine which maddeningly 'would cut in and out, running on two, three and four cylinders', came second, with Crosby fifth and Roberts seventh. Lucchinelli 103, Mamola 94, Roberts 74.

Sweden lacked harmony. The riders, led by Roberts, objected to the inclusion of a national race on the Sunday – pushing the 250 to the Saturday – and objected to the safety of the circuit. They agreed to race only after padding had been added to the armco.

Mamola had tonsilitis and said 'I've felt lousy all week, I've only eaten two meals since Sunday.' He'd go onto mild medication, then stronger medication. Mamola had to win. Sheene took pole from Lucchinelli, with Roberts third and Mamola fourth. *Motor Cycling News* reported that . . .

Roberts opted for wet tyres – rain fell just before the start – but after two warm-up laps the rear tread had been decimated. Roberts, like several top riders, had wanted to change tyres after the warm-up but with half a mile separating the pits from the Anderstorp start line his fate was sealed. Lucchinelli had also wanted to change his tyres and was anxious as he began his cautious ride.

At the start Mamola led Kork Ballington (Kawasaki), Crosby in third place, then Sheene, Lucchinelli and Middleburg. 'My bike was fast enough to win the race but I was so worried about falling off that I took it very carefully, especially in the beginning,' Lucchinelli said. On lap 6, Roberts came in for new tyres, had one changed and decided to retire.

The rain eased, then fell again in a steady drizzle, and Mamola, who'd never liked such conditions, drifted back towards Lucchinelli. Worse, Mamola's bike had broken a fork seal on the warm-up lap and didn't handle properly. On lap 17 of the 30 Lucchinelli caught and passed him. 'It was very difficult to discipline myself to go slowly for the first half of the race,' Lucchinelli said. 'I wanted to change tyres but I had to carry on. Only when I saw Randy did I think I could win the Championship. I felt much happier when I got him behind me. Then I just prayed the engine would keep going.'

Mamola drifted away, drifted away. Lucchinelli continued cautiously, continued cautiously. *Motor Cycle News* reported . . .

Then Mamola's fated ride was really put into perspective when, on the penultimate lap, the factory square four Yamaha bearing number 7 lapped him. The pit lane stood open-mouthed as they saw Sheene fly past the young American, a sight no-one could have expected.

Lucchinelli finished ninth and Mamola thirteenth. Lucchinelli 105 points, Mamola 94. End of story.

Postscript

Sheene won the Swedish Grand Prix from Dutchman Boet van Dulmen (also Yamaha) by 0.82 of a second, Sheene's first win for two years, the nineteenth of his career. Who could imagine on the evening of 16 August 1981 – when Sheene said 'Marco will make a great World Champion, he's been a friend of mine for the past eight years and I really wanted him to win out there today ' – that he, Sheene, would never win another race? Who could imagine on the evening of 16 August 1981 that Lucchinelli would never win another race, either? Who could imagine that Mamola, so strong, would never do what Sheene and Lucchinelli had done: win the Championship?

1982

Uncini's happy road home

Swedish Grand Prix, Anderstorp

HE'D FLOWN BACK to Italy and driven along the autostrada towards the Adriatic. Near the town of Ancona he peeled off and moved onto 10 kilometres of winding side road. He noticed to his puzzlement that 'people stood all along the way.' As he approached home – a community of 18,000 souls called Recanati – he began to realize why they stood. In the piazza Leopardi 'a band played, many, many more people there including the mayor, to greet *me*.'

At this moment Franco Uncini really understood he'd become World Champion. He might have understood it when he reached the first corner of the British Grand Prix a week before, but he didn't, he didn't . . .

A long road home. He'd go-karted from the age of five and his father took him to watch bike races. He'd explored motion on two wheels with a Honda 125. He'd started competing at 14 at Vallelunga on a 750 Laverda and finished third against men. 'A good result,' he'd say more than a decade later, 'considering I raced the last 10 laps without a front brake.' It argues intuitive feel and natural balance. Franco Uncini always intended to be a racer, anyway, and to make a career of it. His father said no; which is curious – however understandable in a paternal, protective sense – because father nursed a lifelong interest in bikes himself.

Evidently, as someone wrote, the Uncini household had been the scene of continuous arguments as Franco tried everything to convince his parents – hunger strike and refusing to attend classes. In the end his father had to give in.

A year after Vallelunga, Uncini won the Italian Superbike Championship on a Ducati, and MV Agusta invited him to test at Mugello. 'Even now I get shivers up and down my spine when I think of the MV. It must be the most fascinating bike that ever existed: an unforgettable experience for me.'

He turned professional in 1976 and, on a 350 Yamaha, beat Agostini twice in the same day during a round of the Italian Championship – a genuine feat. He came second in the 1977 World 250 Championship on a Harley Davidson and rode 500 Suzukis from 1979. By 1982 he was ready.

The battle lines:

On Suzukis: Uncini, Mamola
On Yamahas: Crosby, Roberts, Sheene
On Hondas: Spencer, Takazuni Katayama, Lucchinelli

A close season anticipated, particularly open – the days of Duke lording it, and Surtees, and Hailwood and Agostini long gone. And what might the young American Freddie Spencer do on the Honda – Honda returning for the first time since the Hailwood era? The first couple of races set the tone, Roberts taking Argentina from Sheene, Spencer, Uncini, Lucchinelli and Katayama; Uncini taking Austria from Sheene, Roberts and Crosby. The French ought to have been at Nogaro. *Autosport's* European Circuits Guide describes it as . . .

Ranking with Anderstorp as one of the most inaccesible of racing circuits. It has the glorious distinction of being right in the middle of one of the world's best brandy-producing regions, armagnac. The atmosphere is pleasant, slow Gascon, and if it takes your fancy you can watch the bullfight in the ring in the village. The track itself is curious, with a long back straight running parallel to the nextdoor airport, which can be quite alarming for spectators when a plane seems to be coming in to land with racing cars coming at it.

Ruminating aloud over the choice of Nogaro when France had Paul Ricard and Le Mans, *Motocourse* said . . .

Perhaps, suggested someone, the FIM have moved the race to Nogaro because the region's food is so much better. That, everyone knew, was very important to the FIM and it seemed the only logical answer.

The riders didn't find the atmosphere pleasant and it took their fancy to have a bullfight at the circuit, not in the village. *Motocourse* reported that . . .

Those who were slow getting away (after the Austrian Grand Prix the week before) or took the luxury of a full night's rest on the Sunday arrived to find the paddock filling rapidly. By Tuesday, late arrivals were camping outside and by Wednesday total chaos had descended as the paddock became so packed that there were no roadways and hardly enough room to move a motor cycle. If there had been the smallest fire, which is so possible considering that most teams carry their own welding equipment and their own high octane petrol, there would have been such a rapidly engulfing firestorm that no vehicles and few people would have escaped.

The riders considered the track 'too bumpy and presents serious safety hazards for both riders and machines' – I quote from the riders' statement to the organizers. That statement began . . .

We, the undersigned, have unanimously agreed that for the reasons listed below we will not compete in the French Grand Prix at Nogaro.

The reasons included the toilet facilities – so primitive that they 'are a disgrace and a serious health hazard.'

The 500 race did go on but without any of the leading riders, giving a historical freak like Austria 1977. Michael Frutschi (Switzerland on a Sanvenero) beat Frank Gross (France on a Suzuki) by 9.13 seconds. Frutschi would score only another two points during the season, and Gross none.

An open season? Roberts won Spain from Sheene and Uncini; Uncini won the Nations at Misano from Spencer, Crosby and Roberts; Uncini won Assen from Roberts and Sheene; Spencer won Spa from Sheene, Uncini and Roberts. Uncini won Yugoslavia from Crosby, Sheene and Spencer. Roberts retired, ignition. Uncini 88 points, Sheene and Roberts 68, Crosby 46, Spencer 45 and four rounds to run – the British, Swedish, San Marino and West Germany. The ratchet: all 12 rounds to count.

At Silverstone everything changed. During Wednesday's unofficial practice, bikes from the different categories shared the track together. At 160 miles an hour (255 kph) Sheene could not avoid a fallen 250. His Yamaha was savaged – in photographs it barely resembles a motor bike – and Sheene, flung along the track, broke both legs. They needed so many screws and plates that people wondered (and still wonder) how he gets through metal detectors at airports.

(As an aside, Macauley and the *Daily Mirror* had Sheene under lock and key at Northampton hospital, and he wouldn't talk to anyone else. *The Daily Express,* for whom I worked at the time, had the bright notion of sending me to the hospital to interview Jack Middelburg, who'd been following Sheene and was thrown off, too. With a photographer I penetrated the ward, and there was Stephanie, leggy and lovely, and the photographer tried to persuade her to take the camera and do some shots of Sheene. *No.* Never mind, in a moment I'm going to have Middelburg's graphic account of the crash. I can see him now, a strong man lying awkwardly in bed – jarred vertebrae, back badly bruised. He spoke good English in that guttural accent the Dutch have. 'Sorry' he said, 'I can't remember a thing about it.')

In the race Roberts made a bad start and, hurrying to compensate, went round the outside of the first corner, the right-handed Copse, to pick off as many riders as he could. He rode onto the kerb, which glistened from earlier rain, and went down damaging his hand. Uncini won from Spencer and Crosby.

Sweden at Anderstorp followed a week later. 'I did not know Roberts wasn't coming until I reached Sweden,' Uncini says. 'We heard his broken finger was too painful. I knew for sure when I didn't see him at first practice. How did I feel about that? Not very good because, you know, I prefer to win after a fight, not like this – but it had been a fight at

Silverstone despite the crash of Kenny so I suppose I really won it there.'
Motor Cycle News reported that . . .

Unaffected by the previous night's spaghetti party, Uncini came from behind as he has done before on the works Suzuki this season to snatch the lead from Katayama and an improving Randy Mamola. From a first lap ninth Uncini hit the front on the ninth lap. He led for the next eleven laps until the sprocket moved and threw off the chain. It was Uncini's first machine failure in the ten Grands Prix.

Uncini says 'I was leading the race 10 seconds in front of Katayama and my chain broke, but we'd won the World Championship anyway. Because of that my mechanics were relaxed and they did a mistake. It was an important Championship, especially because the year before Marco Lucchinelli won. I continued the Italian story.'

Did the fact that Lucchinelli won the year before put more pressure on you to do it again? 'Yeah, but I did not feel it so much. There was only winning with my own *feeling* and my own bike, so not such big, big pressure.'

How did you celebrate? 'I remember I rang home.' And caught a plane, and drove the autostrada, turned off for Recanati and saw the people lining the road.

What was it like racing Roberts? 'Ah, ah, very, very good. It was a very, very fantastic year. We are friends a long time, me and Kenny, and only when we used helmet and leather did we fight. After that good friends again.'

You can't put it any better than that.

1983

Spencer – thinking second

San Marino Grand Prix, Imola

PICTURE IT: THE long straight at Anderstorp, the Yamaha of Kenny Roberts, the Honda of Freddie Spencer and a great urgency gripping both men. Rounding the right-hander onto the straight, Roberts, forcing to keep Spencer back from him, accelerated so hard that his front wheel rose. For a milli-second he backed off, enough to let Spencer draw up behind. They fled down the straight nose-to-tail towards the two geometrical corners – both right-hand – which beckoned at the end of it and would feed them into the rush to the line.

They reached towards the first right-hander.

'I think,' Roberts says, 'he made a mistake. He didn't realize what was happening. I left the power on a bit longer than he had anticipated – I hadn't done that until this last lap – and he just let the brakes off in panic mode, he just let the brakes off and took us both off the track. Something I never thought worth doing even for the World Championship, but he did it.'

Roberts turned in, Spencer turned inside Roberts and they went off. 'I made the mistake of watching Roberts,' Spencer said. Spencer re-mounted *faster* and won the Swedish Grand Prix by 0.16 seconds.

'I spoke to him afterwards, oh yes,' Roberts says. 'I didn't say anything you can print. If he'd said a word I was going to knock him off the car' – on the lap of honour. 'I was a little angry. He thought that's racing, but that's exactly the opposite of racing. Yes, that's right, that's what I figure. I had three kids, I didn't need some young guy coming up thinking he could knock people off the race track. Normally you won't get that sort of stuff on a last lap. 500cc riders should not do that kind of stuff.' Circumstances reinforced the words because Roberts planned to retire at season's end.

Spencer 132 points, Roberts 127 and one round remained – the San Marino Grand Prix at Imola. All season they'd grappled and struggled, Spencer rapping off wins in South Africa and France and at Monza,

Roberts taking the West German at Hockenheim, Spencer taking Spain, Roberts taking Austria, Spencer taking Yugoslavia, Roberts taking the Dutch and Belgian.

'When you got to know Kenny,' Nobby Clark says, 'he was a great guy and all the mechanics got along with him. He'd ask a lot of us, from the work point of view, and always said life wasn't easy. I remember Spa. After the first practice he was so much slower than Spencer that I asked him why. He told me he wasn't going to show everyone that he was fast, he had plenty in reserve.

'The Japanese engineers also liked him a lot because he knew which road to take. By this I mean he'd make suggestions for bikes being designed for a new season, if the engine should be more forward, a shorter swinging arm, thicker front forks. If a rider and the designers get together, discuss ideas and, in fact, all aspects, it's an advantage to both.

'There have been riders in the last 10 years who've won Grands Prix but didn't know which road to take. They were lucky the bikes suited them. When their new bikes came along they couldn't always adapt to them with the same flair and aggression. Every rider has his own limit and all the limits are different. Some look like they are riding dangerously but will tell you they feel quite safe.'

Roberts not only observed his own limit, but rarely, if ever, looked dangerous, which makes Anderstorp more poignant.

Roberts took the British at Silverstone, Spencer took Sweden from Roberts and they went to Imola amidst rumours that Yamaha might pluck Crosby from retirement and fly him from New Zealand to help Roberts. Spencer need only finish second to have the Championship whatever Roberts did and an obvious tactic evolved: Roberts to lead and another Yamaha – Crosby – get between him and Spencer. But Crosby didn't come. *Motocourse* wrote that . . .

It may well have had something to do with the fact that Giacomo Agostini, team manager of the Marlboro Yamaha squad, had experienced personal differences with the New Zealander that had prevented Crosby's contract from being renewed after finishing second in the World Championship in 1982.

The full weight fell on Roberts's team-mate Eddie Lawson, and in this his first season of Grand Prix racing. Thus far Lawson hadn't been able to get near Spencer and (in theory) Spencer had Lucchinelli on another Honda to ride shotgun. A problem with that, though. Lucchinelli said crisply that he intended to beat Spencer. Could he? Would he? Moreover, Mamola (Suzuki) lurked as a spoiler again.

Roberts took his children to Imola and said when he arrived 'I've been on a month's holiday, playing golf and taking it easy. I can't get my mind on the race yet. I wish I could. My kids are here because this will be my last race in Europe, their last chance to see their dad as a Grand Prix racer. They need me more than ever now but they live with my ex-wife in California. If I'm racing here I can't see enough of them so there's nothing else to do but retire from the Grands Prix.'

Roberts gripped pole from Spencer, 1 minute 53.49 seconds against 1 minute 54.00. Spencer, looking impossibly youthful, insisted that he'd readied himself just as for any other race and would do his best. These are sentiments sportspeople invariably wield. 'I guess you could say I've spent a lot of time preparing the strategy that I hope to use.' Invariably sportspeople don't divulge what that is.

Spencer led from the start, Lucchinelli behind, Ron Haslam (also Honda) third. By the Variante chicane Roberts passed Haslam but Lawson, further back, had already visibly wobbled as the power came on. Mamola lay seventh.

On lap 4 Roberts moved on Lucchinelli and they waltzed through the chicane in beautiful motion, the bikes tipping in unison, flicking upright. And Roberts passed him, powering towards Spencer, with Lawson fourth but still a long way further back. Roberts needed four laps to catch and pass Spencer. Immediately he tried to break Spencer by hammering out the fastest lap – but he couldn't shed Spencer.

Roberts would have to ride his percentages again, slowing the pace, slowing the pace because, lap by lap, Lawson was catching Lucchinelli for third place and *if* Roberts could slow the pace *enough* Lawson could keep on coming, and might even be able to take second place from Spencer. Spencer knew all that and took the lead back for a lap. Electric moments: in a left-hander Spencer passed Roberts on the outside, the machines close, Roberts dipping hard into the angle of the corner, Spencer dipping harder. Spencer forced Roberts to accelerate to re-take the lead a lap later; then Roberts eased, eased, eased down again.

Motocourse reported that Roberts did this . . .

. . . brilliantly, making full use of the chicanes, slowing through them just enough to knock a fraction of a second off the lap time. If Roberts slowed too much Spencer would overtake, forcing Roberts to increase his speed to repass him.

On lap 17 of the 25 Lawson finally hauled himself past Lucchinelli but that didn't trouble Spencer unduly; nor did Roberts trouble him. 'I knew beforehand Kenny would try to do just what he did. I've run the race so many times in my mind I had all the options covered way before we got to Imola. Kenny obviously tried to slow things up so Lawson could get to me but Lucchinelli had done a good job keeping in third place for half the race and it left Lawson with too much time to catch up.'

On lap 20 Lawson squeezed the gap to five seconds and could now see Roberts and Spencer. Equally Spencer could see him and accelerated, pushing Roberts – and himself – far out of Lawson's reach. On the second last lap Spencer pressed for the lead, Lawson six-and-a-half seconds distant and out of the equation.

Roberts led crossing the line to begin the final lap, Spencer close. They cut cleanly through back markers and came to the left-right before the straight and the line. 'I finally knew I'd got it when I came out of that chicane,' Spencer said. 'I almost got earache on the last lap straining to hear if there was any sign of trouble in the engine.'

There wasn't.

He crossed the line 1.23 seconds after Roberts, and Lawson crossed 7.36 seconds after Roberts. 'Slowing it up was all I could do,' Roberts will say.

When Spencer came back after the slowing down lap his girlfriend Sarie stood in the middle of the tracking waving, rushed up and buried him in an embrace. She made intoxicated noises of triumph. Spencer was mobbed while, almost unnoticed, a Honda mechanic pushed the bike round the rim of the crowd towards the pits. The story of every mechanic, surely.

On the podium Freddie Spencer still looked impossibly youthful. After all, he was only 48 minutes 17.86 seconds older than he had been when the San Marino Grand Prix, 4 September 1983, began.

Postscripts

Roberts, relaxing in the motor home, said he'd go back on holiday. 'I can do the things I want to. Sure I'm disappointed. Sure I could have rode him out today [taken him off!], but that's not my style. We banged fairings and elbows a couple of times but nothing as much as we would have done if he'd had to win the race. The Swedish result narks me because he benefited from his mistake. I won that race . . .'

Spencer said 'I used to watch Kenny Roberts and see the sort of following he had and I didn't really believe one day that could be me, but deep down I knew I could do it. Whatever you take on is a form of expressing yourself and I feel at home on the race track. You have to believe in your own ability. It would be wrong if you didn't. Never at any time did I plan to beat Kenny. I was more worried about Eddie Lawson than him.'

Honda had tried to win the World 500cc Championship in 1966 and 1967, the hallowed days of Redman and Hailwood against Agostini. Hailwood died in a road crash in 1981 and so did not live to see a man utterly dissimilar from him finally achieve it.

Ten years later I'm sitting with Roberts at the British Grand Prix at Donington in a motor home more modern, no doubt, than any at Imola, 1983. Country music – a cascade of stretched, nasal, agonized sounds – echoes from the sound system. What manner of a man was Spencer? Did you *know* him? 'Not much. He was different to the rest of us. He never hung around, he never did what we did, which was a bit peculiar . . .'

1984

The style of Eddie

Swedish Grand Prix, Anderstorp

PICTURE IT: THE long straight and a replay, two riders fleeing down it towards the geometrical right-hand corners and the rush to the line. Whoever reached the first right-hander first would – barring accidents – win the race. Freddie Spencer was not one of those two riders, nor Kenny Roberts. Another generation had risen already, Lawson and Frenchman Raymond Roche. Only the makers' names on the bikes remained constant: Yamaha and Honda.

As Lawson moved down the straight he can scarcely have suspected that by career's end only one man, Agostini, would have more Championships. Lawson, from Upland, California, first raced in 1965 and made his Grand Prix debut on a 250 Kawasaki at Hockenheim in 1981. In 1983, as we've seen, he joined the Yamaha Marlboro World Championship Team and, while Spencer took the title by two points from Roberts, Lawson nestled into fourth place in the table behind Mamola.

The battle lines:

On Yamahas: Lawson, the experienced Ferrari
On Hondas: Mamola, Roche, Spencer, Haslam
On Suzukis: Sheene, British debutant Rob McElnea

Another name ought to be added to the Honda list, that of a gregarious Australian, Wayne Gardner. A journalist friend, Nick Hartgerink, has written that 'Honda Britain wanted Gardner for the 1984 season and offered to seek a sponsor to allow him to do most, if not all, of the World 500cc Championship rounds. However, by the time Gardner returned to Britain in March there was no sponsor and he faced another year of racing in Britain on the same old tracks against the same old faces. He took out his frustrations blitzing the Brits at the opening two rounds of the TT F1 Championship at Cadwell and Thruxton then decided to take matters into his own hands.

"'I was cheesed off, to put it mildly. I had watched the first Grand Prix in South Africa on television and that only made me more frustrated. Guys had done well in that race who I knew I could beat, so I pleaded with Honda Britain to allow me to go to the second round at Misano in Italy on 15 April.'"

On television, Gardner saw Lawson winning from Roche and Sheene. Gardner didn't see Spencer, who'd been lapping Kyalami very, very fast in practice when he reached the esses. 'As I went into the corner the front end just went light and the back collapsed' – a carbon-fibre spoke on the composite rear wheel let go. 'Next thing I knew I was sliding into the straw bales.' Spencer bored deep into those bales, the Honda's rear wheel twisted, as did Spencer's right ankle – the ligaments torn – with extensive bruising to the other foot. By evening he could barely walk and certainly couldn't race.

He recovered for Misano and won from Lawson, with Roche third and Gardner fourth. The winning margin, 19.65 seconds, seemed significant. Clearly Spencer could win all the remaining 10 rounds.

Wrong.

In the Transatlantic Trophy at Donington, Spencer crashed again and missed the Spanish Grand Prix at Jarama, where Lawson won from Mamola. Gardner missed that, too. Honda Britain still lacked a sponsor and Gardner wouldn't be back until the Dutch Grand Prix at Assen in late June, more than half way through the season.

Lawson won Austria from Spencer, and in a gesture of solidarity Mamola, third, slowed markedly on the last lap, allowing Spencer through to the derision of the crowd.

Spencer beat Lawson at the 'new' Nürburgring, Lawson baulked by a back-marker – an 'idiot', Lawson called him – and, slithering onto wet grass, lost so much time he concentrated on second place. Lawson 69 points, Roche 43, Spencer 42. Spencer won France from Lawson and Yugoslavia from Mamola, Roche (third) and Lawson (fourth). Lawson had handling problems, the rear tyre pitching the bike sideways on acceleration. Lawson 89 points, Spencer 72, Roche 53.

Of Assen, Nick Harris and Peter Clifford wrote in *Fast Freddie* that 'you do not win 15 world titles without learning a great deal about how the sport works, and so when Marlboro Yamaha team boss Giacomo Agostini spotted a flaw in Honda strategy at the Dutch TT he exploited it to the full. It was that decision by Agostini which did so much to snatch the World Championship out of Freddie's grasp. Freddie practised on the V4 before the massive Dutch crowds, but at the end of timed practice found himself in fifth position. Freddie decided to go out and try the old three-cylinder machine in the unofficial session before the race, but Agostini had done his homework and stepped in.

'Waving a set of supplementary regulations, he pointed out that Freddie had not practised on the three-cylinder during the timed sessions and so could not use it in the race. There were a few grey areas about the validity of the regulations but Honda could not risk disqualification and out came the V4 onto the grid.'

Spencer led but a plug lead came off. 'While Lawson uncharacteristically sulked in his motor home after only finishing third behind Mamola and Roche, Freddie admitted to the assembled press that his World Championship was slipping away.'

A week later Spencer won the Belgian Grand Prix at Spa, and Lawson was fourth, but in practice for a non-Championship race at Laguna Seca, Spencer's brakes failed and he went down, damaging an old shoulder injury. He'd miss the British and Swedish rounds because he insisted on allowing the shoulder to heal naturally. In his own way Spencer accepted that this would cost the Championship. *Motocourse* reported that . . .

When the bone was X-rayed it turned out that it had broken in almost exactly the same place that it had two years before when he had been brought off at Hockenheim by Franco Uncini on the last lap. According to Spencer's specialist, the bone could not have mended properly then or it would not have broken again in the same place.

Because of this complication the bone would have to be allowed to mend fully this time and no way Spencer would ride at Silverstone or Anderstorp. Even if Spencer could have sat on a bike there was little point in him making the trip to Europe. He wouldn't win unless 100 per cent fit. Lawson was not pleased that Spencer would miss Silverstone. 'I wish he was riding here. I don't want to win the Championship just because he isn't.'

Ah yes, but – Mamola won Silverstone, and Lawson was second at 2.45 seconds. Lawson 119 points, Mamola 96, Spencer 87, Roche 75, and Sweden and San Marino to run. The ratchet: all 12 rounds to count. Only Mamola could stop Lawson.

At Anderstorp Haslam took pole from Roche and Lawson, with Mamola fourth. Haslam led but Sheene fell when a German rider, Klaus Klein (Suzuki), cascaded down in front of him. 'I saw him fall,' Sheene said, 'and I was forced to go inside to miss him. Someone banged into me but I was still OK then. The trouble started when I tried to accelerate away. I gave it some throttle and the engine died. Then, when I whipped the clutch in a bit, the power arrived suddenly, the back end whipped round and I was on the deck. I gave my knee and hip a bit of a clout but the pins seem to have stood up OK.'

Crossing the line to complete lap 1, Mamola led from Haslam, Lawson and Roche. Haslam felt confident, and was going into the corners so much faster than Mamola that 'I was almost running into him.' Haslam tracked Mamola tight, passed him after six laps, Roche moving into second place while Lawson probed at Mamola, occasionally drawing full up alongside.

On lap 10 Haslam dropped out. 'I was just sitting comfortably, everything perfect, then the water pump sprang a leak.' Roche inherited a narrow, perilous lead from Mamola and Lawson, so perilous that Mamola flowed by and at that instant had Roche's Honda as a shield between himself and Lawson. On lap 13 Lawson slipped past Roche and probed Mamola again, passing him on lap 18. Mamola, a man of strong body and mind, hung on across two laps but, nearing the tight left-hand corner half way round, his throttle stuck open. He skittered into the heather which lined the circuit. *Motocourse* reported that . . .

It was a fault almost completely peculiar to Anderstorp, which has very hard braking corners making the rider snap the throttle shut. The cables beat the slides and then they stuck partly open. Mamola battled on for a while but was forced to give up as things got too hairy.

Lawson said 'I wasn't taking any risks right up till I was given the signal that Randy had gone out. Then I decided to go for the win.' Some saw Lawson as a composed man, an extremely composed rider, but not a raw racer who, by temperament, would seize a race and shake it to bits. This charming notion – reticent, rationed Eddie – did not survive the closing laps of the Swedish Grand Prix. He and Roche duelled. Roche took the lead and they came onto the straight – came to the replay – and fled towards the distant right-hand corner.

Lawson said 'I left my braking really late and we both went in really hot. I grabbed the brakes, my back wheel was in the air and I thought I was going to lose it. Then I saw Roche come past me on the dirt and I knew I'd won the race and the Championship.'

Roche said 'as we went into the corner I had a feeling that only one of us would stay on the race track. Unfortunately . . . it wasn't me.'

Postscript

Gardner finished third and, aided and abetted by Roche, observed the great tradition and threw Lawson into the paddock swimming pool. Three years later Gardner would find himself in a swimming pool, but not this one and not even one on this continent. Yes, another generation risen, and rising. The way it was, is and always will be.

1985

Spencer – thinking double

Swedish Grand Prix, Anderstorp

THESE MANY YEARS later the face has filled out into maturity, but the man remains easy and comfortable and perhaps laid-back. When he speaks the drawl is unaltered, a slow warming thing and strictly Deep South, strictly Louisiana or thereabouts. The years have touched Frederick Burdette Spencer, but gently.

He touched immortality. It hardly shows.

He came to motor cycles because it ran in the blood. His father, who ran a corner grocery store in Shreveport, raced them, his brother Danny raced them, his sister Linda raced karts. At the age of six Spencer won his first race on a Honda 50cc. He was naturally gifted, which is a way of saying he could just do it, and a career followed almost inevitably.

A lean 1984 followed his 1983 Championship – only fourth – but during that season 'Honda brought out their 250cc production racer and we talked about it and as the year went on we talked about it more and more.' No man had won the 250 and 500. There had been double champions in many combinations – Redman the 250 and 350 on Hondas, Agostini the 350 and 500 on MVs, for example – but never this one; and there's a clean symmetry about it.

This season there was a major entry by a sponsor, Rothmans, who describe it as 'an historic move' when they and Honda 'joined forces. It was the first time Rothmans had been involved in Grand Prix motor cycle racing and the first time the Honda organization had formed an association with a sponsor.' (Up to now I've given the battle lines in a straightforward way, by makes rather than teams. Because from this moment on there's a subtle interplay between sponsors, teams and riders I'll be giving them more fully.)

Spencer says that 'I rode the 250 for the first time at Suzuka in early December and it wasn't a bad little machine. I tested it again in Australia and then raced it for the first time at Daytona together with the NSR500, and I knew from that moment the double was possible.

'The approach to the 1985 season really started in December with that test in Australia. We were there for seven days – well, six or seven days – and I'd go out on each machine back-to-back. I'd get off the 250 and get straight on the 500, or I'd get off the 500 and get straight on the 250. It meant I couldn't tell Erv Kanemoto (famed and fabled expert technician) what I wanted done to the bikes until I'd ridden both. That made it more difficult.'

To this task Spencer brought formidable intellect and, culled from the intellect, a clear and concise plan emerged. These many years later the man who is somehow easy and comfortable describes it. 'Even though we had separate mechanics for the bikes, Erv was the main guy. We had a set formula we wanted to use and that I could live with and get used to. That's what we started in Australia. I faced races back-to-back during the season so in testing I'd cover 30 lap "races" – get on the 500 and do 30 laps, get right on the 250 and do 30 laps. The objective: to reach the point where I could get off one bike and onto the other and it didn't make any difference.'

Spencer made a conscious effort to make the transition subconscious. He'd need to be able to do that. 'In fact the first meeting where I achieved a "double" – at Mugello (the fourth round) – I got off the 500 and Toni Mang was waiting for me for the 250! By the time I got back to my motor home to change leathers the bikes were going out for the 250 warm-up lap.

'We deliberately tried to get the bikes as close as possible in terms of characteristics so there wouldn't be too much of a contrast between them. We did have a little bit of a problem in that we didn't get the new bikes for '85 until Daytona, so actually in Australia we tried to simulate what it would be like. We had 120 different tyres to test when I was in Australia. How can you remember all that in your mind? It's kinda hard even though I was testing both the 250 and the 500 tyres, of course. There again, we tried to do everything in tandem. That's why testing was so critical.

'Suppose we'd had one bike which was so much different to the other. Disregarding the fact that it rode a lot differently, if we'd struggled with it, if we'd gone way off track trying to develop it, everything would just have been a waste. A struggle with one bike would have taken too much away from the overall effort.'

In South Africa, the opening round, Spencer won the 250 and came second in the 500, but at Jarama – the Spanish Grand Prix – Spencer's personal assistant, Iain Mackay, remembers 'in the morning warm-up he crashed and broke his thumb, cracked it in two places and he had to ride the 250. Claudio Costa (bike racing's resident travelling doctor) froze the thumb with a spray but said he wouldn't give Freddie an injection because then he wouldn't have any feel and wouldn't know how hard he was braking. Costa said "I'll freeze it and the numbness will last for four laps. After that it's up to you to stop or keep on. You'll know how much pain you've got. It's your decision." In the race Freddie's exhaust pipe holed and he went back, back, back, but he'd said he would stay on while he was still in the points and he did – ninth. Freddie didn't shirk his duties.' Moreover, he'd won the 500. Thereafter:

	250	*500*
Germany, Hockenheim 19 May	2	2
Nations, Mugello 26 May	1	1
Austria, Salzburg 2 June	1	1
Yugoslavia, Rijeka 16 June	1	2
Holland, Assen 29 June	1	Crash
Belgium, Spa 7 July	1	1
France, Le Mans 21 July	1	1

The 250 Champioship: Spencer 119, Mang 82, German Martin Wimmer 69 (Yamaha), Venezuelan Carlos Lavado (Yamaha) 67. The 500 Championship: Spencer 111, Lawson (Yamaha) 94, Frenchman Christian Sarron (Yamaha) 62, Gardner (Honda) 61. The ratchet: all 12 rounds to count.

'Freddie took the strain well, very, very well,' Mackay says, 'and it surprised me because he was so young. He isolated himself from the problems of constant travel, different languages, different food. Sure, he'd rather have been at home watching the Oilers or playing golf but he didn't allow that to affect him. He was tough and mentally could be very tough. He kept himself extremely fit, really on top of everything. If he hadn't, the double would not have been possible.

'Even so the double weighed hard on him. I don't think anybody on the outside understood, but people on the inside knew. You had four bikes, you see, two 250s and two 500s at each meeting (one for the race, one spare). They all needed setting up. A lot of things occur to a rider just after he's left a bike and is among the engineers. Freddie didn't have time for that. In normal circumstances he'd have dismounted from the 250 and said *this or that requires doing,* but he needed absolutely to block the 250 from his mind because the 500 waited for him. Very often at one o'clock in the morning in the hotel he'd suddenly say *oh, I've just remembered . . .'*

This was the man who rode the gathering pressure. He compresses it into a few words. 'There were two crucial races, the British at Silverstone and the Swedish at Anderstorp. At Silverstone I needed to finish at least fourth to wrap up the 250. That would allow me to concentrate exclusively on the 500.'

In practice on the Friday Spencer fell. 'I kind of broke my hand and had it frozen (for four laps again!) The doctor said it would hurt and it did. The weather was bad, windy, wet but I knew I was strong enough to finish fourth. That was probably the hardest race for me all year long, one of those where you go just as fast as you need to go. Guys all around me were crashing and my hand was really bad and I had the 500 race next – that was pressure – but as it worked out I did finish fourth. That took a lot of the pressure away.' He won the 500. Spencer 126 points, Lawson 106.

Anderstorp followed a week later.

Mackay says that 'after Silverstone we went down to London, me with my girlfriend and he with his. We took them to show them round, see the sights. We were to leave for Sweden on the Thursday. The night before, he went off to bed and the next morning told me he hadn't slept very well. He said he sat alone in a chair until three o'clock going through every possible permutation, every possible situation which could arise during the weekend. In his mind he'd now fixed how he was going to run the race and all the various ways the race might unfold. *I know exactly what I'll do, I don't have to win the race to win the Championship.'* (Spencer confirms that he examined permutations before races 'a lot'. See Imola, 1983.)

Third place would do, but you have to be careful about that. What if he fell again, hurt himself badly? What if the bike failed? He'd have only one more race, the San Marino Grand Prix at Misano, two weeks further on.

So: he reached Anderstorp prepared for whatever might unfold in the 30 laps, the 75.150 miles (120.930 km). Above the deep, long, packed grandstand a breeze ruffled and teased the flags of 20 nationalities. *The* flag descended and the muscular men shoved off in meaty movements, seven, eight, nine strides, snuggled onto their machines. Haslam (Honda) led into turn one, a right-hander, Spencer moving towards second place. Spencer sliced inside Haslam clean as the cut of a knife, Lawson attacking Haslam. In turn Lawson moved by Haslam and hunted Spencer.

On lap 10 Uncini's Suzuki flung him, knocking him out. The bike, lain nearly mid-track, burst into flames. Spencer missed it, Lawson missed it and Spencer drew away from Lawson whose Yamaha began to slide around when he accelerated: tyres going off. Against Freddie Spencer that left you no chance.

Gardner hustled Lawson and took him at a sharp right, although Gardner ran out of fuel on the last lap which let Lawson finish second. 'There are no excuses,' Lawson said, 'I needed to win and I didn't. It's as simple as that.' In the end it always is.

The climax: Spencer soothed the Honda into a right-hander, soothed it round the next right-hander which brought him to the finishing straight and he hoisted the bike in an enormous wheelie, put the bike back down with a bounce at the instant it crossed the line, took his left hand from the handlebars and punched the air almost horizontally.

Laconically he says that 'in theory I didn't have to win the race but I put the bike on pole and I did win it.' To the great, perhaps in the end it's always as simple as that.

Mackay recaptures Anderstorp crisply. 'We didn't have any real dramas all weekend. It was a little bit like being in a dream. Everything went right.'

They threw Spencer in the paddock's swimming pool and when he surfaced the whole world could see it, the smile on the face of the winner. He flew out of Sweden almost immediately after, a gesture – or action –

which seemed against the spirit of the occasion, against the spirit of the sport. We'll come to that shortly.

These many years later I wonder how winning feels. 'People feel a lot of ways. I was watching Greg Norman's face when he won the British Open a couple of weeks ago (summer 1993 at Sandwich, on the south coast of England) and it wasn't so much happiness as relief. I can understand that. It was very satisfying because so few people believed we could do it. We'd tried to do something that people said you probably couldn't do.

'We had the set plan that we followed and it worked. We pretty much didn't have to vary our course of action although it was real tiring. Looking at it, everything was smooth but there was never a time when you could relax and just enjoy it – never a time where both bikes were perfect. The 500 would be, say, but you'd be worrying about the 250. Like Greg Norman. When the putting is right the drive needs attention, when the drive is right the putting . . .'

In the early and mid-1980s Spencer adorned motor bike racing and intrigued it also. You know the kind of thing, an enigma concealed behind labels so easily stuck on him by others: Bible-belt Christian, teetotal, remote, difficult, private.

Mackay insists that 'Freddie wasn't as he was publicly made out to be. A lot of the stuff you read about him is just not true. You can't put anybody in racing in front of me that Freddie ever said a bad word about. Freddie kept his opinions of other people to himself, didn't bad-mouth anybody.

'Yes, in some ways he was a complicated person but in other ways just a simple man. If you look at almost any sportsman at the top level, or the top level *anybody* in any walk of life, they are complicated individuals. Freddie certainly was. Freddie had his own ideas about lots of things and some of it you could agree with, some not, but I didn't find him difficult.

'As a rider he was unbelievable. There's only one Freddie Spencer like there's only one Mike Hailwood or only one Kenny Roberts. What is it? It's a whole package. Freddie wasn't technical but had tremendous feel. He could tell Erv exactly what the bike was doing, he had total recall of what happened while he was on it. And Erv knew him, Erv could interpret what Freddie said.

'Freddie took winning well, he enjoyed it immensely. He hated losing. *Second place is no place.* He came from a hard school, racing at five or six years old, then dirt track. There is no last chance in dirt track: you lose it, you go home. Disaster. I always remember something he said to Sean Roberts (of Rothmans) the first time he rode the Rothmans Honda. Freddie finished second to Eddie Lawson and asked Sean "I suppose you're going to sack me?"

'You know this wonderful reputation Freddie had of not turning up on time. He never did it to me, he'd be there . . . but after the double season he was invited as guest of honour to the launch of the Rothmans Lite at the National Exhibition Centre, Birmingham. Freddie was the main man. He only flew in that morning and I went to pick him up at the airport. Everybody files out through the arrivals door, no Freddie. I thought *oh dear, oh dear, oh dear me. Here we have a new cigarette, dancing girls, all the executives, the lot – no Freddie.*

'You know where he was? Standing round the corner laughing his head off. He knew I'd seen my life flash before me, knew I'd be dying out there beyond the door. He could do things that way. He had a good sense of humour, that was a lovely thing about him. People didn't see that side of him.'

What Mackay did see, when Frederick Burdette Spencer came through, was a broad smile, the same one everyone saw at the Anderstorp swimming pool on 11 August 1985, the same one I saw in 1993 when he sat and told me about the testing in Australia, the double plan and how it worked.

How do they describe such as he around Louisiana? A Southern gentleman.

1986

Lawson stays on

Swedish Grand Prix, Anderstorp

ON THE FOURTEENTH lap of the Spanish Grand Prix at Jarama on 4 May, the opening round, Freddie Spencer angled his Honda into the pits in 'the worst moment of my career.' It came, as these things do, without warning.

Sinus problems prevented any pre-season practising, but he'd taken pole from Gardner, now his team-mate at Rothmans Honda, and led the race by four seconds after lap 2. It seemed clear then. Spencer would retain the 500cc Championship by bestriding it, lording it, bending it to his will.

Wrong.

On those early laps he looked as he so often did, neat, holding within himself a suggestion that he could go quicker whenever he chose. Lawson lay a long way back battling Gardner, Gardner passing Lawson, Lawson counter-attacking and none of it affecting Spencer so far ahead. In a right-left chicane Spencer slowed visibly and began to coast, gazed wistfully over his shoulder as Gardner came up. Spencer had tendonitis in his right wrist and couldn't operate the front brake. As he dismounted in the pits and made his way quickly to the sanctuary of the motor home the Championship had been decided against him, decided for Lawson.

Hadn't it?

Gardner won Spain, beating Lawson by 2.07 seconds. The battle lines *now:*

Marlboro Yamaha: Lawson, McElnea
Lucky Strike Yamaha: Mamola and fellow American Mike Baldwin
Rothmans Honda: Gardner

Lucky Strike Yamaha? Yes, a new team created in 1984 by Kenny Roberts and now ready, he felt, to contest his 'true love', the 500s. No doubt the fact Agostini ran the Marlboro Yamaha team spiced that.

Meanwhile Gardner, writes Nick Hartgerink, 'began to feel isolated. Suddenly from being very much the No. 2 rider and eager to use his first year as a factory rider to learn and gain experience he found himself virtually Honda's sole chance of taking the Championship.'

The Nations Grand Prix at Monza, second round, proved a disaster. Gardner's bike wouldn't start and he mounted using his right foot to paddle it forward. The grid threaded by, but a Swiss, Marco Gentile, clipped Gardner's leg, forcing it into the gear lever. Gardner clambered off and gave the Honda a push start, the entire grid gone; pitted after one lap, the gear lever bent so that he could only change up. He rejoined hoping he might get a point or two.

Lawson won from Mamola, Gardner sixteenth. Lawson won the West German Grand Prix at the new Nürburgring from Gardner (by 12.08 seconds); won the Austrian Grand Prix at the Salzburgring from Gardner (by 11.50 seconds). Spencer returned there and qualified fifth. On lap 1 Lawson surged past Spencer who had to pit when a steering damper bolt broke. Spencer went out again to see if his wrist could stand a full race distance. It couldn't. He finished sixteenth and caught a plane for Louisiana, not to be seen again.

Lawson won the Yugoslavian Grand Prix at Rijeka from Mamola second and Gardner third. Lawson 72 points, Gardner 49, Mamola 47. A pushover. Assen would be no trouble, Lawson pole with 2 minutes 12.70 seconds, Gardner next with 2 minutes 13.39 seconds. Lawson settled into mid-pack at the start but on lap 1 in a right-hander went wide and onto the grass, the bike digging dust. He put a foot down to steady it but the bike speared away, tripping him. He heaved it upright but too much time had been lost. Gardner won from Mamola. Lawson 72 points, Gardner 64, Mamola 59.

The Belgian Grand Prix at Spa was wet and Gardner 'couldn't get my mind on the job, as simple as that.' Mamola led, Lawson content with second place as riders and bikes slip-slip-slided; Gardner fourth.

The Championship might have opened up between Spa and the French, opened far away at Laguna Seca where Lawson crashed heavily in a domestic race; but rode in France – and won. In the *Rothmans Yearbook* Nick Harris wrote that . . .

. . . just seven days after being told he could not ride for six weeks Eddie Lawson displayed all the qualities of a true champion with a superb victory in the vital 500cc race. The 28-year-old Californian dislocated his collar bone in a crash at Laguna Seca a week earlier and was told to rest for six weeks. He visited a sports clinic who got him fit and strapped up for his most important win of the season in the 21-lap race. Even a fracas with an official, which left him with a cut eye, two days before the race failed to dampen his resolve and courage.

Lawson beat Mamola, with Gardner fifth – 'the low point of the season, so depressing to have no answer to the Yamahas.' It rained hard during the British at Silverstone and someone described the conditions as monsoon.

Gardner rode the spray superbly, Lawson at a distance. Didier De Radigues (Honda) pressured Lawson, at one moment trying to pass him on the outside at Woodcote. Lawson wasn't unduly concerned when De Radigues did go by . . . Lawson 109 points, Gardner 93, Mamola 92.

The ratchet: all eleven rounds to count and two rounds to run – the Swedish at Anderstorp and San Marino at Misano. Lawson needed to finish in front of Gardner at Anderstorp to have the Championship. Gardner stated his intentions by taking pole (1 minute 36.35 seconds), Lawson next (1 minute 36.64). By his nature, by every fibre of his being, Gardner would play it to the end, tough it out, concede nowt. No surrender. You want the Championship? Come and get it.

The trees round the circuit smothered the skyline, sombre as the old Nürburgring. A crowd of 22,000, most in high-banked stands which reached back towards the trees, watched a flurry of a start, Haslam and Belgian De Radigues (Honda) away fast. Soon Haslam drifted back – the front suspension unit failed – and Lawson tucked in behind De Radigues, Gardner tucked in behind Lawson – a race poised, positions to be established.

Lawson slipped inside De Radigues at a right-hander at the end of lap 2, Gardner copying, and lap after lap Gardner forced the Honda taut onto the Yamaha: lose a bit along the straight, regain it by late braking, circle, lose a bit along the straight, regain it. A contrast in styles: Lawson economic in each corner, hugging the inside, Gardner describing wide expansive arcs as if trying to pump more and more power from the Honda and harness it when he got it. Mike Hailwood would have understood. Gardner stayed with Lawson, yes, toughing it out. No surrender.

After 16 laps they moved among back markers and one of them briefly baulked Gardner. Maybe in the whole history of our story to this moment – all the bravery and sadness, the great rides and improbable, imperious races – this moment was *necessary.* Someone entirely anonymous, so anonymous that nobody I've met knows who, may not even have made a mistake; just happened to be in the wrong place at the wrong time for a very short space of time; and unwittingly, unknowingly decided the World Championship. It stands as a great contrast to – selecting a big example – Agostini winning Championships by inter-stellar distances and with plenty to spare; it also represents another facet of the sport. You'd need Jodrell Bank to track Agostini; you'd need a microscope to dissect Gardner behind the back marker.

In a contest so perfectly matched it cost Gardner dear. Lawson set fastest lap (1 minute 36.59 seconds, 93.35 mph/150.23 kph) and drew away. Gardner, held by being so perfectly matched, could do nothing. Lawson won by 16.04 seconds. As he crossed the line he raised a clenched fist and then unknotted it so that a single finger stabbed, signifying number one.

'Wayne made me work for it,' he said 'and I feel just great. The second title is every bit as good to win as the first and the third will be even better.' Gardner said with undisguised candour – after Lawson tipped a large glass of champagne over him on the podium – that 'the best man won the race and he deserves the title. I was with him until the back markers started coming up and then he had the better run which broke my slipstream. After that it was better to settle for a second to help sew up runner-up spot in the series.'

Then, Lawson into the swimming pool. He emerged, clambered out and went back to his motel. *Motor Cycle News* reported that . . .

At the victory dinner party it started very formally with toasts for the new champion. Then all hell let loose. A diversion while his Italian Marlboro Yamaha team staged a fireworks display outside the restaurant gave Lawson a chance to team up with Rob McElnea and sneak a couple of bottles outside. When everyone was back in the room (after the fireworks) they let loose with a couple of well-shaken bottles. It was an uncharacteristic display from the normally quiet and reserved Californian who's not known for his outrageous outbursts.

'At last I'm entitled to let my hair down,' said Lawson who'd won title number two with a near faultless display of the motor cycle racing art. 'People will say it's been easy but I don't care. You have to show up to win and I've been showing up all year.' The champ dodges questions about the man who ducked out of Sweden on the first plane after he'd clinched the title here last year. Ask him directly about Freddie Spencer and he simply says 'who? I don't recall anyone of that name scoring any points this year.'

Lawson 139, Gardner 117. Mamola 105, descending to M. Papa (Italy, Honda) 1, Spencer 0. The year before Spencer had had 141 in the 500, 127 in the 250. A year may be a long time in motor sport, just as, reaching a back marker, a moment may be a long time. Ask Wayne Gardner.

1987

Gardner, zoom, zoom

Brazilian Grand Prix, Goiania

'FIFTEEN MINUTES LATER Gardner emerged in the grandstand opposite the pits flanked by 25 armed policemen, still wearing his leathers but covered with a Rothmans tee-shirt proclaiming he was the 1987 World 500cc Champion. Amidst the mayhem which his arrival created he spotted me and my microphone. Earlier in the week he'd promised to do a live interview with the BBC in London after the race whatever the result.

'Even the BBC's insistence on going round every cricket ground in the country while the sweating and now totally exhausted World Champion had to wait failed to break his resolve. More than a few Australian swear words were uttered and the tee-shirt had to be taken off and used as a towel as we checked on the exploits of Glamorgan and Somerset before the new Champion was finally interviewed by Stuart Hall. Hours later, when champions in other branches of motorsport would have been flying home to secluded and heavily fortified homesteads, Gardner minus a shirt was leading the dancing and drinking at Goiania's Zoom Zoom Club.'

Thus Nick Harris on the essence of the Aussie, afternoon, evening and late night 27 September moving towards morning 28 September. Hall, incidentally, had long been a Gardner admirer and their live cross-talk during his sports programme – Hall at the BBC in London, Gardner wherever he happened to be racing – became richly irreverent, spicy, honest and wonderful listening. A long journey to here.

The battle lines:

Rothmans Honda: Gardner, Spencer
Marlboro Yamaha: Lawson, McElnea
Lucky Strike Yamaha: Mamola, Baldwin

Japan on 29 March was wet, and Mamola's Dunlops coped better than Gardner's Michelins, Gardner settling for second place. Lawson, who'd picked the wrong compound, pitted after lap 1 to change his rear and later retired.

Gardner found his stride, winning Spain at Jerez from Lawson. At Hockenheim for the West German Grand Prix he stormed pole position just under two seconds quicker than Sarron (Yamaha), and on lap 5 led Lawson by seven seconds, but an electrical problem made the four exhaust valves stick open. 'The power loss was dramatic. It felt like two cylinders had been disconnected.' Gardner gestured for Lawson to go through and limped to tenth.

Gardner won the Nations at Monza from Lawson (and by 15.66 seconds) but rode virtually the whole race with a headache and a nosebleed. Under braking, when he rose from the seat, the wind pressed the blood into his eyes and across his visor. In Austria Lawson retired early – carburation problems – and Gardner wrestled Mamola to the end, beating him by 2.37 seconds. Gardner won Yugoslavia from Mamola and Lawson; Lawson struck back at Assen beating Gardner by 6.67 seconds. Gardner 85 points, Mamola 66, Lawson 64.

A three way split: Mamola took France at Le Mans; Lawson took the British at Donington; Gardner took Sweden and Czechoslovakia; Mamola took San Marino at Misano. Gardner 145 points, Mamola 124, Lawson 115. The Portuguese Grand Prix was held at Jarama, Spain after concerns about the safety standards at Estoril. Gardner led, but a balance weight came loose and punctured the radiator. 'It was like a slow dying process. By the time I finished I'd lost two cylinders and the mechanics said the bike was lucky to make it home. In another lap or two it would have seized solid. As it was I had blisters on my left hand from the intense heat coming up from the engine.' Lawson won from Mamola, and Gardner was fourth. Gardner 153 points, Mamola 136, Lawson 130 and two rounds to run – Brazil at Goiania and Argentina at Buenos Aires. The ratchet: all fifteen rounds to count. Gardner needed only finish in front of Mamola in Brazil.

Harris wrote that . . .

Goiania, which is situated 100 miles west of Brasilia, had never seen anything like a motorcycle Grand Prix before, while a motorcycle Grand Prix had never seen anything quite like Goiania! The result was an incredible combination of parties, dancing and singing that threatened to engulf the racing.

While everyone was full of praise for Goiania, racing in Brazil does have its problems. The British-based Dunlop tyre factory provided Mamola's Lucky Strike team with tyres and had been rapidly improving all season to match the dry-weather Michelins used by the rival Honda and Yamaha teams. Dunlop flew 50 special tyres into Brasilia for the race, but they were stolen at the airport and so Mamola was forced to use the Japanese Dunlop counterparts.

Gardner had problems of his own in the final practice session. Watching the rev counter of the Rothmans NSR Honda and a slower rider in front of him he missed his braking point at the end of the main straight at around 180 mph (290 kph). He went off the track and through the grass but managed to stop a metre short of the armco barrier without falling off his bike.

Nick Hartgerink wrote that . . .

. . . from the opening qualifying session Gardner set about his goal with single-minded determination and was rewarded with his ninth pole position of the season – 0.77 of a second ahead of Mamola. The American spread a story around the pits that Gardner had used a special qualifying tyre that wouldn't be suitable for the race. It wasn't true, so Gardner knew his rival was rattled.

That 27 September was hot, humid, cloying, sticky after heavy overnight rain. The riders faced 32 laps (76.25 miles/122.72 km) on a bumpy circuit. At the start Gardner sliced down the inside clear of the pack and turned the bike mid-track, seized the first right-hander in the lead, Lawson second, Roche third, De Radigues fourth.

'I got my head down and didn't look back once,' Gardner said. 'I wasn't confident that the rear tyre would last the distance so my strategy was to go hard from the start and try to build up a cushion that would give me the luxury of being able to back off towards the end. Completing lap 1 my pit boards told me I was almost a second ahead. I thought *that's nice, I can win it from that* and put my head down and went harder.'

Mamola, slow away, caught Lawson and took him, tried to catch Gardner and couldn't. Lawson moved back into second place, Mamola's rear tyre spinning badly. Harris reported that . . .

. . . even an amazing mini-whirlwind which sent columns of litter spiralling across the track failed to halt Gardner's progress, although nervous start-line officials thought about stopping the race.

'When I was eight seconds ahead at half distance I could afford to relax a little bit, but I was trying desperately *not* to think about the Championship,' Gardner said. 'I concentrated harder than ever trying to put together consistent laps and then keep the gap, but with two laps to go the whole thing hit me. I realized I was just three minutes away from the World Championship. These last two laps were hell, the longest of my life. I did slow down, desperate for nothing to go wrong. That chequered flag was the best thing I have ever seen.'

The slowing allowed Lawson to reach within six seconds of him but Lawson suffered 'the same problem I'd had in Sweden. When the tank is full I can't flick the bike into the corners quick enough.'

Gardner lifted both hands and shook them into fists as he passed that chequered flag, pounded the fists ahead like pistons above the fairing. Even into that first right-hander, where he'd taken the lead 47^{1}/2 minutes before, he kept his left hand off the handlebars, pounding and pounding and pounding like a man dissipating enormous energy.

'I don't know whether to cry or laugh,' he'd say. He thought it *nice* to win it with a win, and on the podium tears welled. Then he spoke to

Harris, and spoke to Hall so far away.

Iain Mackay judges the win as 'wonderful. I mean, he was head and shoulders above everyone else and he deserved it. He went mad, he was in tears – what you would expect from Wayne. He had a whale of a party and went in the swimming pool at the hotel. Everybody went in, two or three hundred people! Kenny Roberts and Wayne threw me in. People were going back to their rooms to change – girls taking their frocks off and putting on jeans – because they knew they were going to end up in the water.

'There is no-one you can compare Wayne with: a one-off, a totally different person to the rest, a real racer and a split personality. He's lovely and friendly with the lads, easy going but really tough on the bikes. He could be a very, very emotional person and he rode emotionally as well. Emotions carried him through on some occasions and they brought him to grief on others.

'He was also extremely professional in his own way. He'd ride through problems where a lot of people might say "I can't ride with this" or "I can't ride with that." Wayne would get on with it, a bit like Mike Hailwood in that respect. They thought *this is what we have got, the only thing to do is to go out and fight it round*. That's what the job is about.'

1988

Lawson floats it

Czech Grand Prix, Brno

THE HAND-PICKED hand-maidens, each with a classically sculptured figure and face you could drown in, had brought the costumes of men's dreams: the Lucky Strike girls with very short white skirts and skimpy sleeveless blouses, a Lucky Strike girl in black with a tanned midrift and blonde hair which whispered and tumbled in a cascade. A Team Pepsi Suzuki girl wore a leotard stretched so tight it clung to each undulation. They'd decorate the grid before the race on the Sunday.

A wonderful contradiction, that.

To the circuit of Brno, some eight miles from the be-spired town of the same name, columns of Trabants and Wartburgs, some panting under the weight of box-like caravans they towed, put-put-puttered on their journey from East Germany for their annual, and only, taste of the big bikes. The Sachsenring had passed into memory, no race there since 1972. These cars bore within them solid families in their plain workers-state clothing, the husbands sweating under a fierce sun in vests – how many remembered Hailwood, remembered Agostini? – the women often heavy, the kids on the back seat strong-boned. They'd be in the stands for the race on Sunday.

The riders themselves weren't so sure what they'd be ready for, what might happen next or if anything would happen next. Brno, on the afternoon of Friday, 26 August – as the maidens checked the cut of their costumes and the Trabbies panted on towards the Czech border – existed as a place of very great uncertainty.

The Sunday ought to have been the third last round of the season and important, although not in the proper sense of the word crucial, with Argentina and Brazil to follow; but the uncertainty revolved precisely there.

Argentina had proved an extremely unpopular place, putting it diplomatically, for the final race of 1987. Two descriptions are worth quoting, the first from *Rothmans Yearbook.*

While everybody enjoyed their stay in Brazil the season reached a very disappointing end in Argentina. Chaotic organization and a slippery track should have led to a riders' strike. Instead, with the threat of no air ticket to get them and their machinery home, they reluctantly agreed to race.

Nick Hartgerink wrote that . . .

The track was a shambles and the organization almost non-existent. The riders were appalled by the safety standards and went on strike in protest. They eventually agreed to ride when the organizers said they would withold payments to ship the teams back to Europe. The riders had to work on the circuit themselves, dismantling a chicane and other obstacles while their mechanics erected hale bales in front of the fences that were perilously close to the track.

Twelve months later and the week before Brno, the organizer in Buenos Aires, Renzo Cozzanic, faxed the FIM to inform them that the promised work on the track had not been completed and that new tarmac was breaking up.

Cozzanic said the race could be held but on the track the way it was in 1987. Would a single rider tolerate that? Unlikely, putting it diplomatically. On top of this, rumours ebbed to and fro that financial difficulties hung over the Brazilian race and it, too, might be cancelled.

That Friday night at Brno the riders met and decided no to Argentina, although Lawson felt it 'very bad for the image of the sport that the decision had been left so late' – not an implied criticism of the riders, who'd only discovered the position a few days before. That Friday night Lawson went to bed possibly World Champion for the third time. He led Gardner by 23 points and under the new scoring system – 20 for a win, then 17, 15, 13, 11, 10, 9, 8, 7, 6, 5, 4, 3, 2, 1 – could not be caught if Argentina and Brazil melted into nothingness. The ratchet: all fifteen rounds to count.

On Saturday that altered. The riders announced their decision on Argentina but the FIM announced they'd put money in to support Brazil. Gardner, unrepentant about Argentina, openly complained of the 'dreadful facilities and the complete lack of enthusiasm of the organizers. To renege on my promise not to go back after the organizers had not carried out any of our demands would have been disgraceful.'

This stance minimized Gardner's chances. He sat relaxed, hair shorn towards a crewcut, wearing jeans and a sleeveless tee-shirt and faced a microphone. 'In one way it's the worst thing that could happen, but in another way it's the best thing because the organizers have had a whole year to do it and they haven't, and we've got to start drawing the line somewhere. Otherwise we're going to be taken advantage of and basically be asked to race on anything. It's the right decision as far as that goes, but unfortunately the sad part is it gives me less chance of retaining the title. Professionally, however, it's the best answer.'

Lawson, more circumspect, murmured that he liked the track – he'd won there in 1987 – but 'if everyone agrees it's not ready, it's not ready.' Unlike the others he'd been looking forward to going.

Now Lawson needed only second place at Brno. Lawson's lead of 23 plus 17 for the second created an impregnable total because *if* Gardner won Brno and Brazil and Lawson got nothing there, Gardner could only equal Lawson's total; Lawson had it on the tie-break of most wins, six-five.

The battle lines:

Marlboro Yamaha: Lawson
Lucky Strike Yamaha: Wayne Rainey, Kevin Magee
Gauloises Yamaha: Sarron
Rothmans Honda: Gardner
Pepsi Suzuki: Kevin Schwantz
Corse Cagiva: Mamola, Roche

Lawson confessed that his tactics would be conservative but did permit himself some sharp observations about Gardner. 'Our relationship hasn't really been any different this year. Wayne's using his mouth a lot, bad-mouthing me, but I guess that's his way. He stopped me doing a good qualifying lap here. It's things like that which get to me. He's much more aggressive on the track than me, but who's to say which is better?' That qualifying:

Gardner	2m 05.55
Rainey	2m 06.80
Sarron	2m 06.86
Mackenzie	2m 07.05
Lawson	2m 07.20

Sunday 28 August, and they came to the grid. One of the maidens offered Lawson a drink as he sat astride his Yamaha but he declined it. Nearby, Rainey accepted one while the girl in black with the cascading hair held a parasol over him against the sun which shimmered from a sky flecked by trails and whisps of cloud. Rainey's team-mate Magee had a Lucky Strike girl holding a parasol for him while a dusky maiden in identical costume positioned herself at the other side of the bike not doing much except stun men at 20 paces. The Yamahas had no team orders.

Team manager Roberts spoke urgently to Magee who nodded, ingesting the instructions. The girl in the leotard held a parasol over Schwantz and his Suzuki, Schwantz who felt he was riding for his place in 1989, and said so. Gardner said he liked the Honda's handling and the bike had a new suspension which he liked, too.

They faced 23 laps, 77.09 miles (124.06 km) on a track so new it had only been used for the first time the year before: smooth, certainly, but turning across difficult off-camber corners. A crowd of 166,000 sat in stands or on banks framed against a backdrop of forest-clad hills.

Moving into the warm-up lap Gardner spent an instant or two adjusting his visor while other riders set off sharp and hard, engines gurgling to a growl. They came round, settled, waited. The man with the red flag, holding it taut in both hands, moved like a matador across the front row and moved away, the flag falling slack once the grid had formed. The green light took a long time, so long that Mamola gestured towards a television camera *start it now.* The wait stretched to 15 seconds, the bikes on the front row nibbling forward, the riders impatient under the constraint of the wait.

The American Rainey got onto the power first and led. Behind him riders weaved and danced and darted. By the time they'd moved through the sweepers at the back of the circuit Gardner had slipped past and so had Tadahiko Taira (Yamaha), giving: Rainey, Sarron, Pier-Francesco Chili (Honda), Schwantz, Lawson.

Gardner constructed a significant lead, less a tactic than a necessity. He flowed and skimmed hard into the corners while a necklace of riders pursued, Lawson still seventh after lap 2; still seventh after lap 3. Then Lawson moved, Schwantz falling away on lap 4, Taira falling away on lap 5 when Lawson took Chili, too. Order: Gardner, Sarron, Rainey, Lawson. On lap 7 Rainey angled inside Sarron – Lawson spectating, Gardner alone at the front, the construction of the lead growing. Almost imperceptibly Lawson increased the pressure on Sarron, once, twice, thrice positioning himself out of corners to strike, tucking down again, waiting again.

A contradiction, that.

On lap 8 Magee sliced inside *Lawson,* thrusting Lawson to fifth. Magee sliced past Rainey and a curious thing was born. Magee and Rainey, both Lucky Strike Yamaha, seemed to be trying to stop Lawson on the Marlboro Yamaha. 'I raced for Lucky Strike, not Marlboro,' Rainey would say, but he dropped away and Magee sliced past Sarron to take second place – Lawson fourth. 'It looked like I wasn't going to get second, it was me against the rest of Yamaha,' Lawson said.

A bunch and a gaggle gathered so far from Gardner, moving within move and counter-move: Magee, Sarron swarming him, Lawson screwing his bike onto Sarron, Chili lurking here and there, looming, travelling within striking distance of Lawson. On lap 10 Sarron and Lawson moved past Magee and on lap 11 in a right-hander Sarron – albeit on a Gauloises Yamaha – moved aside. 'I opened the door to let Eddie through,' Sarron would say, 'but the rest all came past, too . . .'

Magee took second, Lawson third, Chili fourth, Rainey fifth, poor Sarron sixth and with the touch of a master Lawson outbraked Magee into a left-hander. Move and counter-move. Magee stayed the length of three, perhaps four bikes away but the master smoothed away from him. Sarron, struggling to retrieve anything, lost control and the bike bucked pitching him into the air. Lap 16: Gardner, Lawson, Rainey, Magee, Chili, De Radigues. Magee crashed a lap later. 'I was coming up real well and then I came down real well.'

They held station, Gardner safe and clear, Lawson safe and second, although towards the end Gardner eased in an attempt to lure Lawson into a trap, goad him to accelerate and try for the win, maybe force an error. 'I slowed so they'd close a little and maybe crack.' Lawson habitually saw traps. In the right-hander before the finishing line Gardner looked once, twice over his shoulder to verify that Lawson remained second.

What Gardner saw was not just Lawson comfortably holding Rainey but Lawson in his full majesty, drawn in on himself, the bike moving at one with the rider. Gardner took his left hand off the handlebars and tucked it into his waist, a casual posture, no hurry now, nothing more to be done; and at the instant of crossing the line he looked back again to be absolutely sure. 'That was the easiest race ever,' he'd say. Or, if you wanted to retain a Championship, the hardest.

Gardner	49m 11.06
Lawson	49m 12.97
Rainey	49m 13.54

On the slowing down lap Gardner took both hands off and fashioned twin thumbs-up signs although there seemed to be a different connotation to the gesture, might have been indicating *well, what more could I have done?*

When Lawson dismounted a happy throng surrounded him in the afternoon sunshine and he slipped a Marlboro World Championship Team tee-shirt on before he moved to the podium. Because of the confusion over Argentina and Brazil there had been no time to prepare a proper conqueror's tee-shirt so someone had written it in heavy felt-tipped pen across the front:

1988 World Champion

'I didn't think we were going to get second place,' he said, a blue cap at a jaunty angle on his head, a hand smoothing sweat from his chin. 'It looked like Lucky Strike Yamaha against me but we came out on top and I'm happy for the team. The Marlboro team did a great job once again.'

What does it feel like to be champion for the third time?

'Better than the other two.'

Later, sanguine and reflective, Lawson added a homily. 'Wayne had bike troubles at the beginning of the season and of course I've had bike problems. He's fallen down, I've fallen down. I've got more points, he's got less points. That's kinda the way I look at it. I enjoy the racing very, very much. The travelling I don't enjoy – sitting on a plane, all the rentacars, it's really tiring. Anybody who's done it a lot will know what I'm talking about. It's a hassle, not pleasure. I have to get home whenever I can, I have to. I just take the boat, float down the river, shut my brain off and don't do anything. It's nice.'

Postcript

The Brazilian Grand Prix did take place, 17 September, and Lawson won from Gardner, 47m 06.32s against 47m 19.68s. *If* Lawson had fallen into Gardner's trap at Brno, had overstretched and crashed, it wouldn't have mattered, wouldn't have mattered a trice. He'd still have had the three.

1989

The merry-go-round

Brazilian Grand Prix, Goiania

THE WHISPERED STORIES could barely be heard above the samba music, and anyway nobody believed them. The stories said that Eddie Lawson might be leaving Marlboro Yamaha, where he'd spent the whole of his Grand Prix career, to join Rothmans Honda. That was Goiania, 17 September 1988, after the Brazilian Grand Prix which – as we've just seen – Lawson won from Gardner.

Long before, Lawson expressed discontent with what someone described as the 'moral support' he received at Yamaha, discontent that his efforts against Gardner in 1987 received less than their due. Lawson had requested a transfer to the Roberts Lucky Strike team for 1988 but this was refused and Lawson tentatively approached Honda.

A lot of whispered stories, in fact, as the samba music drummed on into the night of 17 September. Schwantz expressed discontent at Suzuki and had approached both Yamaha and Honda. Certainly Yamaha wanted Schwantz as No. 2 to Lawson, and Honda wanted Schwantz, too – Schwantz had hinted as much at the British Grand Prix at Donington, six weeks before Brazil. Suzuki assured Schwantz they'd make a reliable and competitive bike for him in 1989, and he stayed.

Lawson, meanwhile, negotiated with Honda. Mat Oxley wrote in the seasonal preview published by *Motor Cycle News* that . . .

It took until mid-October for the news to break for real. Even then some refused to believe it. Ironically Lawson was working on a Marlboro publicity video at Laguna Seca, California, when the news reached America. He'd not told Ago or Kel Carruthers about the deal and Lawson left the States for the Fuji International in Japan like a ship heading for a storm.

Japan was already alive with the story when he arrived at Tokyo. Lawson had given his manager Gary Howard power of attorney in the final negotiations with Honda and it's likely that Howard signed on the dotted line in the week before Fuji. Yamaha were so offended they didn't bother meeting Lawson at the airport and when he asked for a lift they suggested he made his own way to the track.

He arrived two days later. Lawson petulantly burnt his last boat with Yamaha by sulking to tenth (two laps adrift) in the Fuji race on 23 October after leading from the start. Not everyone heard the news at the same time, though. Wayne Gardner got the shock of his life when he read the papers at Heathrow while waiting for a flight to Japan.

That begged the big question: how would Gardner and Lawson co-exist? And it led to another question. Could Lawson tame what has been described as 'the evil-handling NSR500?'

The battle lines:

Rothmans Honda: Lawson, Gardner, Australian debutant Michael Doohan
Lucky Strike Yamaha: Rainey, Magee
Marlboro Yamaha: Spencer, Mackenzie
Gauloises Yamaha: Sarron
Pepsi Suzuki: Schwantz, Haslam
Corse Cagiva: Mamola

In Japan, Rainey led from Schwantz and they duelled, Schwantz winning, Rainey second, Lawson a distant third. Then 'we had a bad race in Australia,' Lawson would say. In practice Lawson followed Magee and Magee's bike suddenly slowed. Lawson clipped the back of it, forcing him onto the grass. He ran along it, the Honda bucking and bounding and weaving until it cast him off. He lay spreadeagled five or six yards from the bike, stunned.

In the race Schwantz, chasing Rainey for the lead, lost control in the tight right-left corners and the rear tyre slewed, the bike corkscrewed and pitched him up, up, up. Schwantz somersaulted *in the air* and landed splayed across the track. The bike, rearing like a frightened horse, plunged off by itself. This moment distilled much of Schwantz, the precious talent which sometimes went frantically wrong. The presence of Schwantz in any race gave it the unknown, the deliciously unexpected, the terrifying; and often all arriving at the same instant. Chewing through his Texas drawl – a real one, a rumble-grumble of a thing – he'd vouch that what he had to do was learn to stay on the darn things.

Rainey went clear but Gardner caught him, took him, Lawson sixth and a place behind Spencer. Rainey re-took Gardner, Sarron led briefly and Spencer fell. A race among races, really. Gardner won; Lawson nowhere.

Then, says Lawson, 'we went to Laguna Seca and got third and won in Spain, and from that time on we were always in the hunt.' Schwantz crashed in Spain when he held a comfortable lead; crashed in another brutal ballet of movement. Lawson, smooth, won it from Rainey.

The surface of Misano lacked adhesion and the riders agreed that if rain fell during the Italian Grand Prix they'd stop and change to wet tyres. It rained. Schwantz gave the signal and, in a ripple, the riders peeled off to the pits. Plump raindrops drummed onto the circuit and the riders demanded a practice session rather than race again immediately. It was refused and they refused to resume.

'Well, this place is unique in that the surface is very, very slippery,' Lawson said. 'If there's water on it you can't ride on it. All the top riders felt that it was too dangerous, and it is.'

At Hockenheim Lawson led, but Rainey took him at the mouth of the stadium 'complex' and won by the length of a bike. Rainey 91 points, Lawson 78, Sarron 58. At the Salzburgring Schwantz stayed on and won from Lawson and Rainey. At Rijeka, Yugoslavia they circled in a trio – Lawson, Rainey, Schwantz – but Lawson went wide approaching a right-loop, drifted across the grass and rejoined. Schwantz won from Rainey with Lawson third. At Assen Rainey won from Lawson: Rainey 143 points, Lawson 127.

This mid-season Lawson revealed his full maturity. Every race is a sudden, sharp thing, milli-second piling on milli-second in what can be a great blurr. Maturity allows the rider to slow this, measuring all the factors in the race and placing them in the context of a whole season. Push hard here, back off there, go for the win here, take a third place there. The mature rider does not just see the next corner coming so quickly at him, he sees the Championship, still perhaps several months away. Lawson, circling Assen, knew that six rounds remained.

At Spa Lawson cut past Rainey and it rained. Rainey gestured for the race to be stopped, Sarron overtook Lawson who began signalling himself. Sarron skidded off and the riders came in after five laps. At the re-start Lawson led, but Schwantz took that from him. A rider crashed and they slowed again, stopped, re-started a third time, the track drenched. They tip-toed, ghostly figures in the spray, and on the last lap Schwantz's Suzuki skimmed away from him. Not that that mattered – the third leg would be declared void, giving Lawson the win and cutting the Championship deficit to $14^1/2$.

At the French Grand Prix Lawson won, Schwantz nearly went to the ballet again on the last lap but held second, and Rainey was third. At the British Grand Prix it didn't rain and Schwantz won from Lawson. Rainey $180^1/2$ points, Lawson 174. At Anderstorp Schwantz retired, Lawson tracked Rainey, took him with the purest of pure power plays down the straight and, with two laps left, Rainey's bike reared in a right-hander, casting him away like a plane crash, cartwheeling him onto the adjacent runway. Lawson won and went to the Czech Grand Prix at Brno with a $13^1/2$ point advantage. The ratchet: all 15 rounds to count.

An important race, only Brazil to follow. Rainey led immediately from Schwantz. Schwantz needed that lead and got it, Lawson spectating. Lawson took Rainey into a right-hander, poise and balance and control, tucked his head into his shoulder for a brief glance back at the prey he'd despatched. He took Schwantz the same way but Schwantz struck back and Lawson followed him home, Rainey third because Sarron slowed to allow him through. Lawson 211, Rainey 195^{1}/2. Lawson needed no more than eleventh in Goiania, while Rainey needed the win.

It provoked Rainey to declare before the race 'I feel like I've been beat up by everybody in the world.' A percentage race from Lawson? No, sir. Taking the outside line at the green light he angled across into turn one clear, Schwantz hovering, Rainey searching. Rainey struck past Schwantz (who, inevitably, almost fell when the bike oscillated). As the race unfolded they scythed through the back markers and 'we were dirt track riding out there,' Lawson said. 'In the back of my mind I was telling myself *don't fall down, dummy.*'

Lawson led to lap 19, Schwantz wobbling and weaving a path behind Rainey in second. Schwantz took him on the inside at a right-hander, Rainey responded instantaneously and they moved side by side, almost welded, almost touching. Two laps later Schwantz took Lawson at the end of the start finish straight, a manoeuvre Lawson chose not to contest. The maturity allowed him that. Lawson did not contest the remainder of the race, either, but followed at a prudent distance. The maturity allowed him that, too. How could he know a nightmare would rear at him, sudden as a spectre?

A couple of laps to run, a right-hander and a Chilean, Vince Cascino, tumbled directly in front of Lawson, the impetus of the fallen bike casting if fractionally left, left, left. It gave Lawson a gap if he twisted right, right, right and hugged the inside – but could he, all in the milli-second? 'I saw him go down and I thought *Jeez, oh no* but I kept a real tight line.' This moment distilled much of Lawson; not just reaction-time but what you are able to do within the reaction time. He described it almost humbly. 'I got through.'

He moved back into his maturity, stroked the Honda home. 'I wanted to win but Kevin was just too fast.' The tension reached Schwantz. 'When I was just behind Eddie looking for a gap to get through I was real worried (that he'd touch Lawson and bring him down) but once I got ahead I thought I was safe.' He was and so was Lawson. Duke won the Championship on two makes of bike (Norton, Gilera) and so did Agostini (MV Agusta, Yamaha) but no-one else – until now.

Postscript

There's a political echo which travels back down our story all the way to the Sachsenring and the races there from 1961 to 1972. That important Czech Grand Prix at Brno took place on 27 August, but against a backdrop heaving with politics. Ordinary East Germans were using Czechoslovakia and Hungary as escape routes: they either camped in the West German embassies or crossed the (now open) Hungarian border to Austria. The East German government panicked and forbade all travel to Czechoslovakia. Brazil, so impossibly far away for any East German, had been 17 September. Seven weeks later the Berlin Wall opened, releasing a mighty torrent of people. From this milli-second on they could go wherever they wanted – even Goiania.

1990

Rainey day people

Czech Grand Prix, Brno

'I JUST RAN out of brakes. I'd been having trouble with them since the second lap. I pulled in the lever and it went to the bar. By the time I pulled it in the second time I was going too fast and lost the front end. The worst thing was that I also took out Eddie Lawson and I'm so pleased he wasn't badly hurt.' This is how Michael Doohan described the events of lap 5 of the Japanese Grand Prix at Suzuka, opening round of the season. Lawson had returned to Yamaha but to Kenny Roberts's team, not that of Agostini.

The battle lines (and note that Roberts now enjoyed unique direct support from the Yamaha factory):

Marlboro Roberts Yamaha: Lawson, Rainey
Rothmans Honda: Gardner, Doohan
Lucky Strike Suzuki: Schwantz, Magee
Gauloises Yamaha: Sarron
Corse Cagiva: Mamola, Haslam

Lawson, unknowing and helplessly, began to lose the 1990 Championship as Doohan ploughed into him, and did lose it at Laguna Seca where he fell himself and broke his heel. He didn't compete again until the eighth round, the Dutch at Assen, and by then the season had devolved to Rainey and Schwantz.

Of handling a 500cc bike Roberts would say (maybe untypically) 'you've got to have the talent to ride the thing out of control.' Whatever, it was precisely what Schwantz so often didn't have. He'd get it out of control and it wouldn't come back. That's what happened at Laguna Seca when he disputed Rainey for the lead.

A hard season, a bone cruncher.

Gardner won Spain and said, sharp as you like, 'it was easy. Once I had caught Rainey it was just a matter of getting past him. Once I'd done that I could pull away easily.'

In practice for the Italian Grand Prix at Misano, Gardner crashed and cracked two ribs. 'At one stage I thought it was impossible that I was going to ride but they did a lot of work on me in the warm-up. It was very, very painful without drugs so Dr Costa fitted me up with one. I was catching Mick towards the end, and I wish it had gone the extra 15 laps. I'm pretty sure I would have caught him then but the race was stopped because of rain. It was restarted as a 12-lapper and I finished second to Schwantz in that. I probably rode better because I was a bit more in tune and more motivated, a bit more confident in my own ability by then. It's one of those weekends . . .'

Gardner finished third overall, but Rainey seemed to have the Championship in an arm-lock: he'd won Japan, Laguna Seca, been second in Spain, now won Misano. Rainey 77 points already, Gardner 50, Schwantz 47, Doohan 45.

Approaching Germany, Gardner said that 'Dr Costa told me the pain will be even greater but I'm prepared to ride through it. I must keep going and hope that Wayne Rainey has a few problems.' In practice Gardner crashed again, breaking three bones in his right foot. Schwantz won, beating Rainey by nearly 12 seconds.

Gardner missed Austria where Schwantz won from Rainey, with Doohan third. Rainey 111 points, Schwantz 87, Doohan 60. Rainey struck back at Rijeka in the Yugoslavian Grand Prix, beating Schwantz by 10 seconds, but Schwantz tightened it by taking Assen with Lawson, returning, third. He could disturb the balance of the Championship. Schwantz fell back on the same philosophy as Gardner, the philosophy of the inevitable and used almost exactly the same words. 'All I can do is keep winning the races and hope that Wayne Rainey has problems.'

Rainey didn't. In the rain at Spa he made the right tyre choice and caressed the bike gently round the circuit, beating Jean-Philippe Ruggia (Gauloises Yamaha), Lawson third again, Schwantz maddeningly seventh. Rainey 168, Schwantz 133, Doohan 96. In the French Grand Prix at Le Mans, Schwantz – on pole – started slowly and then stormed it, Gardner hounding, Rainey happy with third. In the British Grand Prix at Donington, Gardner had pole, but on the opening lap his Honda suffered a broken piston ring. Schwantz won from Rainey. In Sweden Schwantz went to the ballet again, crashing after three laps, and Rainey won it from Lawson. Czechoslovakia, Hungary and Australia to run, Rainey leading Schwantz by 47 points. The ratchet: all 15 rounds to count.

Before Brno, uncertainty threaded into it. Nick Harris wrote that 'a decision whether the penultimate round of both the 250cc and 500cc World Championships will be held at the Hungaroring will be taken later this week. If the track is not safe the event will be cancelled, leaving Wayne Rainey the 1990 World Champion.' As it happened, the Hungarian Grand Prix would be held . . .

'Well, Brno was my first World Championship attempt,' Rainey says, 'and we'd already had a good season up till then. I was on the rostrum every race (and never lower than third) and we had a huge lead but you know *there was still some way I thought I was going to lose the Championship*. At that race I was probably the most nervous and excited I've ever been. I don't usually get nervous but I do usually get a lot of excitement. This time I felt nervous because of the final outcome and what that could be. I wanted to clinch it at this race, I didn't want to go through this feeling of not knowing it was going to happen any longer, didn't want to delay it, didn't want anybody to catch me in the race. I think I qualified on pole, and in the race Schwantz fell down.'

That was moments after the start.

'I was World Champion right then and there so I decided to win the race anyway: a very strange feeling because usually when you race you race to win, but in a sense I'd already done that. We'd achieved what we'd set out to achieve and yet the race was still going on. Double double strange.'

Gardner, riding with a cracked bone in his wrist after a practice fall, led for the first 10 laps. Rainey pressured him. 'My hand was really swollen,' Gardner said, 'and I only had the use of two fingers to operate the brake lever. I was having to roll the throttle back with the palm of my hand.'

Rainey said that 'Gardner was fast and I decided to follow him for a while before I made up my mind to go past. I set the fastest lap late in the race because Gardner was still pushing. I wanted to let him know I had something left for the finish.' He had.

Rainey   47m 50.847s
Gardner   47m 52.850s

Postscripts

A question to Rainey. We understand that World Champion bike racers are not famous in America, even American World Champions. 'Yeah, that's right. People are not like they are here in Europe, but it's comin' and it's going to be five years more before they get as big. As soon as we get the races on TV live and not with a two-week delay or a three-week delay – and we keep having the Americans do good – it's going to go well; but right now I think American riders will fade away and European riders will start dominating. When I look at what I've done and what Schwantz has done, I don't see any Americans coming up.'

As if to emphasize that, The Lawson Era had reached (in reality) its end, though he'd compete in 1991 and make an effort to become unique, winning the Championship on a third make of bike, the Cagiva. An unusually complex man, this Lawson. Dean Miller, a sports medicine specialist, has said that 'working with Eddie is like reading a series of novels. His character changes all the time. It is as if he has some secret that he doesn't want to share. He can go away, analyse a problem and almost re-create his mind.' Maybe Freddie Spencer was straightforward; and his era was at an end, too.

Another forethought. On the afternoon of 16 August 1992 the driver of a Canon Williams Renault car – Riccardo Patrese – rounded a right-loop at the end of a straight. The car brushed a minor dust storm at the rim of the track and spun off in a flurry. Nigel Mansell became Formula 1 World Champion there and then, barring accidents. We are at the Hungarian Grand Prix at the Hungaroring. The dust lay on the rim of the track because the kerbing had been removed at the insistence of the bike riders for their race on 12 July. Kerbs throw bikes. Kerbs contain cars: no kerbs and you're into the dust.

This had cast the Hungarian bike race into doubt in 1990, the race after Rainey did it. Rainey contested the Hungarian Grand Prix of 1990, of course, but dropped out two laps from the end. If he'd needed to finish . . .

1991

It's funny, because . . .

Grand Prix de Vitesse, Le Mans

IT'S FUNNY BECAUSE the race shouldn't have been here, nor even on the European continent, funny because what kind of name is that, anyway – Grand Prix of Speed? There's a third reason, but all in good time.

Eight men – Duke, Surtees, Hailwood, Agostini, Read, Sheene, Roberts and Lawson – won the 500cc Championship two years running; Duke, Surtees, Hailwood, Agostini and Roberts added a third (genuine hat-tricks, three consecutively). Could Rainey at least get the two? No laughing matter.

The battle lines:

Marlboro Team Roberts Yamaha: Rainey, American John Kocinski
Lucky Strike Suzuki: Schwantz
Rothmans Honda: Gardner, Doohan
Cagiva: Lawson

Schwantz held off Doohan in Japan, Rainey and Kocinski heavily involved but third and fourth. Rainey struck back at Eastern Creek in Australia, holding off Doohan by 2.54 seconds, with Schwantz fifth. Next, America. *Moto Grand Prix* reported that . . .

Racing in the 'land of the free' should be something the GP paddock looks forward to but Laguna Seca has become the jinx event of the World Championship circuit. In a freak post-race incident at the '89 race Bubba Shobert ended his career there, and Kevin Magee and Wayne Gardner were both badly hurt. A year later Magee suffered serious head injuries which put him in a coma for 10 days. What, everyone wondered, could go wrong this time?

The worst happened to John Kocinski. Going like a bat out of hell in pursuit of Wayne Rainey in the 500cc race, he looped his YZR and bashed his head but the pushy 250 champ didn't end up in intensive care. Instead he ended up behind bars. Chased and caught by local Feds after a minor traffic misdemeanour, Kocinski's mouth finally got him into real trouble. He was sentenced to five days in jail.

Before the race Gardner said 'the most important thing for me is to get

227

through it in one piece. I don't like the circuit and I have bad memories of the place.' Rainey won by a distance from Doohan and said 'I went out and ran my own race. Everybody knows the way I like to do it now. It's no secret.'

Doohan blitzed Spain. 'I got a good start for a change and I was fortunate enough to get by John Kocinski before the first corner. I noticed that Wayne Rainey's tyres were going off, and the main thing I had in mind was to conserve my front tyre. I can live with rear tyre problems but when the front end starts to slide it becomes impossible to go hard into corners. I was particularly careful for the first 10 laps or so with a full tank of fuel. Once I got the lead I did not put on any pressure but I seemed to pull away from the Yamahas all the same. It's nice to be leading the Championship but that doesn't mean much at this stage.'

Doohan 71 points, Rainey 70, Schwantz 46, Kocinski 45, Gardner 42, Lawson 41.

In the Italian Grand Prix at Misano, Lawson led the first lap on the Cagiva, provoking hysteria, but Doohan won from Kocinski, with Lawson third, while Rainey – hobbled by the rear tyre which 'chunked', and a pitstop which cost him a lap – came in ninth. In the German Grand Prix at Hockenheim, Schwantz threw the Championship into turmoil by beating Rainey. 'I decided at the beginning of the season that I wasn't going to ride the bike 120 per cent and get slagged off every time I fell,' he said. Now, presumably, he contented himself with 110 per cent.

He and Rainey took and re-took each other, Schwantz attacking at the approach to the 'complex' on the final lap – and, approaching it, Schwantz received a dire warning of the risk. He saw a '200 metre skid mark' left by some other rider. 'I had the front stopping well but the rear locked solid. I looked at Wayne and thought *it's just you and me, buddy.'* It was Schwantz by 00.01 of a second.

Doohan said 'it was a hell of a race until things started to go wrong for me. I am certain the Honda had the speed advantage but the pace was just too hot and in the end the rear tyre went off.' He still led the Championship with 106 points, Rainey 94, Schwantz 75, Lawson 69, Kocinski 62.

And Doohan took Austria at the Salzburgring from Rainey. 'I'd been trying to get away,' Doohan said. 'but when I had a slide with three laps to go he got back at me and caught up about half a second. I was lucky because I ran with him a bit in the morning warm-up and he came past me on the inside going up the hill. That made me think about things and I changed my line going up there in the race. I ran in the middle of the track so he wouldn't have an easy way past me either side.' Doohan 126, Rainey 111, Schwantz 90.

Rainey took Jarama from Doohan but made a genuine error at Assen. Leading into the final chicane he over-cooked it and went onto the grass. 'A rookie's mistake. Really, really, really stupid.' It let Schwantz through. Doohan crashed – 'the front end folded under and away I went, nothing I could do about it. It seemed to slide for ages and luckily the end of the slide wasn't too hard. As I walked back I realized I had lost the lead in the Championship.' Rainey 148, Doohan 143, Schwantz 123.

Then France. *Moto Grand Prix* reported that . . .

With five races to go the balance of power was now Rainey's. His Marlboro Team Roberts YZR was undoubtedly the best motorcycle on the race track, his Dunlops the best tyres and he never gave Doohan a chance to worry him. Doohan led from the start on the shortened, castrated Le Castellet track (see postscript) ahead of Kevin Schwantz and Rainey, but it wasn't long before Doohan was in trouble, taking ultra-wide lines as he scrabbled for front tyre grip. Rainey bided his time before moving ahead at one third distance.

Doohan conceded that 'Rainey had the best tyres. I tried as hard as I could, and on certain parts of the circuit I could match his speed or even go quicker, but when the bike started to slide I faced an impossible task. I settled for second. Rainey rode really well and I was not prepared to do anything silly in a bid to beat him.'

At Donington, Schwantz stirred the fires again, beating Rainey and, incidentally, taking Rainey on the *outside* at the hairpin, a move which evidently 'blew the champ's mind.' Doohan came third.

Doohan said 'I was out there trying to stay upright and keep things together. The front wheel folded under when I pushed hard out of corners or put in some aggressive riding. The bike slid around so much at times that it was like racing in the wet. I nearly crashed more times than in the other 10 rounds.' Rainey 185, Doohan 175, Schwantz 156.

Rainey closed his grip at Mugello, Schwantz coming second, and a combustible Doohan third. 'My chances were ruined by backmarkers. These sort of riders should not have an international licence. But there are three more rounds to go and as far as I am concerned the Championship is not over. If I thought it was I'd pack my bags and go home.'

In Czechoslovakia Rainey showed his tactical awareness. 'When Doohan came by I had no problems staying with him. I kept showing him my front wheel which made him push. As soon as I saw him sliding around I knew it was time to go.' The tyres had claimed Doohan again, and he confirmed it. 'There are no excuses, just the fact that I had tyre problems. The front end started to go when I was leading and Rainey said afterwards that I left a big black line right round a fast corner. It is the story of the last few Grands Prix once again, with the Yamaha and Dunlops working well. I'm not giving up although I must admit I do need a little luck now. If he stays on board and has no trouble it's going to be tough.'

On the podium Rainey said 'there is no talk about the World Championship from this particular rider. Everything is working well at the moment but we will just treat the race at Le Mans like any other.' Rainey 225, Doohan 207, Schwantz 184 and over and out for him. Rainey needed only third place at Le Mans.

The race ought to have been at Interlagos, Brazil, but Schwantz visited it earlier in the season to inspect safety improvements and (surprise, surprise) found they hadn't been done. Hence the Grand Prix de Vitesse, a hand-me-down name of convenience and, frankly, a silly one.

The ratchet: 13 best scores from the 15 rounds to count. That gave Rainey a working total of 203, Doohan 192, and it favoured Rainey more than the obvious. Only Malaysia remained after Le Mans and if Rainey didn't score there all he'd have to drop from his seson's harvest would be seven points from the Italian Grand Prix: the zero and seven his worst results. Doohan hadn't scored at Assen, a handy zero *but* if he won Le Mans he'd have only 227 points and *if* he went on to win Malaysia he'd have to discard one of three third places. His maximum 232. *If* Rainey finished third at Le Mans he'd have 233 . . .

'Well, it's funny because Le Mans is a race track that I didn't particularly like,' Rainey says. 'I only had to finish that third and my team-mate John Kocinski was going well. He said "look, I really want to help you" and I said *no, no, no-no-no. The best way you can help is by forgetting me and winning this race* but it happened that he couldn't hang on there out in front. Schwantz and Doohan ended up getting first and second and I ended up getting third.

'It was a race where I really didn't have to think about the Championship because I was racing with all those guys. Sometimes it can be easier if you know you have to win, but you've also got to think you don't have to win it. You don't want to take the risk. If you're tempted to stuff a guy, get him on the last corner of the last lap you don't. It might cost you the World Championship. You'll have that even if you finish second. The smart guy will say *hey, OK, you* – whoever the other rider might be – *are you going to win this race and I am going to win this Championship*. Nobody remembers who won the race but everybody remembers who won the World Championship. And that's what I set out to do, that was my ultimate goal.'

Doohan said 'I kept battling to the end. The result was not so bad, really, after a very tough race with Schwantz. Although his corner speed and possible acceleration were not as good as mine, there is no getting away from the fact that the brakes on his Suzuki are much better, and they helped him to win the day. I knew that if I passed him by the pits on the last lap he would have got back in front almost immediately so I hung back and planned to have a go at the back of the course.' *Moto Grand Prix* reported that . . .

The last 10 laps were unforgettable as Doohan went head-to-head with Schwantz knowing he had to win to have any chance of keeping his title hopes alive. Schwantz finally got ahead but came close to falling on the final lap when he locked the front tyre entering a hairpin. Then he nearly ran out of fuel. Doohan was still right with him as they crossed the line, Rainey, Kocinski and late-charger Gardner a few seconds adrift.

Schwantz   47m 37.76s

Doohan	at	00.15s
Rainey	at	03.46s
Kocinski	at	03.70s
Gardner	at	03.96s

Postscripts

If Rainey had wished to joust with Schwantz and Doohan, front brake problems would have inhibited him. 'The fluid must've boiled,' he said impishly. 'I was thinking about adjusting the brake but I didn't know which way the adjuster went!'

Spare a thought for Kocinski, helping the best way he could, keeping Rainey just there, just in front of him, just in third.

Testing at Shah Alam for the Malaysian Grand Prix, the final round and now irrelevant to the Championship. of course, Rainey 'high-sided' and sustained a broken femur, a broken bone in his left hand and three broken ribs. *If* . . .

The Paul Ricard circuit had been truncated for safety reasons and the length of the immense Mistral straight curtailed.

1992

Climbing Doohan's monument

South African Grand Prix, Kyalami

A LITTLE MOMENT, it seemed, nothing more. The final qualifying session for the German Grand Prix at Hockenheim and two bikes – the Rothmans Honda of Michael Doohan, the Marlboro Team Roberts Yamaha of Wayne Rainey – threaded through the chicane and burst towards the stadium 'complex'. As they reached the complex Doohan sat clearly ahead.

Rainey banked the Yamaha hard right, brought it vertical, rose in a jerk as he braked for the spoon of a left, banking hard over for that. He came round the spoon in the most ordinary, unremarkable way holding the bike on the inside rim of the track. A handful of people, scattered across the infield, watched without particular interest. Just riders, another lap. The concrete bowls of grandstands were virtually empty.

Doohan selected a wider line and, emerging from the spoon, Rainey had come closer to him. At that instant the Yamaha dipped and Rainey's knee brushed the surface of the track. The bike no longer turned out of the spoon but at a diagonal within it. Rainey, it seemed, caught this slide, and for an eyeblink the Yamaha pointed more or less straight ahead. An eyeblink later the front wheel reared, Rainey in mid-air.

Like a gymnast on a 'horse' he did a handstand on the top of the Yamaha and fell back onto the tank, striking it with his head. He landed on the track on his back and rolled, spinning, to the grass. He crawled – a bike passing in the background – then tottered, brushed a marshal away and walked now, walked stiffly. He'd damaged his wrist and ankle.

Irony and pathos, irony and pathos. At this point Rainey still felt the direct effects of Shah Alam 1991 and would say then 'it's always going to play a part in my lifestyle. I'm still restricted doing things that I used to take for granted, that's the way it's always going to be and I've learnt to accept it.'

He urged himself to half distance in the Grand Prix and retired. In the pit he found difficulty in dismounting. From the first corner, he'd say, he thought 'this probably isn't the place where I should be racing. I went from third place to eighth in three laps and I couldn't do what the bike demanded so I just pulled in.' It didn't matter. Doohan, who won from Schwantz, was building a monument. He'd already won Japan, Australia, Malaysia, Spain. Leaving Hockenheim Doohan had 130 points, Schwantz 77, Rainey 65. The ratchet that all rounds counted didn't matter a cuss, nor that the scoring had been revised in a major way to 20, 15, 12, 10, 8, 6, 4, 3, 2, 1. Doohan could scarcely be caught with only six rounds to run.

Between Hockenheim and the Dutch TT at Assen, Rainey found medical treatment didn't help, and even riding a bicycle hurt so much he had to take his hand off the handlebars. He hoped the suspension of a 500cc machine might not be as violent . . .

Friday practice at Assen told him what he suspected, his body nowhere near well enough to cope and he decided to fly home to California, nothing to lose because he'd lost it already. Better to rest, recuperate, forget about a third Championship.

Assen to Amsterdam is no great distance so Rainey flew from there, unaware of the second qualifying, and settled into a long flight which stretched deep into Saturday and the race. When Rainey arrived home and checked his fax machine he might have received an electric shock.

In second qualifying and on only his third lap, Doohan went down hard enough to break his right leg in two places, 'my foot trapped under the bike as it slid along the track and I am sure that is why I broke the leg.' Rainey, ruminating on the consequences of Doohan's crash, underscores how precarious bike racing really is. 'One mistake was all it took.'

The season developed and dissolved into complete uncertainty and the Dutch Grand Prix compounded that. Schwantz and Lawson duelled, Schwantz lost control of his Lucky Strike Suzuki and fell in Lawson's path, breaking his left arm and dislocating a hip. The Championship lay in hospital wards and treatment centres, and was held in the hands of physiotherapists but, 'with these guys out,' Rainey thought – maybe, just maybe – he could catch up. 'A heck of a way to do it, but . . .'

Rainey returned for the Hungarian Grand Prix, wet-dry and a race for hard men. Lawson won, Schwantz (astonishingly) fourth, Rainey (astonishingly) fifth. Rainey experienced 'a strange feeling' seeing others on the podium, 'didn't feel like the season had turned around yet.' The absence of the ratchet – all rounds counting, remember – could save him.

He won France, but Gardner pushed him back to second at Donington, the meeting where Gardner announced his retirement and gave his emotions full rein when he won. Wonderful to do it here, he'd say, in my adopted country in front of all the people who mean so much to me; and meant it. Doohan 130 points, Rainey 108, Schwantz 87.

Rainey said 'we will just keep the pressure on Doohan as much as we can although I was disappointed not to win. I wasn't too happy about the end of the race because I thought there was still one lap to go when they hung out the chequered flag and I also got caught among the backmarkers which really messed things up.' Worse, Rainey had to be taken to the medical centre for an X-ray on his knee after an exuberant spectator knocked him over. Schwantz, running second, hit oil and crashed, isolating Rainey as the only rider who could still climb Doohan's monument. 'It'll be interesting in Brazil,' Rainey said, 'because nobody has raced at the circuit (Sao Paulo) before and we certainly haven't given up our chances.'

Doohan 130, Rainey 108 and two rounds to run – Brazil and South Africa. A mere eight weeks after his crash Doohan returned and, while Rainey won, finished twelfth (astonishingly). 'I gave it my best shot and as you can imagine the whole team is bitterly disappointed that we didn't score any points. However, by tomorrow we will be putting the disappointments behind us and working flat out at Dr Costa's clinic in Italy to build the strength of my right leg for the final race in two weeks. At least I proved today I can ride a 28 lap race and I am sure the two weeks will enable me to gain a great deal more fitness and strength.' Doohan 130, Rainey 128.

The emotion of Gardner hadn't diluted over all these years. 'Most of my family and friends are coming to South Africa to watch my last race and I expect I will shed a few tears when I cross the line for the very last time.'

Rainey says 'I could see the Championship. I didn't worry about qualifying. I just wanted to get out there and race.' He did. He led from the start but at a left-hander 'Kocinski came by (deep to the inside) and I just followed him. There were no team orders. It depended really on what Doohan did' – and Doohan pushed and grappled, but down the field. 'Then Gardner started catching me at a tenth of a second a lap, it seemed like for 20 laps.' Gardner, pugnacious to the end, would make the final gesture of his career: to help Doohan.

'I finally caught Rainey, who was riding really well, just like a Champion, and I managed to get by,' Gardner said. A backmarker loomed as they reached for that left-hand corner, Gardner close to Rainey. The backmarker drifted wide, Rainey went with him and the mouth of the corner opened for Gardner who cranked the Honda hard over, knee caressing the surface of the circuit – the angle of man and machine seeming to disprove the theory of gravity. Rainey tucked in behind.

'Obviously,' Gardner says, 'he wasn't going to risk anything that would spoil his Championship chances because he knew where Doohan was. I kept up as much pressure as I could in the hope he might just make a mistake, letting Michael in for the Championship.'

Yes, of course Rainey 'knew where Doohan was at, I knew he was in sixth place and I knew I had to be third to win the Championship. That's where I finished.' In the pits they hauled the door down and Rainey, astride the bike, murmured *oh man,* lowered his head, shook it slowly from side to side. *Did we win?*

'Three times,' someone said. Yes, 1990, 1991, 1992.

He clenched his eyes shut, no doubt to stem tears.

He was there now, there with Duke and Surtees and Roberts on genuine hat-tricks. Only Hailwood with four consecutively, and Ago with the impossible seven-in-a-row, bettered it.

Doohan masked *his* emotions as best he could. 'Congratulations to Wayne Rainey winning the championship but as you can imagine I'm feeling pretty fed-up at the moment. The basic difference was that I could not use the rear brake. Other riders may tell you it's not important, but there are plenty of black marks on the track and you see plenty of riders with the rear wheel in the air. Obviously the race did not go as planned and I settled into some consistent times but in the end it was very lonely: going as hard as I could, nobody passed me and I didn't pass anyone. At least I'm pleased I didn't go any slower as the race progressed.

'Dr Costa and his team did all they could to get me ready, a year's work in nine weeks, but I've spent so much time working on my leg that I have neglected my fitness programme. Now I intend to ride bikes and go testing as much as possible and get myself in peak condition for the start of next season. As far as I'm concerned, today was only another motor cycle race. I've got a few years left . . .'

Some half a season later I invited Rainey to review it. 'After Le Mans in 1991, we went to that race in Malaysia and I think I was a little bit relaxed for some reason. I made a mistake, I wasn't focused nearly as much as I had been and I forgot I was still doing 180 miles an hour. *It hit me and I paid for it.* It's the last time I've thought that way.

'Doohan didn't have to put himself in that position at Assen, not in qualifying. I fell off at the Nürburgring in I think '90 and hurt my finger and it's these situations that you put yourself in mentally. You have to ride like this because this is how you've always done it, and then it bites and you think *why did I have to do that?*

'Doohan was in a position where he had the best bike because he was winning the races. I was injured, Schwantz would be injured and Doohan had a second on the field. Maybe his guard came down a little bit because he had such an advantage and it bit him just like it bit me in Malaysia.

'After the South Africa race, I didn't know what to say to him but I had to go up and say, you know, *hey Mick, I'm glad you're OK, you've done a hell of a job to get back to where you have and obviously you've proved you want to be World Champion very bad. I worked my ass off to get it but I congratulate you on the season. You had it but we ended up with the most points.*

'It was a tense race. I had Gardner catching me, Kocinski pulling away. They put out the board when I crossed the line to say I was Champion but I didn't know until I turned around and actually saw Chandler and Schwantz come by before Doohan.'

1993

Schwantz – bitter sweet

American Grand Prix, Laguna Seca

DONINGTON IN AUGUST, lap 1, the crocodile of bikes threading into a left. Maybe Alex Barros, a Brazilian on a Suzuki, braked late, maybe not. 'There was just nowhere to go and we all went down,' Doohan said. 'I am bitterly disappointed.' Barros fell, Doohan fell, Schwantz fell, a mad mêlée. Luca Cadalora on a Roberts Yamaha felt 'lucky to get through' and made it with no more than a cracked windscreen.

Cadalora set off after and caught Rainey, his team-mate, and everyone understood that this was to put a bit of a show on, offer some racing to a vast crowd who'd paid hard money to be here, although clearly Cadalora would defer to Rainey before the end. If Rainey won the British Grand Prix he overtook Schwantz in the Championship, and Cadalora had to be mindful of that, not to mention his future within the team.

A couple of laps to go and Cadalora moved into the lead, *a very good show, lovely to see, your money's worth*. We waited for Cadalora to slow, dice, return the lead to Rainey. He didn't. The Italian won his first Grand Prix, beating Rainey by three seconds.

Kenny Roberts muttered that he'd need some time in the solitude of the motor home before he'd comment. During a Press Conference conducted with a deep undercurrent of understatement, Cadalora seemed not to understand what the fuss was about, and Rainey adopted a diplomatic pose. 'Luca was able to get out of several of the corners quicker than me.' On team-orders, or the absence of them, Rainey made a joke or two.

Schwantz said 'it's down to a four-round Championship and I still feel I can make it.'

The battle lines:

Marlboro Team Roberts: Rainey, Cadalora
Rothmans Honda: Doohan, fellow Australian Daryl Beattie
Lucky Strike Suzuki: Schwantz, Barros
Cagiva: Kocinski

Schwantz 192 points, Rainey 189, Beattie 126, Doohan 120 under a new scoring system embracing the first 15 finishers in the races: 25, 20, 16, 13, 11, 10, 9, 8, 7, 6, 5, 4, 3, 2, 1. The ratchet: all 15 rounds to count. Thus far Schwantz had taken Australia, Spain, Austria and Holland, Rainey had taken Malaysia and Japan. An intriguing balance. Had Donington disturbed it?

Rainey now took the Czech Grand Prix at Brno – Schwantz fifth. Rainey 214, Schwantz 203. In the Italian Grand Prix at Misano, Cadalora led. Rainey took that from him, but on lap 10 Rainey crashed with extreme ferocity. Cadalora said that 'Wayne braked very late, then ran wide and hit a bump. His rear suspension bottomed out and he lost the back end, followed by the front.'

Nightmarish pictures showed Rainey being lifted onto a stretcher, his head cast back; showed the urgent hands of medical staff arranging him in the ambulance while Cadalora battled Schwantz for the lead. He had to do that, had to prevent Schwantz having the full 25 points. In fact Doohan came past Schwantz, who finished third. Schwantz 219, Rainey 214.

First Team Bulletin: 'Rainey was taken by helicopter to a local hospital where he underwent tests, and on Sunday night doctors reported the Californian had damaged his sixth lumbar vertebrae. Rainey's life is not in danger but, according to latest reports from the hospital in Cesena, his spinal column was broken in the fall, causing paralysis from the middle of his chest down. Rainey's mentor and Team Roberts team owner Kenny Roberts is with him, and his wife Shae flew from their home in Monterey, California to join him today (Monday).'

Second Bulletin: 'Wayne Rainey is in a stable condition and was released from intensive care on Tuesday afternoon. He remains in hospital near Cesena. He is expected to stay in Italy until the weekend, when he will be flown to a hospital near his home in California.'

Third Bulletin: 'Wayne Rainey arrived in the United States on Friday and is now at Centinella Hospital, Inglewood, Los Angeles. Rainey is about to begin the lengthy rehabilitation process and wide consultations have been made with physicians throughout the USA and Europe as to the best methods. The Centinella Hospital is well-known for its work with many famous sportsmen, including members of the LA Lakers basketball team, the LA Kings hockey team, the Los Angeles Dodgers baseball team and the Los Angeles Rams football team. Two attending physicians have now been assigned to the Californian – Drs Watkins and Williams, both experienced in working with top athletes.

'"A lot of our purpose in bringing Wayne to Los Angeles was that he and Shae have a lot of family and friends in the vicinity," said Dean Miller, Rainey's long-time trainer. "And being in an atmosphere where other athletes are rehabilitating was something he wanted to do. Other consultations were made last week with Peter Richards, a neurosurgeon, and IRTA medical officer, Dr Giancarlo Caroli from Bologna, Professor Sailliant who worked with Clay Regazzoni, and Bernie Ecclestone put us onto Professor Sid Watkins, the Formula 1 doctor. They've all spoken to one another, and through their experience and understanding of the case they are all in agreement on the stability procedure that needs to be performed.

"'Drs Watkins and Williams are expected to perform the spinal stabilization procedure this week, which will allow Rainey to sit up comfortably. On Monday afternoon, myself and team orthopaedic surgeon Arthur Ting will explain the pre-rehabilitive surgical procedures and post-rehabilitation procedures to Wayne, Shae and the family. It could be a lengthy process but knowing Wayne and his drive we'd hope him to cut the programme shorter than expected."

'Roberts visited Rainey in hospital last night (Saturday). "Mentally he's very, very strong, much stronger than we are, and he's got a very strong wife," said Roberts. "But we all know there will be highs and lows. We want Wayne to get on with his life, we love him and we're just glad he's here. It could have been worse, that's what we have reflected upon. And it could have happened on a scooter on the way to the shops. Wayne knows he went out leading a race, hard on the gas. Guys like Wayne are one in a million. He's got a lot to look forward to. He's very positive, he wants to stay in the sport, build riders and run a team."'

That was Saturday, 11 September. Irony and pathos, irony and pathos. At Laguna Seca, on the Monterey peninsular some two hours drive south of San Francisco, Doohan had pole from Kocinski, Barros and Schwantz. And Schwantz had the Championship. That may seem impossibly pedantic, but up to here *in theory* he didn't because *in theory* Rainey might compete. However academic this appeared – absurdly academic – it had to be enacted so.

On Sunday 12 September Doohan led, crashed and broke a shoulder bone. Kocinski won, and Schwantz was fourth. 'I knew I had to stay consistent,' Kocinski said, 'because that's the way Wayne did it. I felt him there with me.'

Schwantz said 'it's great to be champion but I wish it didn't have to be this way. I know Wayne would have fought it out right to the end – that's the kind of guy he is – but I still feel I deserve to be champion. I've earned it.' Schwantz revealed that he'd suffered injuries in that crash at Donington and not said a word. 'My right hand has started playing up again here. A bone is fractured and seems to have worked itself into an awkward position. I can run for three laps then it seems to cut off the circulation. I expect to have surgery when the season has finished.'

Fourth Bulletin: 'Wayne Rainey has undergone spinal surgery at Centinella Hospital in Los Angeles. The surgery performed by Dr Robert G Watkins of the Kerlan-Jobe Clinic was a reduction and fusion of his fractured, dislocated thoracic spine. The reduction was carried out using the TSRH internal fixation system in which metal rods are used to obtain a reduction of the dislocation and to maintain the position of the reduction until the fusion heals. The spinal canal has been realigned and held in place.

'Wayne's condition is extremely serious but stable. The triple World 500cc Champion has been completely paralysed from the chest down since the accident, and because of the complex nature of the paralysis he is not expected to recover movement. The plan is to work for his recovery from surgery and return him to as high a functional level as possible. Wayne is in good spirits and has shown tremendous strength and courage throughout this difficult ordeal.'

A postscript to the postscripts in this book

All motor sport used to be nakedly dangerous, and the Clay Regazzoni mentioned above chugs round in a wheelchair after a Formula 1 crash more than a decade ago, but the darkened days of unprotected circuits – Clady, Dundrod, the Ring, Spa, the Sachsenring and the rest – seemed far away, dangerous only in memory. A rider or driver might expect a broken bone or two, a sequence of real frights, concussion and a bit of battering one way and another, but not worse. He might gaze forward with great confidence to a career spanning a decade and then ripe middle-age, with time to reminisce, to savour.

The moment Rainey went down at Misano, memory shuddered. It's still there, this transition from absolute control to no control. It always had been there, bearing its consequences. It is true: the consequences had been minimized but not eliminated and never would be.

The spectre of this physically unites every man who ever hoisted himself onto a racing bike, twisted power from it, put his head down and angled into the first corner of the race, because all had confronted it, just as they had on 21 August 1949 when Les Graham twisted power from his AJS, put his head down and angled into the first corner of the Clady circuit, Belfast.

Statistics

The Showdown races
(Names in italics are the Championship winners)

1949 Ulster Grand Prix, Belfast-Clady, 15 laps, 247.5 miles (398.30 km)
1 *L. Graham* (AJS) 2h 34m 04.50s (96.49 mph/155.28 kph)
2 A. J. Bell (Norton) 2h 35m 44.40s
3 N. Pagani (Gilera) 2h 35m 54.00s
4 W. Doran (AJS) 2h 36m 00.00s
5 J. M. West (AJS) 2h 40m 21.00s

1950 Nations Grand Prix, Monza, 31 laps, 120.9 miles (194.56 km)
1 G. Duke (Norton) 1h 11m 06.30s (102.34 mph/164.69 kph)
2 *U. Masetti* (Gilera) 1h 11m 57.00s
3 A. Artesiani (MV) 1h 12m 43.00s
4 A. Milani (Gilera) 1h 12m 43.20s
5 C. Bandirola (Gilera) 1h 13m 06.10s
6 R. H. Dale 1h 13m 06.48s

1951 Ulster Grand Prix, Belfast-Clady, 15 laps, 247.5 miles (398.30 km)
1 *G. Duke* (Norton) 2h 36m 06.30s (95.18 mph/153.17 kph)
2 K. Kavanagh (Norton) 2h 38m 56.00s
3 U. Masetti (Gilera) 2h 39m 31.20s
4 A. Milani (Gilera) 2h 42m 45.00s
5 J. Lockett (Norton) 2h 46m 30.00s
6 W. Doran (AJS) one lap

1952 Spanish Grand Prix, Barcelona-Montjuich, 48 laps, 124.8 miles (200.84 km)
1 L. Graham (MV) 2h 06m 18.30s (59.54 mph/95.81 kph)
2 *U. Masetti* 2h 06m 45.20s
3 K. Kavanagh (Norton) 2h 06m 48.50s
4 N. Pagani (Gilera) 2h 07m 19.20s
5 H. R. Armstrong (Norton) 2h 07m 40.00s

6 S. Lawton (Norton) 2h 07m 41.30s

1953 Nations Grand Prix, Monza, 32 laps, 125.2 miles (201.48 km)
1 *G. Duke* (Gilera) 1h 10m 18.30s (106.84 mph/171.93 kph)
2 R. H. Dale (Gilera) 1h 10m 59.40s
3 L. Liberati (Gilera) 1h 11m 10.10s
4 H. R. Armstrong (Gilera) 1h 11m 19.00s
5 C. C. Sandford (MV) 1h 12m 00.40s
6 H. P. Muller (MV) one lap

1954 Swiss Grand Prix, Berne, 28 laps, 126.58 miles (203.70 km)
1 *G. Duke* (Gilera) 1h 21m 04.60s (93.68 mph/150.75 kph)
2 R. Amm (Norton) 1h 21m 08.30s
3 H. R. Armstrong (Gilera) 1h 22m 03.10s
4 J. Brett (Norton) 1h 22m 22.90s
5 R. W. Coleman (AJS) 1h 23m 52.90s
6 D. Farrant (AJS) one lap

1955 Ulster Grand Prix, Belfast-Dundrod, 25 laps, 185 miles (297.72 km)
1 W. A. Lomas (Guzzi) 2h 00m 31.00s (92.30 mph/148.53 kph)
2 J. Hartle (Norton) 2h 00m 37.00s
3 R. Dale (Guzzi) 2h 03m 44.00s
4 B. McIntyre (Norton) 2h 04m 52.00s
5 G. A. Murphy (Matchless) one lap
6 J. Clark (Matchless) one lap
   Geoff Duke did not take part

1956 Ulster Grand Prix, Belfast-Dundrod, 27 laps, 205 miles (329.90 km)
1 J. Hartle (Norton) 2h 20m 14.60s (85.66 mph/137.85 kph)
2 R. N. Brown (Matchless) 2h 23m 02.00s
3 G. A. Murphy (Matchless) 2h 23m 03.00s
4 G. B. Tanner (Norton) 2h 23m 44.20s
5 R. W. Herron (Norton) one lap
6 J. Brett (Norton) one lap
   J. Surtees did not take part

1957 Nations Grand Prix, Monza, 35 laps, 125.05 miles (201.24 km)
1 *L. Liberati* (Gilera) 1h 04m 49.30s (115.75 mph/186.27 kph)
2 G. Duke (Gilera) 1h 05m 13.30s
3 A. Milani (Gilera) 1h 95m 13.70s
4 J. Surtees (MV) 1h 05m 22.50s
5 U. Masetti (MV) one lap
6 T Shepherd (MV) one lap

1958 West German Grand Prix, Nürburgring, 9 laps, 127.56 miles (205.28 km)

1 *J. Surtees* (MV) 1h 50m 51.60s (69.96 mph/112.58 kph)
2 J. Hartle (MV) 1h 51m 35.90s
3 G. Hocking (Norton) 1h 52m 23.10s
4 E. Hiller (BMW) 1h 57m 01.30s
5 D. Dale (BMW) 1h 58m 09.70s
6 R. Brown (Norton) 1h 58m 10.30s

1959 Dutch Grand Prix, Assen, 27 laps, 129.18 miles (207.88 km)

1 *J. Surtees* (MV) 1h 31m 20.20s (84.91 mph/136.64 kph)
2 R. Brown (Norton) 1h 33m 12.60s
3 R. Venturi (MV) 1h 34m 12.90s
4 D. Dale (BMW) 1h 34m 36.90s
5 J. Redman (Norton) one lap
6 R. Miles (Norton) one lap

1960 West German Grand Prix, Solitude, 18 laps, 127.6 miles (295.34 km)

1 *J. Surtees* (MV) 1h 22m 32.10s (92.83 mph/149.39 kph)
2 R. Venturi (MV) 1h 22m 50.80s
3 E. Mendogni (MV) 1h 24m 07.20s
4 D. Dale (Norton) 1h 25m 17.60s
5 J. Hempleman (Norton) 1h 25m 28.30s
6 R. Glaser (Norton) 1h 26m 02.00s

1961 Ulster Grand Prix, Ulster-Dundrod, 20 laps, 148.32 miles (238.69 km)

1 *G. Hocking* 1h 38m 20.40s (90.49 mph/145.63 kph)
2 M. Hailwood (Norton) 1h 40m 14.40s
3 A. King (Norton) 1h 40m 15.60s
4 R. Langston (Matchless) 1h 42m 50.00s
5 P. W. Chatterton (Norton) one lap
6 T. Thorp (Norton) one lap

1962 Nations Grand Prix, Monza, 35 laps, 125.05 miles (201.24 km)

1 *M. Hailwood* (MV) 1h 04m 22.70s (116.54 mph/187.54 kph)
2 R. Venturi (MV) 1h 04m 23.20s
3 S. Grassetti (Bianchi) one lap
4 P. Read (Norton) one lap
5 P. Driver (Norton) one lap
6 B. Schneider (Norton) one lap

1963 Finnish Grand Prix, Tampere, 35 laps, 78.49 miles (126.31 km)

1 *M. Hailwood* (MV) 59m 49.60s (78.78 mph/126.78 kph)
2 A. Shepherd (Matchless) one lap

3 M. Duff (Matchless) one lap
4 F. Stevens (Norton) two laps
5 S. Mizen (Matchless) two laps
6 N. Sevostyanov (CKB) two laps

1964 West German Grand Prix, Solitude, 18 laps, 127.6 miles (205.34 km)
1 *M. Hailwood* (MV) 1h 18m 25.20s (97.68 mph/157.19 kph)
2 J. Ahearn (Norton) 1h 21m 03.50s
3 P. Read (Matchless) 1h 21m 04.40s
4 G. Marsovsky (Matchless) 1h 22m 56.30s
5 M. Low (Norton) one lap
6 F. Stevens (Matchless) one lap

1965 East German Grand Prix, Sachsenring, 20 laps, 107.5 miles (172.99 km)
1 *M. Hailwood* (MV) 1h 08m 33.80s (93.64 mph/150.69 kph)
2 G. Agostini (MV) 1h 09m 32.00s
3 P. Driver (Matchless) one lap
4 J. Ahearn (Norton) one lap
5 F. Stevens (Matchless) one lap
6 I. Burne (Norton) one lap

1966 Nations Grand Prix, Monza, 35 laps, 125 miles (201.16 km)
1 *G. Agostini* (MV) 1h 03m 4.00s (118.97 mph/191.45 kph)
2 P. J. Williams (Matchless) two laps
3 J. Findlay (Matchless) two laps
4 F. Stevens (Paton) two laps
5 W. Scheimann (Norton) three laps
6 E. Lenz (Matchless) three laps

1967 Nations Grand Prix, Monza, 35 laps, 124.97 miles (201.11 km)
1 *G. Agostini* (MV) 1h 00m 17.20s (124.45 mph/200.27 kph)
2 M. Hailwood (Honda) 1h 00m 30.40s
3 A. Bergamonti (Paton) one lap
4 F. Stevens (Paton) one lap
5 G. Mandolini (Moto Guzzi) one lap
6 J. Hartle (Matchless) one lap

1968 East German Grand Prix, Sachsenring, 20 laps, 107 miles (172.19 km)
1 *G. Agostini* (MV) 1h 00m 39.40s (105.86 mph/170.35 kph)
2 A. Pagani (Linto) one lap
3 J. Findlay (Matchless) one lap
4 J. Cooper (Norton) one lap
5 B. Nelson (Paton) one lap

6 G. Nash (Norton) one lap

1969 East German Grand Prix, Sachsenring, 20 laps, 107 miles (172.19 km)

1 *G. Agostini* (MV) 1h 08m 09.70s (94.23 mph/151.64 kph)
2 B. Nelson (Paton) one lap
3 S. Ellis (Linto) one lap
4 W. Bergold (Matchless) one lap
5 T. Dennehy (Honda) one lap
6 J. O'Brien (Matchless) two laps
7 M. Hawthorne (Matchless) two laps
8 P. Lehtela (Matchless) two laps
9 J. Linah (Seeley) two laps
10 P. Kiisa (Vostok) two laps

1970 East German Grand Prix, Sachsenring, 21 laps, 112.4 miles (180.88 km)

1 *G. Agostini* (MV) 1h 03m 45.10s (105.78 mph/170.23 kph)
2 J. Dodds (Linto) 1h 06m 55.50s
3 M. Carney (Kawasaki) one lap
4 A. Barnett (Seeley) one lap
5 C. Ravel (Kawasaki) one lap
6 B. Nelson (Paton) one lap
7 E. Offenstadt (Kawasaki) one lap
8 D. Simmonds (Kawasaki) one lap
9 G. Nash (Norton) one lap
10 T. Robb (Seeley) one lap

1971 East German Grand Prix, Sachsenring, 21 laps, 112.39 miles (180.86 km)

1 *G. Agostini* (MV) 1h 04m 47.80s (104.20 mph/167.68 kph)
2 K. Turner (Suzuki) 1h 07m 36.70s
3 E. Hiller (Kawasaki) one lap
4 H. Brungger (Bultaco) one lap
5 K. Koivuniemi (Seeley) one lap
6 K. Auer (Matchless) two laps
7 J. Campiche (Honda) two laps
8 R. Bron (Suzuki) three laps
9 P. Lehtela (Yamaha) eight laps
   (only nine finishers)

1972 Belgian Grand Prix, Spa, 13 laps, 113.84 miles (183.20 km)

1 *G. Agostini* (MV) 56m 04.70s (121.86 mph/196.10 kph)
2 A. Pagani (MV) 56m 37.60s
3 R. Gould (Yamaha) 57m 23.40s
4 H. Kanaya (Yamaha) 57m 23.70s

5   B. Granath (Husqvarna) 59m 33.40s
6   E. Offenstadt (Kawasaki) 59m 33.60s
7   J. Lancaster (Yamaha) 1h 00m 03.20s
8   B. Nelson (Yamaha) 1h 00m 08.10s
9   C. Bourgeois (Yamaha) one lap
10 L. John (Yamaha) one lap

1973 Swedish Grand Prix, Anderstorp, 26 laps, 64.58 miles (103.92 km)

1   *P. Read* (MV) 47m 00.00s (82.86 mph/133.34 kph)
2   G. Agostini (MV) 47m 00.50s
3   K. Newcombe (Konig) 47m 58.00s
4   B. W. Nielsen (Yamaha) 48m 11.40s
5   W. Giger (Yamaha) 48m 16.80s
6   C. Bourgeois (Yamaha) 48m 17.10s
7   B. Nelson (Yamaha) 48m 29.40s
8   S. Gunnarsson (Kawasaki) 48m 39.70s
9   K. Kangasniemi (Yamaha) one lap
10 B. Brolin (Suzuki) one lap

1974 Finnish Grand Prix, Imatra, 20 laps, 74.94 miles (120.60 km)

1   *P. Read* (MV) 46m 45.00s (96.17 mph/154.76 kph)
2   G. Bonera (MV) 46m 45.20s
3   T. Lansivuori (Yamaha) 46m 46.90s
4   J. Findlay (Suzuki) 48m 02.30s
5   P. Korhonen (Yamaha) 48m 29.50s
6   J. Williams (Yamaha) 48m 39.40s
7   C. Leon (Kawasaki) 48m 55.90s
8   W. Giger (Yamaha) 48m 57.10s
9   P. Coulon (Yamaha) 48m 57.30s
10 K. Auer (Yamaha) one lap

1975 Czech Grand Prix, Brno, 17 laps, 115.34 miles (185.64 km)

1   P. Read (MV) 1h 04m 23.90s (107.47 mph/172.95 kph)
2   *G. Agostini* (Yamaha) 1h 05m 24.30s
3   A. George (Yamaha) 1h 06m 16.00s
4   K. Auer (Yamaha) 1h 06m 50.00s
5   O. Chevallier (Yamaha) 1h 07m 00.90s
6   C. Mortimer (Yamaha) 1h 07m 42.50s
7   M. Ancone (Suzuki) 1h 07m 57.60s
8   H. Braumandl (Yamaha) one lap
9   B. W. Nielsen (Yamaha) one lap
10 A. Resko (Yamaha) two laps

1976 Swedish Grand Prix, Anderstorp, 28 laps, 69.91 miles (112.50 km)

1   *B. Sheene* (Suzuki) 48m 20.73s (86.75 mph/139.60 kph)

2   J. Findlay (Suzuki) 48m 54.91s
3   C. Mortimer (Suzuki) 48m 54.96s
4   T. Lansivuori (Suzuki) 48m 55.60s
5   S. Avant (Suzuki) 48m 56.67s
6   P. Coulon (Suzuki) 48m 58.08s
7   V. Palomo (Yamaha) 49m 07.47s
8   K. Auer (Yamaha) 49m 36.85s
9   T. Herron (Yamaha) 49m 36.85s
10 J. Newbold (Suzuki) 49m 48.42s

1977 Finnish Grand Prix, Imatra, 22 laps, 82.43 miles (132.66 km)

1   J. Cecotto (Yamaha) 46m 50.00s (105.60 mph/169.94 kph)
2   M. Lucchinelli (Suzuki) 47m 33.00s
3   G. Bonera (Suzuki) 47m 41.60s
4   M. Rougerie (Suzuki) 47m 54.70s
5   S. Parrish (Suzuki) 48m 07.20s
6   *B. Sheene* (Suzuki) 48m 08.70s
7   T. Lansivuori (Suzuki) 48m 46.50s
8   A. Toracca (Suzuki) one lap
9   J-P. Orban (Suzuki) one lap
10 K. Auer (Yamaha) one lap

1978 West German Grand Prix, Nürburgring, 6 laps, 85.13 miles (137.01 km)

1   V. Ferrari (Suzuki) 51m 21.70s (99.45 mph/160.04 kph)
2   J. Cecotto (Yamaha) 51m 22.40s
3   *K. Roberts* (Yamaha) 51m 55.60s
4   B. Sheene (Suzuki) 51m 57.70s
5   T. Katayama (Yamaha) 51m 58.00s
6   M. Rougerie (Suzuki) 52m 17.70s
7   S. Baker (Suzuki) 52m 19.20s
8   B. van Dulmen (Suzuki) 52m 29.80s
9   T. Lansivuori (Suzuki) 52m 31.70s
10 J. Steiner (Suzuki) 53m 32.10s

1979 French Grand Prix, Le Mans, 29 laps, 76.41 miles (122.96 km)

1   B. Sheene (Suzuki) 48m 06.80s (95.30 mph/153.36 kph)
2   R. Mamola (Suzuki) 48m 09.20s
3   *K. Roberts* (Yamaha) 48m 20.69s
4   F. Uncini (Suzuki) 48m 26.51s
5   J. Cecotto (Yamaha) 48m 26.82s
6   P. Coulon (Suzuki) 48m 27.46s
7   S. Parrish (Suzuki) 49m 03.12s
8   M. Rougerie (Suzuki) 49m 20.87s
9   J. Woodley (Suzuki) one lap
10 P. Sjostrom (Suzuki) one lap

1980 West German Grand Prix, Nürburgring, 6 laps, 85.13 miles (137.01 km)
1 M. Lucchinelli (Suzuki) 50m 38.33s (100.87 mph/162.33 kph)
2 G. Crosby (Suzuki) 50m 58.04s
3 W. Hartog (Suzuki) 51m 02.00s
4 *K. Roberts* (Yamaha) 51m 26.23s
5 R. Mamola (Suzuki) 51m 28.06s
6 J. Cecotto (Yamaha) 51m 30.03s
7 F. Uncini (Suzuki) 51m 52.07s
8 J. Middelburg (Yamaha) 52m 13.94s
9 C. Perugini (Suzuki) 52m 16.93s
10 G. Reiner (Suzuki) 52m 18.69s

1981 Swedish Grand Prix, Anderstorp, 30 laps, 75.15 miles (120.93 km)
1 B. Sheene (Yamaha) 55m 24.04s (87.43 mph/140.70 kph)
2 B. van Dulmen (Yamaha) 55m 24.86s
3 J. Middelburg (Suzuki) 56m 02.56s
4 K. Ballington (Kawasaki) 56m 14.52s
5 G. Crosby (Suzuki) 56m 15.32s
6 M. Fontan (Yamaha) 56m 20.14s
7 F. Uncini (Suzuki) 56m 20.46s
8 S. Rossi (Suzuki) 56m 21.06s
9 *M. Lucchinelli* (Suzuki) 56m 44.52s
10 B. Fau (Suzuki) 56m 49.96s

1982 Swedish Grand Prix, Anderstorp, 30 laps, 75.15 miles (120.93 km)
1 T. Katayama (Honda) 50m 29.05s (89.30 mph/143.71 kph)
2 R. Mamola (Suzuki) 50m 36.97s
3 G. Crosby (Yamaha) 50m 38.57s
4 M. Fontan (Yamaha) 50m 38.63s
5 M. Lucchinelli (Honda) 50m 58.72s
6 K. Ballington (Kawasaki) 51m 21.70s
7 B. van Dulmen (Yamaha) 51m 22.29s
8 P. Coulon (Suzuki) 51m 33.83s
9 S. Pellandini (Suzuki) 51m 45.00s
10 S. Parrish (Yamaha) 51m 56.83s
   F. Uncini (Suzuki) did not finish

1983 San Marino Grand Prix, Imola, 25 laps, 78.30 miles (126.00 km)
1 K. Roberts (Yamaha) 48m 16.63s (97.30 mph/156.58 kph)
2 *F. Spencer* (Honda) 48m 17.86s
3 E. Lawson (Yamaha) 48m 23.99s
4 M. Lucchinelli (Honda) 48m 36.02s
5 R. Mamola (Suzuki) 48m 42.71s

6 M. Fontan (Yamaha) 48m 43.24s
7 R. Roche (Honda) 48m 43.82s
8 B. van Dulmen (Suzuki) 49m 50.72s
9 R. Haslam (Honda) 49m 55.20s
10 A. Mang (Suzuki) 50m 05.43s

1984 Swedish Grand Prix, Anderstorp, 30 laps, 75.15 miles (120.93 km)

1 *E. Lawson* (Yamaha) 50m 01.03s (90.14 mph/145.06 kph)
2 R. Roche (Honda) 50m 04.17s
3 W. Gardner (Honda) 50m 20.51s
4 T. Katayama (Honda) 50m 37.39s
5 R. McElnea (Suzuki) 50m 54.46s
6 V. Ferrari (Yamaha) 50m 56.73s
7 B. van Dulmen (Suzuki) 50m 58.95s
8 W. von Muralt (Suzuki) 51m 18.75s
9 K. Huewen (Honda) 51m 38.77s
10 E. Hyvarinen (Suzuki) 51m 44.17s

1985 Swedish Grand Prix, Anderstorp, 30 laps, 75.15 miles (120.93 km)

1 *F. Spencer* (Honda) 49m 26.73s (91.18 mph/146.73 kph)
2 E. Lawson (Yamaha) 49m 49.53s
3 R. Haslam (Honda) 50m 04.64s
4 C. Sarron (Yamaha) 50m 18.97s
5 R. Mamola (Honda) 50m 33.21s
6 D. De Radigues (Honda) 50m 35.27s
7 M. Baldwin (Honda) 50m 36.10s
8 R. Roche (Yamaha) 50m 58.43s
9 T. Espie (Chevallier) one lap
10 M. Messere (Honda) one lap

1986 Swedish Grand Prix, Anderstorp, 30 laps, 75.15 miles (120.93 km)

1 *E. Lawson* (Yamaha) 48m 59.33s (92.03 mph/148.10 kph)
2 W. Gardner (Honda) 49m 15.37s
3 M. Baldwin (Yamaha) 49m 17.77s
4 R. McElnea (Yamaha) 49m 18.89s
5 R. Roche (Honda) 49m 41.57s
6 D. De Radigues (Honda) 49m 49.06s
7 N. Mackenzie (Susuki) 49m 57.79s
8 R. Mamola (Yamaha) 50m 08.74s
9 R. Haslam (Honda) one lap
10 W. von Muralt (Suzuki) one lap

1987 Brazilian Grand Prix, Goiania, 32 laps, 76.25 miles (122.72 km)

1 *W. Gardner* (Honda) 47m 39.57s (95.99 mph/154.47 kph)
2 E. Lawson (Yamaha) 47m 44.76s
3 R. Mamola (Yamaha) 47m 52.18s
4 D. De Radigues (Cagiva) 48m 03.99s
5 C. Sarron (Yamaha) 48m 05.16s
6 S. Yatsushiro (Honda) 48m 21.90s
7 T. Taira (Yamaha) 48m 31.28s
8 N. Mackenzie (Honda) 48m 36.26s
9 P. F. Chili (Honda) 48m 40.69s
10 M. Baldwin (Yamaha) 48m 43.29s

1988 Czech Grand Prix, Brno, 23 laps, 77.09 miles (124.06 km)

1 W. Gardner (Honda) 49m 11.06s (94.04 mph/151.33 kph)
2 *E. Lawson* (Yamaha) 49m 12.97s
3 W. Rainey (Yamaha) 49m 13.54s
4 P. F. Chili (Honda) 49m 26.74s
5 T. Taira (Yamaha) 49m 30.97s
6 N. Mackenzie (Honda) 49m 40.50s
7 R. Haslam (Honda) 50m 08.50s
8 R. McElnea (Suzuki) 50m 09.30s
9 P. Igoa (Yamaha) 50m 10.42s
10 F. Barchitta (Honda) 50m 57.02s

1989 Brazilian Grand Prix, Interlagos, 33 laps, 76.25 miles (122.70 km)

1 K. Schwantz (Suzuki) 46m 44.39s (97.88 mph/157.51 kph)
2 *E. Lawson* (Honda) 46m 46.09s
3 W. Rainey (Yamaha) 46m 55.60s
4 M. Doohan (Honda) 47m 03.51s
5 R. Haslam (Suzuki) 47m 08.64s
6 K. Magee (Yamaha) 47m 17.81s
7 W. Gardner (Honda) 47m 18.02s
8 C. Sarron (Yamaha) 47m 23.00s
9 N. Mackenzie (Yamaha) 47m 51.03s
10 A. Morillas (Honda) 47m 54.40s

1990 Czech Grand Prix, Brno, 23 laps, 77.09 miles (124.06 km)

1 *W. Rainey* (Yamaha) 47m 50.84s (96.67 mph/112.11 kph)
2 W. Gardner (Honda) 47m 52.85s
3 E. Lawson (Yamaha) 48m 10.37s
4 N. Mackenzie (Suzuki) 48m 26.02s
5 J. Garriga (Yamaha) 48m 33.46s
6 C. Sarron (Yamaha) 48m 37.09s
7 S. Pons (Honda) 48m 42.23s
8 J-P. Ruggia (Yamaha) 48m 57.09s

9   M. Doohan (Honda) 48m 58.76s
10 C. Fogarty (Honda) 49m 10.26s

1991 Grand Prix Vitesse du Mans, Le Mans, 28 laps, 77.02 miles (123.94 km)
1   K. Schwantz (Suzuki) 47m 37.76s (97.03 mph/156.15 kph)
2   M. Doohan (Honda) 47m 37.91s
3   *W. Rainey* (Yamaha) 47m 41.22s
4   J. Kocinski (Yamaha) 47m 41.46s
5   W. Gardner (Honda) 47m 41.72s
6   J. Garriga (Yamaha) 47m 75.61s
7   D. Chandler (Yamaha) 47m 76.10s
8   D. De Radigues (Suzuki) 47m 76.96s
9   S. Pons (Honda) 48m 68.31s
10 A. Morillas (Yamaha) 48m 82.20s

1992 South African Grand Prix, Kyalami, 28 laps, 74.11 miles (119.28 km)
1   J. Kocinski (Yamaha) 47m 00.72s (94.58 mph/152.20 kph)
2   W. Gardner (Honda) 47m 03.66s
3   *W. Rainey* (Yamaha) 47m 05.69s
4   D. Chandler (Suzuki) 47m 13.30s
5   K. Schwantz (Suzuki) 47m 22.77s
6   M. Doohan (Honda) 47m 31.04s
7   A. Criville (Honda) 47m 34.59s
8   N. Mackenzie (Yamaha) 47m 35.24s
9   M. DuHamel (Yamaha) 48m 03.85s
10 J. Garriga (Yamaha) 48m 10.95s

1993 American Grand Prix, Laguna Seca, 33 laps, 72.46 miles (116.62 km)
1   J. Kocinski (Cagiva) 48m 17.16s (90.04 mph/144.90 kph)
2   A. Barros (Suzuki) 48m 23.54s
3   L. Cadalora (Yamaha) 48m 27.65s
4   *K. Schwantz* (Suzuki) 48m 35.43s
5   D. Beattie (Honda) 48m 36.65s
6   S. Itoh (Honda) 48m 54.45s
7   A. Criville (Honda) 48m 56.48s
8   N. Mackenzie (Yamaha) 49m 00.01s
9   J. Reynolds (Yamaha) 49m 33.34s
10 J. Mella (Yamaha) one lap
11 J. Kuhn (Yamaha) one lap
12 J. McWilliams (Yamaha) one lap
13 S. Emmett (Yamaha) one lap
14 S. David (Yamaha) one lap
15 L. Naveau (Yamaha) one lap

Index